KINSHIP WITH
THE ANIMALS

KINSHIP WITH
THE ANIMALS

Edited by
Michael Tobias and Kate Solisti-Mattelon

BEYOND
WORDS
Publishing
I N C

Beyond Words Publishing, Inc.
20827 N.W. Cornell Road, Suite 500
Hillsboro, Oregon 97124-9808
503-531-8700
1-800-284-9673

Editor: Ann Granning Bennett
Design: Robin Weiss
Typesetting: William H. Brunson Typography Services
Proofreaders: Margaret Willis Tusko and Marvin Moore
Managing editor: Kathy Matthews

Printed in the United States of America
Distributed to the book trade by Publishers Group West
First published in Germany in 1997 by Kosmos

Library of Congress Cataloging-in-Publication Data
Kinship with the animals / edited by Michael Tobias and Kate Solisti-Mattelon.
        p.   cm.
    ISBN 1-885223-88-9 (pbk.)
    1. Human-animal relationships.   2. Animal psychology.   I. Tobias,
Michael.   II. Solisti-Mattelon, Kate.
QL85.K535   1998
591.5—dc21   98-24950
                                                                                        CIP

The corporate mission of Beyond Words Publishing, Inc.:
   Inspire to Integrity

For Jane Gray Morrison, the wildest animal
in my life—my true love, soul mate,
and editorial inspiration

To our children, Miranda, Alex, Anais, and
Adrien—may the world you grow up in be rich
in kinship with all life. To the animals who
have taught me so much, I am eternally grateful.
And to Patrice, my partner, my husband,
my love—thank you

CONTENTS

INTRODUCTION

Despite the world's love affair with such great animal stories as those of Beatrix Potter and Hugh Lofting, science still chooses to dismiss most deep personal intuitions and feelings about animals as merely "anthropomorphic." In *Kinship with the Animals* we have expressly sought out extraordinary stories, anecdotes, and the rich, subversive science of encounters between humans and other life forms that might truly expand and accelerate the vocabulary of interspecies dialogue and empathy.

These exquisite tales of revelation, discussion, research, and miraculous accident are all real; they happened. The exchanges occurred in the earth's wildest places and in the most familiar homes. In every case their presentation here suggests a new and critical wave of emergent understanding that has gained considerable stature among an ever-increasing range of caring individuals in all countries. Those individuals' views regarding animal awareness, cognition, and communication form the backbone of a new human consciousness which is surfacing at the very moment that more species are being driven to extinction than at any other time in biological history, a time when so many millions of animals are being killed every year for human consumption.

It is the intent of the book to make potently clear that the joys, significance, and possibilities for interspecies relationships through communication, empathy, and mutual understanding should constitute one of the most important and shaping imperatives for all human behavior, now and forever more. It is our hope that these consistently personal and subjective stories and insights will help shed new light on the behavior, thinking, and feelings of other creatures and, perhaps, of the biosphere herself.

Contributors to *Kinship with the Animals* come from numerous countries and traditions. Together, we raise a united voice to push the limits of the possible within scientific circles and currently accepted "norms" by offering and exploring alternative explanations for personal experiences and revelations amid the cornucopia of other animal and plant species surrounding us. We wantonly suggest companionship and affiliation with such creatures, both in the wild and at home, that challenge traditional views regarding animal intelligence and emotional refinement. Finally, each of us recounts and reveals moments in our lives where the inexplicable occurred, leading our minds toward new awareness, our hearts toward deeper wellsprings, our communities—if they will listen—toward a path of ecological sanity, our species—if only it will agree to wake up—toward an embrace of its own humanity.

If the massive amount of pain inflicted upon other life forms is to cease and if the tide of habitat loss and lineage extinction in the coming hours, days, and years is to be reversed, human ethics, behavior, and science must accept its humble place in the world. We have no other choice. Our muscleman mentality is an anachronism; our outbreaks of violence absolute throwbacks to a churning cauldron of evolution we should long ago have transcended. Evolution does not dictate the possibilities for virtue and compassion. Only our individual choices can do that. Our kinship with all other life forms, as suggested in this modest volume, offers up a path directly before us, and to all sides: the path of biophilia, the love of nature, and the hope—well documented—for having most meaningful encounters with other species. We need not seek one-celled organisms beneath the seas of Jupiter's moon, Europa, to remind us that we are not alone in the heavens. The Earth herself may comprise as many as fifty million currently co-habiting species, of which fewer than 1.6 million have ever been identified by *Homo sapiens*. The possibilities for forming new friendships are staggering. But with between seventy and eight hundred species going extinct, or being driven to the brink of extinction, every day—a rate and figure that is fast increasing—there is not much time left to unleash this renaissance of empathy and gentle inquiry.

Nonetheless, there is still time, and we ask our friends and readers of this volume to meditate deeply on ways that they might help engender paths of nonviolence and compassion, paths of love toward our kindred plant and animal friends, all of whom came before us, all of whom depend upon the vulnerable benevolence of this miraculous planet, which is presently dominated—overrun by any other name—by one species.

Michael Tobias
Kate Solisti-Mattelon

PART 1

BEYOND SCIENTIFIC RELATIONSHIPS

THE DRAGONFLY'S GIFT

JANE GOODALL

To begin at the beginning: I think it began when I was about one year old—but I only found out recently when my mother was writing an account of my childhood. She said that I was fascinated by animals from the time I could crawl. Once, aged about eighteen months, I took earthworms to bed. When she found me intently observing as they wriggled around my pillow, she told me they would soon die if I did not return them to the earth. Quickly I ran back with them to the garden. I don't remember that.

I do remember going to stay in the country, where my father's family owned a farm—what a treat for a little girl from London who loved animals. Cows, pigs, and horses. And hens. I collected the eggs each day, from the little henhouses—no battery units in those days. Apparently I kept asking where the eggs came out—I could not see a big enough hole! As no one explained, I hid inside one of the stuffy henhouses, in the straw, and I waited and waited and waited. For more than four hours! And then, as dusk was falling and my family was searching everywhere, my frantic mother saw a small figure, covered in straw, rushing back toward the house. How lucky I was that, instead of scolding me for making everyone so worried, going off without telling anyone, my mother saw the excitement in my eyes and sat down to hear the story of how a hen laid an egg. To this day I can remember that hen and how she rose a little with her back to me so that I could watch the slightly soft white egg gradually emerging until—*plop!*—it landed on the straw.

But the crucial incident that I had completely forgotten occurred when I was less than a year old. I was in my pram outside the grocery store, guarded by our bull terrier, while my nanny made a purchase inside.

3

A dragonfly began swooping around me, and I screamed. So a well-intentioned passerby hit the dragonfly to the ground with his newspaper and crushed it with his foot. But I continued to scream all the way home. In fact, I became hysterical, and my puzzled mother had to give me a sedative to calm me down (something she almost never did).

Forty-five years later, as I read my mother's account, I was suddenly transported back in time. I remembered lying in my nursery and watching a dragonfly which had come in through the window. As my nanny shooed it out, she told me that it had a sting the length of its tail. That is a *long* sting! No wonder I was scared when that dragonfly zoomed around my pram. But being afraid of something does not mean we want it dead. If I close my eyes I can see, with almost unbearable clarity, the glorious quivering wings, the blue tail gleaming in the sunlight, the head crushed on the sidewalk. Because of me, perhaps it had died in pain. I screamed in helpless outrage from a terrible sense of guilt.

All through my childhood I learned about animals and wrote down my observations. My heroes were Doctor Dolittle and Tarzan. I had dreams of living with animals in Africa. My teacher was Rusty, my childhood companion, my best friend. He was a mutt—an utterly engaging mixture of cocker spaniel and poodle (at least, so I assumed after meeting one other dog that looked like Rusty and who was, his owners assured me, thus pedigreed). From Rusty I learned so much about animal behavior; he demonstrated daily the amazing cognitive abilities of the canine mind. Rusty's personality was vivid and unforgettable, so that even now, forty years later, I can see him lying at the foot of my bed, following me up a ladder, scrambling with me up and down the wild cliffs that rose up from the seashore. He showed me, again and again, that dogs are capable of planning.

For example, on a hot day he would set off for the sea alone, a ten-minute walk. At the main road he would pause, check the traffic, then trot down for a swim. Then, after a good shake, he returned, cool and satisfied. (I knew this because I sometimes spied on him, as he set out and returned, from my bedroom window.) He loved to play games like "hunt the thimble," quickly differentiating between "you're getting hot" and "you're getting cold." He would even pretend to hunt for me.

He would face away while I hid in the bushes and then told him to search. Of course he knew exactly where I was—he had his nose as well as his eyes and ears. But he would rush in a frenzy back and forth, often going right by me, until, after about three minutes, he would decide it was OK to "find" me. Once, when I had to go away for a week, I left Rusty limping with a hurt foot and, of course, much sympathy. When I returned, I was shocked to find he was still limping. "Oh, *poor* Rusty!" I was down on my knees commiserating. Then I saw the family laughing. He'd been limp-free for days but started again as soon as he saw me!

Rusty was my first real mentor in my ongoing effort to understand, ever more clearly, the true nature of nonhuman animals. He provided me with an intuitive awareness of the subtleties of animal behavior, very different from what I would have learned during a conventional undergraduate education. In fact, I had not been to university when, in 1960, the late Louis Leakey gave me the chance to observe wild chimpanzees in Tanzania's Gombe National Park. Thus I set off unbiased by the ethological thinking of the time. And so, as I learned to identify the various chimpanzees, I named them rather than giving them numbers, which would, I was told, have been more scientific. As I realized how they differed from one another, I described their vivid personalities, even though in those days nonhuman animals were not supposed to have personalities. I referred to them as "he" or "she" rather than "it." I also credited them with the ability to reason, and I described their emotions. After all, Rusty had demonstrated those things, and the brain of a chimpanzee is more similar to our own than that of a dog.

Rusty was a dog among dogs. His counterpart, in the chimpanzee world, was David Greybeard. "Do you have one favorite chimpanzee?" I am often asked. David Greybeard is my reply. There will never be another quite like him, with his broad intelligent face, his large, widely spaced brown eyes, and his calm, gentle personality. Yet he was also a very determined sort of individual too and usually managed to get his own way. It was he who helped me open a door into a magic world not previously explored—the world of the wild chimpanzees.

When I arrived at Gombe, the chimpanzees were terrified of the peculiar white ape who had invaded their territory. But David Greybeard, for some reason, was less afraid of me than were his companions. When they fled, he often stayed, provided I was not too close. Not surprisingly, then, he was in the small group on the very first occasion that I was able to get really close. David, and his closest friend, Goliath, just looked up as I emerged from some bushes. And instead of running off, they continued to groom each other. I had been accepted! The sheer ecstasy of that moment is as pure today as it was all those long years ago.

So often it was from David Greybeard that I learned new and exciting facts about the Gombe chimpanzees' way of life. It was David who gave me that first thrilling observation of tool use, as he fished termites from their underground nest with pieces of grass. And I watched in disbelief as he picked leafy twigs and stripped the leaves or trimmed wide blades of grass. He was modifying objects, making them suitable for his purpose. He was making tools. At that time, humans and only humans were supposed to be able to make tools—it was the most important distinction between ourselves and the rest of the animal kingdom. When I sent a telegram to my mentor, Louis Leakey, he beamed and said, "Now we must redefine *Man*, redefine *tool*, or accept chimpanzees as humans!"

David was also the first chimpanzee whom I saw feeding on meat, sharing the body of a young bushpig with an adult female in response to her begging. And some months later, he was part of a group that showed sophisticated cooperation during a hunt.

Gradually David introduced me to his companions. In addition to Goliath, he often spent time with Mike, JB, Mr. McGregor, Leakey, and Mr. Worzle. And then there were also Melissa, Olly, Marina, Sophie, and their families. And so many more.

And, of course, there was Flo, that most famous matriarch, known all over the world thanks to the National Geographic Society documentaries and articles. Flo and her frequent companion, Olly, were the first adult females to tolerate my proximity, and from them I learned so much about the importance of the family bond in chimpanzee society. I spent hours in their company: watching, recording, and wondering. From them I began to learn something of the tremendously important role played by mother

and family in molding the behavior of the offspring. I found that while a full-grown son (like Flo's Faben) played a part in educating his young siblings, there was no equivalent, within the close-knit family group, of the traditional human father. Instead, as I would eventually learn, all community males spent time together and protected the resources of their territory for the females and youngsters of their community.

There was another moment, during those early days, that I can never forget—the first time I actually made contact with a wild chimpanzee. And of course, it was David Greybeard again. It was as he sat, quietly grooming Flo, that I ventured, one day, to make a grooming movement on his back. He glanced at me—but then continued his own grooming of Flo. What magic: a fully grown male chimpanzee allowed me to groom him! Soon he gently pushed my hand away. But he allowed me the same liberty on other occasions—and for longer.

Then, when Flo's infant, Flint, was about five months old, just beginning to totter about under his own steam, she allowed him to come right up to me one day. He reached out and touched my knee, looking up at my face with his wide-eyed, wondering gaze. And although she kept a restraining hand around him, Flo permitted the contact. Soon after that, her two elder offspring, Figan and Fifi, sometimes allowed me to join their games. And these were individuals who, for months, had been so fearful—avoiding me, hiding in the vegetation, silently vanishing in the forest. Now I had gained their trust.

As time went on, though, I realized that contacts of this sort would have to cease. Hugo van Lawick had been sent by the National Geographic Society to film the chimpanzees, funding was assured for the next few years, and students had joined us to help collect data. Obviously, repeated interactions with human observers would seriously affect the behavior of the chimpanzees. Yet, even if I were given the chance to go back and do things differently, I would not. Those friendly contacts were a fantastic reward for all the long hard months that had gone before.

Interestingly, as time went on, I found that I no longer even *wanted* to interact physically with the Gombe chimpanzees. My relationship with these amazing beings is hard to define. "They must seem like family to

you?" people will ask. But no, not like family. Not like pets, either. A little while ago one of my dogs was very sick, and I was distraught. "If you feel like this about a dog," said a man, who was visiting the house in Dar es Salaam, "I certainly hope I won't be around when one of your chimpanzees is sick."

Well, the thing is, they are not "my" chimpanzees. They are not dependent on me for anything. They are wild and free. I help them when they are sick, if I can, but they do not expect it. I am very upset when one of them is hurt or in pain—but I do not feel responsible. That is the difference between a free, wild animal and a domesticated animal. If my dog is hurting, and I cannot help, that is a betrayal. A good master is a god in the eyes of his dog. I am not a god for the Gombe chimpanzees. My relationship with them is one of mutual respect and trust. Some of them I love—I loved David Greybeard and Flo, Olly, and Gilka, as today I love Gremlin and Galahad, Prof and Pax, and Skosha. But there is no reciprocal love from them. It simply is not, could not be, that kind of relationship. Whereas the dogs whom I love also love me in return.

At Gombe, I am happiest when I sit among a group of chimpanzees, disregarded and ignored, while they carry on with their lives around me. I almost cease to exist. I am a conduit, observing and recording that which takes place. Outside their society, yet somehow living it, my every sense is attuned to the nuances of their behavior. As soon as another human enters the picture, the feeling is gone, the spell broken. Then I become a mere human watching a group of chimpanzees.

Over the years, more and more researchers have spent time at Gombe, collecting data, watching, learning, and pondering. At one time there was a team of young people from North America and Europe; today most of those observing are Tanzanians from the surrounding villages. They collect sophisticated information, use 8-mm videocameras, are proud of their work, and talk about it with families and friends. Most important, they care about the chimpanzees as individuals. There is no poaching at Gombe. And so, thanks to the supportive attitude of the Tanzanian government toward my work, and the fact that Tanzania has been the most politically stable country in Africa after independence, we

are, as I write (June 1995), one month away from the thirty-fifth anniversary of my arrival at Gombe. What a huge and rich store of information we have gathered!

We have recorded youngsters of five to ten years old, juveniles and adolescents, caring for their infant siblings after the death of a mother. A young male may be an excellent caretaker and will wait for and carry an orphaned sibling, share his food and his night nest, and do his best to protect his young charge from danger. In this way, Prof adopted four-year-old Pax. And Sniff tried to care for his little sister, but she was only just over one year old when their mother died, absolutely dependent on milk, so she only lived two weeks.

Adoptions are mostly family affairs, but this is not always the case. One middle-aged female, Gigi, who had been sterile all her life, looked after no less than three small orphans when their mothers died in an epidemic. For years she had tried to make friends with first one mother and then another, apparently so that she could play with and carry their infants. Now, finally, she had full responsibility for three of her own.

One of the most touching stories is that of a twelve-year-old adolescent male, Spindle, who adopted a sickly infant of just over three years old. We all thought Mel would die when he lost his mother, for he was alone in the world. But Spindle cared for him day after day, carrying him, sharing his food and his nest, and protecting him from danger. Almost certainly Spindle saved Mel's life—yet they were not even related. Why did Spindle take on this task? Could it have been because during the epidemic that claimed the life of Mel's mother, Spindle also lost his? Was there an emptiness in his life, despite his adolescent status, that was in some way filled by the close relationship with a dependent youngster? Maybe we shall never know. There are many unanswered questions, many mysteries.

Why did Passion and Pom, mother and daughter, start to cannibalize the newborn infants of other females in their community? For four years it was unsafe for new mothers to walk the forests of Gombe by themselves. Eleven infants were born to the community during those years, and ten died. Five of those infants were definitely victims of the killer females; we suspect the others suffered the same fate. Only when each of

the females gave birth to their own young did the killings stop. Aberrant behavior, we thought. But was it?

Just recently, three of our senior females, who always seemed so respectable and concerned with child-raising, ganged up on a young female, Gremlin (who happens to be my favorite), and tried (but luckily failed) to seize her newborn. The four females had known each other for years. Their children had played together. It was a sudden and horrifying eruption of violence. And then, two days after the attack, they were seen together again, Gremlin seeming quite calm. Indeed, we still have much to learn.

The thing is, with chimpanzees, they are so similar to humans that while there are individuals I love, there are also others I dislike intensely. I utterly disliked Passion until just before her death. She was so sick and in such pain, yet as she still attempted to care for her four-year-old son, Pax, I forgave her. She was, after all, a chimpanzee, not a human. Surely a chimpanzee is less aware of the suffering of a victim than we would be. Surely her behavior had been less deliberate and less calculated. Or not? These are the questions that perplex the mind in the dark hours of the night, when one is contemplating the mystery: the meaning of life on earth and the part we humans play.

Over the years, the chimpanzees have taught me a great deal about their place in nature—and just as much, perhaps, about our own place in nature. The most important lesson I have learned from the chimpanzees is humility. We humans, after all, are not so different from the rest of the animal kingdom as we once believed. The gradual revelation of the complex natures of chimpanzees, our closest living relatives, has helped to bridge the supposed gap between "man" and "beast." It now appears that there is an evolutionary continuity of mind as well as structure. After all, it has been shown that chimpanzees are capable of intellectual abilities once thought unique to ourselves. They can, for example, be taught to understand and use signs (ASL, or American Sign Language, as used by deaf people), or lexigrams on computer keys. They can then use these signs in new contexts and in different combinations. Whether or not this research provides evidence of linguistic ability per se, it certainly teaches us a good deal about the capabilities of chimpanzee cognition. Chimpanzees have proved their ability to understand and use abstract

symbols in communication and to make generalizations and abstractions. It has also been shown that chimpanzees have a sense of humor and a concept of self.

In the wild, chimpanzees communicate with a variety of calls, as well as a repertoire of postures and gestures. Many forms of chimpanzee communication are uncannily like our own and elicited in similar contexts. Chimpanzees hold hands, pat one another on the back, kiss, and embrace when greeting, reassuring or calming each other. They swagger magnificently to intimidate. They punch, hit, and kick when fighting. Moreover, they fight for many of the same reasons we do: food, sex, territory, and to protect family and friends. They have a long childhood, during which, as for human children, learning is important. And, like their human counterparts, chimpanzee youngsters learn a good deal by observing and imitating the behavior of others.

In all areas where chimpanzees have been studied, they show variations in behavior. Sometimes these can be described as cultural differences—behaviors that are passed from one generation to the next through observational learning. They are like us in other ways, too. Supportive, affectionate bonds between family members and friends may persist through a lifespan of fifty or more years. Chimpanzees are capable of compassion, altruism, and love. And, just as we humans have a dark side to our nature, so do the chimpanzees: like us they are capable of brutality and intergroup conflict that may, on occasion, escalate into something similar to primitive warfare.

Chimpanzees are too much like us. They share some 99 percent of our genetic makeup, their blood composition and immune responses are amazingly like ours, and the anatomy of the chimpanzee brain and central nervous system is more like ours than any other living creature. This is why they are imprisoned in medical research laboratories to serve as living test tubes for the investigation of certain diseases that other primates, less like us, cannot catch or be infected with. AIDS and hepatitis are a couple of examples. Hundreds of chimpanzees are confined in steel-barred cages that are no more than five-by-five feet and seven feet high. Highly sociable, they are alone in their confinement—and usually their sentence is for life.

The first adult male I met in an American laboratory was named Jojo. I knelt, looking into his eyes, while he looked back, not in anger or hatred, which I could have endured, but with what seemed like bewilderment and utter resignation. Already he had spent at least ten years in his little prison. I thought of the chimpanzees at Gombe and their rich lives filled with excitement, stimulation, and variety, enjoying the freedom of the forest, the siestas in the shade while stretched out on the leafy ground or on their soft, springy beds in the treetops. Very gently Jojo reached toward me through the bars, touched the tear that was trickling down under my mask and then stared intently at my face. Today, Jojo is infected with the HIV virus. Almost certainly, he will always be a "dirty" chimpanzee, for the rest of his life.

Because chimpanzees can be taught to do so many things that humans do, they are sold as pets in order to serve as surrogate children or to act in circuses or various other forms of "entertainment." All of these unnatural conditions are cruel, as is both the training and the ultimate fate of these hapless and exploited creatures. By the time chimpanzees are between four and seven years old, they are as strong as a person, resent discipline, and are potentially dangerous. What will become of them? Zoos don't want such individuals, for they do not behave like normal chimpanzees. They have had no chance to learn. As a result, they often end up in medical labs.

In Africa—where ever-increasing human populations compete for ever-shrinking limited resources and struggle to survive—chimpanzees are disappearing across their range, either from the destruction of their forests, from hunting, or both. Sometimes female chimpanzees are shot deliberately and their infants sold to dealers who ship them out of Africa for the entertainment and medical-research industries. Infants sold in the market places are usually by-products of the bushmeat trade. Their mothers have been shot (usually illegally) for food. They have been killed not just to feed family and friends in the village, as in the old days, but to be chopped up, smoked, and trucked to the towns.

Little Jay was the first infant whom I saw with my own eyes offered for sale in a big tourist market in central Africa. Tied to the top of a tiny cage in the hot sun, surrounded by a noisy crowd, Jay, dehydrated with

dull and glazed eyes, seemed close to death. Yet when I knelt and made the small panting sound of greeting, he sat up, stared at me, then reached to touch my face. If you buy one of these pathetic infants you perpetuate the trade. Yet how could I abandon him? Luckily, we were able to persuade a government official to confiscate him. (There was a law prohibiting the sale of chimpanzees without a license, but it had never been enforced.) A Belgian woman, Graziella Cotman, offered to nurse him back to health.

Today, Graziella represents JGI in the Congo. And now that the government is cooperating by confiscating other illegally captured infants, her "family" is growing. She and our Congolese staff are trying to cope with forty-eight young chimpanzees in a nine-acre sanctuary built for us by Conoco, one of the few oil companies having a strong environmental ethic, even when working in third-world countries.

Neither shall I forget my first sight of Gregoire. When I met him he was an emaciated skeleton. His bones were held together by the skin, and he was almost hairless. Gregoire had been in his bleak, dark cage in the Brazzaville Zoo since 1944. How was he still alive—and why? I looked into his old eyes, and he reached out and, mumbling his jaws like an old man, tried to undo a button on my sleeve. As we established friends, gradually conditions began to improve for the other wretched zoo prisoners.

Should we continue accepting the challenge of caring for the Little Jays and Gregoires of Africa? Many conservationists suggest that it is irresponsible to "waste" money on a few individuals; rather we should use our limited resources to protect the species in the wild. Other people ask how I can justify spending money on animals when people are starving. We are doing what we can in the field of conservation. Working with villagers, working with governments, and offering jobs, we try to help the situation of the chimpanzees. Using our orphan chimpanzees to attract tourists, we capture their foreign exchange. We also use the chimpanzees as a focus for conservation education so that local people, especially children, start to realize that we are all in this together. If the forests and the animals go, the desert will creep across the land, and people will be doomed as well.

Yet quite apart from all the justification, and it is real, I cannot turn my back on individuals. My research has always focused on the importance and value of the individual. Once we are prepared to accept that not only humans have personalities and are capable of reason, and above all, not only humans have emotions and can feel pain, our attitude toward many of the nonhuman beings we share the planet with will change. This new understanding will lead to a new respect, which, in turn will raise many difficult ethical questions relating to the way we use and abuse so many animals in our daily lives (human as well as nonhuman, incidentally). These are questions for each one of us to answer for ourselves.

The other day I was giving a talk at a zoo. At the end, a student asked me, rather pompously, if I wasn't being somewhat irresponsible, committing myself to the well-being of so many young chimpanzees. As I was preparing to give a reasoned reply, the door opened, and a young woman walked in with an infant chimpanzee in her arms. His mother had rejected him, and he was being hand-raised. Of course, everyone crowded round, wanting to touch his hands, look into his eyes, and stroke his sleek black hair. When they had all sat down again, I took the infant, returned to the podium, and, looking slowly round the room, asked if anyone there would be able to kill the little chimp—because when the governments cooperate with us by confiscating, we have only two choices: to take and care for, or take and kill. There was dead silence, and I saw some tears.

In fact, there is no choice. Certainly not for me. After all, I have to assuage the guilt of the one-year-old child who caused the death of a dragonfly.

ON TORTOISES, MONKEYS, AND MEN

ANTHONY L. ROSE

Here in dark subthalamic pools of archetypal memory echo the voices of those cold- and hot-blooded ancestors who invented the harmony of individuality and community that every animal descendant seeks, to this very day. We humans, off-balance and retreating from our natural history, look back in terror. Fear drives our ambitions and schemes to subdue and conquer nature. Scientist, teacher, politician, parent—all are afraid of being consumed in the potent exuberance of this elaborate and unknowable universe. Wilderness scares us. We hide from its truth.

We also hide its truth. A few years ago I talked to ethologists and conservationists at an international conference. My main thrust was to encourage them to loosen up, to report the personal aspects of their involvement with wild animals. When we describe how we face our fears and talk openly about our personal encounters with wildlife, we help the layperson experience the scientist as a fellow human and establish the groundwork for an informed sense of interspecies kinship. One scientist declared, "If taking a politician to meet a gorilla gets a vote for conservation, it's worth the risk of a little anthropomorphic thinking." Many agreed.

Still, a few argued that "we must never think of animals in human terms. It's unscientific." Ironically, this narrow-mindedness has undermined the natural sciences. Like all forms of ritualized simplicity, the law of parsimony and its correlated demand for severe detachment from and objectification of animals has hamstrung research, dehumanized animal caretaking, and dampened the spirit of conservation.

Fortunately, recognition of the value of personal experience in these domains is growing. Empathy and intuition are again becoming legitimate factors in the understanding and support of other species. This allows us to attest to the secret truth of the scientific community—most people who study wildlife have experienced profound connections with animals and are deeply aware of the mysterious hidden lives of their animal subjects.

I have collected and analyzed hundreds of anecdotes describing such natural epiphanies. In addition to being self-defining for the individual humans involved, *Profound Interspecies Events* (PIEs) inspire a transformed worldview that is essential to the reunion of man and nature.

At our core, all living beings are endowed with an innate affinity for the organisms and landscapes through which we evolve. That core must be reached in order to energize the reunion. This means plunging past the cortex to the midbrain, past the exquisite human elaborations of our mammalian mind to the sublime remnants of our reptilian heritage. Some of the most hardheaded scientists have made this plunge. Many know that the laboratory rat, the desert tortoise, and the wild gorilla are loving, spiritual, thoughtful beings. We are just scared to admit it or talk about it.

After fear, the greatest obstacle to understanding these potent events is their ineffability—the best of poets struggle to record them. The autobiographies of scores of natural scientists are marked with quick and fitful allusions to these experiences. "Words can't describe how I felt" and "I'll never forget this incident" are used to signify the occurrence of a life-changing natural epiphany. It's not enough.

Having studied with poets and fiction writers, trying to develop my ability to signify these events, I can tell you it's the hardest work I've ever done. When one has been bred on concise ideas and concrete observations aimed at cool impersonal rhetoric, one finds it difficult to produce the prose and poetics that evoke the actual experience in the reader, as if it were happening now, in the moment. This is especially true for the ephemeral spiritual and emotional epiphanies that highlight our lives with other animals.

Some years ago in a fiction workshop, after reading an excerpt in which I tried to display an orangutan communicating with a human, a

more experienced novelist criticized, "Orangutans don't talk." My first reaction was, "Of course they do." The workshop leader corrected me— "Yes, but not like that." I had not yet found the words, style, and syntax to evoke a believable sense of "orangutan language" in the reader. But I keep trying. Very few people will meet the ape in its rain forest or talk to the tortoise as it crawls from its desert burrow. But many can read, empathize, and act with compassion evoked by those of us who are blessed with such experience and the will to express it.

It is that will, that desire to let the truth be known, that compels this essay. With humility, I shall weave together a few tales, starting with my own, to inform and arouse the love and reverence for the animal world that is our heritage and our hope.

My interspecies life began at age seven when I got a turtle named Rocky and learned the meaning of perseverance. Then I thought that the creature inside that hard shell sat still on the palm of my hand in order to survive, waiting me out, balancing against the tilts and twitches of my shaky arm. As a child I could only sense the reptile's stability. I was hot blood, and he was cool bone. I could not find our common voice.

Thirty years and many moves after Rocky, a big healthy twelve-pound male California desert tortoise wandered into the park behind my home in Hermosa Beach. No one in the neighborhood claimed him, so I installed him in the garden and named him Sydney after my dad. Four years later folks moved next door with a half-blind crack-shelled old tortoise of questionable age and life history. "Let's put them together—if they get along, you can have her," they said. I was quick to accept the offer.

We sat close by, in the event of hostilities, and gingerly placed her in the dirt by his side. He sniffed. She retracted. He bobbed his head. She blinked. He nipped gently at her shell. She turned. Bob, blink, nip, turn—they carried on with increasing intensity. We humans chatted about life and love in our garden. The tortoises did the same.

Suddenly Sydney was hefting himself up her shell. Her turning hastened at first, but he stayed front feet up, rear legs on the ground, and maneuvered like an agile athlete, steadily tracking her turns. She slowed. He took position at her rear. She lowered her head and raised

her aft, ever so slightly. A penis emerged from his underside, beneath his tail, and in it went. Less than fifteen minutes after meeting, after years of solitude, these ancient beings were working, amiably, to ensure their species' survival.

I ran into the house, brought out glasses and champagne, and with new neighbors, human and tortoise, I celebrated a reunion that would change my view of life.

I named that old tortoise Lolita, after my mother. Ten years of summer mating and winter hibernation passed—five clutches of eggs pulled from the dirt in June, forty embryos incubated, thirteen hatchlings nursed and sealed, grown to healthy youngsters. Burrows were built, stone enclosures and work sheds constructed, trails of fruit, vegetables, water, vitamins, and fecal matter laid out and cleaned up, tortoises lost and found, measured and monitored, studied and ignored day after day from then to now.

Yet with all this opportunity in my own backyard, I remained an outsider. I avoided attachment, objectified observation, stifled interpretation, conducted the most practical of experiments, carried on business as usual, as if everybody in Southern California were breeding a 200-million-year-old endangered species in their gardens.

Then, one summer night, it all changed—events forced me to switch from a detached scientist to a deeply involved humanist and beyond into the naturalistic discovery of my reptilian heritage. I write this story with all my values showing. This is not a simple tale about a man and his tortoise. It is about how I was confronted with the overwhelming mystery of these stoic beings who live in a world that my species only knows in its bones and brainstem. This is an allegory about humankind losing and finding the reptile voice.

VOICES WE MUSTN'T HEAR

There are voices we mustn't hear. In that wind, an aroma. In that leaf, a sigh. Behind that shadowed knoll, where the green turns to a battered transparency, an untimely death delivers its canto. I am gone, I am gone. This winnowed testament awakens me from a night of tossing. It

isn't just the fireworks, ratcheting crackles like my grandmother pouring chestnuts into an iron bucket. The explosions are only cover. Something unspeakable wakens me. The hidden moon, I think at first, then know better.

It's pitch-black this July 4 morning, and the spirits are up and about. Kids with restless loins. Lanky poltergeists in torn pants and white T-shirts, up and out on the railroad tracks, lighting cherry bombs to start the celebration of a biological impossibility. Independence—the word tumbles over my thick tongue. Peering west, across the balcony railing, into night, a smell of fish salt convinces me that Santa Monica Bay is still there, though I cannot see it. The sticky fog wall says I could be in Kansas, on a cornfield outside Wichita. The collision of water and sand in my ears, and this trickle of brine on my beard say otherwise.

Voices or not, I'm home in Hermosa Beach and will sleep till first light. I barefoot back to bed, toss another three hours, then pull on shorts to start an early day. We'll be heading for the desert at 7 A.M.—got to beat the sun to Tehachapi. Chores to be done, kids to dress, animals to feed, tortoise burrows to clean. Down the stairs and out into the yard.

I feel it again. A soundless voice, but palpable. Pepper on my tongue. A burning sensation in the soles of my feet. Something is very wrong. I want to swallow but cannot. I squint and scan the lawn, a yellow-olive tube of dull light slashes by, and I blink at the strange flat stone in the dirt just below the back hedge. A flat stone.

We have only round stones, walking stones, stones of Triassic origin pressed in hard shell and thick leather legs like logs, stones that fold their bones and flesh inside at night, stones that dig in before Thanksgiving and don't come out till Valentine's Day. Round stones that never show themselves in twilight and don't like to expose their flat sides.

At once I know—that voice, that pepper, that tube of light. That flat stone is Lolita overturned, the mama of all our hatchlings on her back, weak side up and resigned to it, given over to the impossibility of independence. Out I tread, cool feet on damp grass, kneel down, peer in. Then the stench hits me, and I see the bubbling liquid in a dark hole where her tail should be. See viscous liquid splattered on dirt under her. See a trail of stringy flesh stretching across the lawn. Liquid and skin

and entrails and God knows what meat and gore that I try to deny—try to think is some misplaced garbage dragged out by the cat, some lamb flank or ham hock shredded by another carnivore's tooth—try to believe it's anything but the ripped out vitals of Lolita. Half-blind, crack-shelled Lolita who came to me ten years ago, the same year Annie, my wife, came to me. Lolita who took big Sydney on her back within a quarter hour of bobbing heads, circles, and bangs, and gave us eight eggs every other summer.

Yes, it is Lolita, and she has been dragged from her lair by some eager claws under cover of fireworks and night. Dragged five yards, hissing first like a snake in the box, then squeezing herself small, to make a rock of her, to become an image of invulnerable. Lolita, torn from her burrow, dying.

I turn her over. She gargles, huffs, hangs out her head, heaves in a breath, gargles. I bend down close, look straight into her face. She blinks, shuts her eyes. I run for a carton, return and gently put her in, climb in the car. With Lolita wheezing in the passenger seat I speed to the only veterinary hospital open on July 4. In the exam room I take her out, place her on the metal table. As I lift her, blood spills from her shell, splashes the metal, my hands, my trousers. I talk to her—"It's OK, mama tuga, we'll do what we can, we'll keep you if we can." Her neck stretches out, eyes open, and she bobs her head up and down, up and down—a greeting tendered to other tortoises, never before to me.

"Yes, I'm here, I'm with you." Head bobs again. I find myself nodding back, breathing slow, keeping time with my bones. Thinking, how strange—she's never looked at me, always shied away, more than ten years shied away. Now we stare straight at one another, no blinks, no withdrawal into the pseudosafety of round-shell back-house. No business as usual. Staring brown eye into brown eye, reptile into mammal, blood into blood, being into being, and I feel a pain in our hot and cold hearts, smell the aromas of nightfall and birth, musk of clawed feet scratching a deep hole in the dirt, honey breath of eggs, white and round—dropping . . . one, two, three . . . four, five, six . . . seven . . . eight.

I see cracked-open egg shells, tiny flat heads poking through, thumb-sized replicas of grown tortoises, pulling for life. I see a dozen orphaned

Lolitas, hatchlings grown bigger than fists, scratching their own holes in dirt. I see the eyes of this shy mama tortoise peering into my soul, thanking me for my part in her destiny. I hear the voice, still small, of primordial earth. Then an eerie creaking call bubbles through her throat, mouth opens, a gasp, a bob, a choke, a bob. Mouth closes. Her head drops. She's dead.

My tears are not for Lolita alone, nor just for me, my family, her companion, their offspring, our loss. I cry for all the lost offerings, the beings we've brushed souls with and not allowed ourselves to know, except in their utility, their service to our trivial tasks.

Lolita the tortoise is all the swamp and savanna of natural history, leaving us behind. She wandered in and out of places like streams and the wind. She lived as part of nature, no matter how civilized the terrain around her. She died the same, preyed on by starving raccoons, strangers in a strange land. Ten years of living epiphany flowed through her, right in my own backyard, and I did not hear her voice till the hour of her death.

I stare at her fallen head, my blood-soaked hands. How easily we die. How fast the breath passes. At once I realize that Lolita and all her kind are the most vulnerable animals alive. She cannot run, or fight, after all. She can only stay and hide. Put up a strong front—seem solid, unsavory, impenetrable. When threatened, hiss like a snake. Then pull inside herself, hide her holes, and pretend she's a rock. I know some people like that. Lots, in fact. I spent years trying to be just like that. A hard-shell, stuck-in-burrow techno-scientist who seemed like a rock but was truly the most vulnerable of beings.

Science is a special kind of construction that cuts off the mind below the cortex, to avoid pain, confusion, excitement, love, fear, elation. It's an adaptive architecture for the very sensitive in a world where vulnerability is not allowed—the "think-and-act" world. It promotes a kind of hibernation, a mental regimen to keep us cool, no matter how hot the reality. It produces hardheaded rationality and rock-bottom reductionist methodology. We use this thick armor to protect our soft underbellies from detection by prowling raccoons. But it has severe consequences— we become cortical tortoises.

Without the reptilian brain we lose the fundamental faith that everything, one way or another, returns to earth. The desert tortoise, and the natural human, suffer mortality without fear. Somewhere below the corpus callosum, between thalamus and medulla, is the locus of awareness that life is transformation from flesh to dirt, dirt to flesh. When Lolita dug in each winter she reentered the womb-grave of our mother, turned cold, and became again the earth. Buried alive for three months, she resurrected in spring. And in her brain, reverence for the transcendence was fixed. Would that it were so for us, warm-blooded scientists, terrified of the cold, the dark quiet earth.

For over two decades my most constant involvement with any living being has been with the California desert tortoises that have been breeding and burrowing in my backyard. I thought for much of that time that all we had in common was our will to live. Now I know that our underground ancestors have a power far stronger than the simple survival motive. Now I know that these ancient creatures carry out their long and fruitful lives with an unshakable and abiding faith.

My involvement with tortoises is on their terms. They are in their element, their earth, and I watch, awestruck by their resilience. To be buried and resurrected every year. To lay eggs without attachment. To eat and fast at the whim of time, at the rise and fall of the sun and prosperity. To die without fear. These are realities that I longed for but could not find as a scientist. It took a fundamental shock to my humanity—the overturned stone, entrails, a shell-backed mentor's nod of farewell—to open me to the brilliant earth-life that only the reptile voice can articulate.

I walk onto my balcony, peer at the yard below, and see Sydney, grown large as a watermelon, bathing in the first triangle of sunlight. When Lolita died, he dug in and hibernated. Did he find her there, underground, spirit to dirt, regenerating? I had to pull him out of the earth eight months later. Now he is back on cycle—warming, grazing, warming, sleeping. Perhaps dreaming of his lost companion and waiting for another. And across the yard, Lolita's children crawl from their burrows, greet the light of another day. What a blessing to have nature, so pregnant with historic faith, in my own backyard.

Colors We Mustn't See

When I look beyond my backyard, I am blessed with views of sea and sky. Living at the edge of the Pacific Ocean, I am reminded daily of the depths of our natural heritage. I have swum these cold waters since childhood, skimming the surface. I leave underwater exploration to more adventuresome souls. But I know those who dive beneath the surge have had their interspecies encounters. A friend, Dr. Randy Harwood, told me about an event that occurred while he and a diving buddy were returning to shore from a dive on a sunken ship off Guadalcanal in the Solomon Islands.

"I spotted five squid floating in shallow water, near shore. We immediately switched to our snorkels, to avoid scaring them with noisy scuba regulators. There were four small six-inch-long individuals and one squid nearly two feet in length, perhaps a mother and her offspring. We slowly approached the group until we got about ten feet from them. In unison they all quivered when they saw us and went from pale gray to colorless. The larger one then pulled away and momentarily displayed a spotted-brown pattern of blotches to the group. They immediately responded with a similar pattern. All then went transparent again and the four retreated, while the big squid slowly approached to within four feet of us, tentacles first. She was inspecting us, looking us over, while the little ones watched at a safe distance.

"Suddenly the big squid began displaying with all sorts of spots, stripes, and patterns—colors shifting from a blush of red, to gray and brown, to metallic blue. She was trying to communicate with us, greeting, questioning—*Nice day, huh? What are you and what are you doing here? Why can't you speak?* We hung motionless, unable to respond.

"After two minutes of questioning, the big squid became pale gray again, turned around, and slowly bobbed back to the others. She then displayed in deep reds and browns with large blotches and spots. The leader was reporting on the reconnaissance. The little ones replied, reproducing her messages, matching her colors.

"All five went transparent and slowly, tentacles first, approached us. At four feet distance they stopped and as a group, large and small,

repeated the brilliant displays of the first encounter. It was incredible! They had discussed us and decided to try again. In all the colors of their rainbow, five self-aware aliens from another world talked to us. As they repeated the inquiry with exquisite precision, the message boiled down to a simple one—*Hey stupid, who are you?* It was magical—if only we could have replied.

"Eventually they gave up or got bored and slowly drifted off. My partner and I jumped out of the water and breathlessly told our friends on the beach what had transpired. We were received with skepticism by some and envy and laughter by the others. The experience confirmed my belief that these animals have individual feelings, personalities, and are much more than we normally credit them."

Dr. Randy Harwood has seen colors we are not supposed to see. The corporate powers that harvest the sea, sending squid and countless other beautiful and intelligent beings toward extinction want us to believe that what's fried on the platter is just protein. Harwood makes his living as a dentist, enriches his life as an underwater adventurer, and is in every way a traditional citizen. He doesn't march or lobby for animal rights, condemn medical research, or eat only vegetables.

But if his friends and patients ask him about the uncanny experiences he's had diving the reefs and wrecks of the world, he tells them about the time a family of squid showed him their colors and hopes they get the message. Harwood says: "We humans must open our minds about all living beings—not be so quick to destroy their homes and lives for our own pleasure, greed."

The fact that these hard-shelled ancestors are cold-blooded does not mean they are without affinities. Harwood's squid are as curious as the family dog. Once they recognize that we are not predators, that we care to know them, they return the compliment. That the big old tortoise who lives in my garden appreciates me is apparent to any who see him amble over and sun himself at my feet. He's taking my companionship, nothing more. And in so doing, he prepares my eyes and ears for the colors and voices of nature. Secret hues and silent symphonies that the fearful and greedy say we mustn't see or hear. Sights and sounds that rob us of our false sense of independence and deliver us back to nature.

The Fastest Route

The fastest route back to nature occurs when animals we consider dangerous, distant, or disinterested surprise us. Wild creatures that *seek a friendly encounter* with a human produce most profound interspecies events—in my research I call this the SAFE scenario. It's rare for squid to do this with humans; not so rare for our fellow primates. Because monkeys and apes are so much like us, we recognize their shows of interest and concern more easily and respond more openly than with less familiar beings. The real power behind Dr. Dolittle was, after all, a monkey named Chee Chee. It is through these kindred spirits that many scientists learn to talk to the animals.

My first profound interspecies event occurred in 1963 while working as a research fellow at the UCLA Brain Research Institute. We young scientists were encouraged to experiment with anything, with soft-furred rodents, with a lost dog, a litter of alley cats. Most of all we wanted close kin—chimpanzees. But we'd settle for monkeys: rhesus and nemestrina, cynomolgus, and the red-faced Japanese macaque. Settle for distant cousins in gunmetal cages, a meter square; tree swingers boxed with barely room to stand.

I remember tough-muscled monkeys pacing in small circles, rocking on red rumps, sucking thumbs. Hear them chatter high pitch at me in the morning when I troop into the lab. I inhale the thick brown musty smell of flaked skin, matted hair and sawdust soaked in urine, caked to lumps of feces, burnt-bronze, texture of wet Purina monkey chow. I snicker back, smile my big teeth, huff thanks to turned backs, their shows of submission. If time allows I accept their invitations to put a forearm against the links, let brown fingers scratch for invisible ticks, let pink tongue lick salt from my skin. Those monkeys taught me how to talk with animals. For years we groomed and gestured, cooed and smacked. And for years I also restrained, invaded, implanted, and shocked.

Then one day a frightened janitor tracked me down in a colleague's office to tell me that a pigtailed macaque had escaped from his cage and was ransacking my lab. This had never happened to me before. Handling a scared monkey in a cage or experimental chamber was one thing:

catching an escapee was another. I became terribly nervous as I walked through the long dingy corridor. I entered the room and peered through the haze and clutter; a familiar smacking sound drew my eyes to the far wall. Snicky, a three-year-old male, stared down at me from atop a bookcase, hair on end, eyes wide, teeth bared. Half terrified and thinking him hostile, unsure what to do, I mechanically smacked my lips at him, our usual morning greeting. He shuddered through a kind of tension meltdown and at once jumped from the shelf, leapt into my arms, and held on.

In the distance he had seemed so huge, imposing, wild. Now in my arms he was small, vulnerable, dependent. I sat on the linoleum floor with this animal in my lap—cleaned the scab that edged his dental-cement skullcap, checked his implanted electrodes to be sure they hadn't loosened, and examined his dilated eyes. I remember thinking, "After all I've done to him, he wants my friendship more than his freedom." I cried. This profound experience turned me away from medical research. I had become too bonded to continue. How could one experiment on his friends? I managed to complete my research and moved into a field where I could work with people in creative innovative endeavors—as far as I could get from the laboratory lives of trial and tragedy.

Scientists who study monkeys and apes in the wild have a better chance of keeping detached and staying focused on their inquiry. But epiphanies come rarely to the scientific mind-set. For years Professor Carl van Schaik has been tracking wild animals across the Indonesian archipelago. I was thrilled by his precision when he described orangutan tool manufacturing—a behavior never before seen in the wild. It takes particular knowledge and experience to empathize with the profundity of a discovery such as his.

Van Schaik reports that, in the peat swamps of western Sumatra, when conditions are right—enough holes in trees; enough sweatbees, ants, and termites in the holes; enough hunger to stir the curiosity—then an orangutan will manufacture chisels. He describes with a palpable excitement how he and his assistants watched wild apes perform this chain of behavior time after time: break twigs off just the right size, chew one end into a sponge, bite a wedge off the other end, grip the wedge end in front teeth, push the sponge into the hole to sop up insects, and drag out and

gobble up enough soaked ants to fill the belly with protein to last till the fig trees go to fruit. Carl's hard-sought findings about the conditions for invention in our ape ancestors are fantastic, but what I find equally exciting is the relentless appetite Dr. van Schaik has for discovery that sends him scurrying deep into the rain forest, slugging through mud, liana, and leeches for days and months and years upon years just to watch orange apes poking around for bugs.

The scientist's appetite for discovery was rewarded by observation of wild orangutan behavior that has been missed by all other observers. This is the kind of epiphany that scientific researchers live for, in which the animal *Exhibits Natural Reactions which Illuminate Crucial Hypotheses* (the ENRICH scenario). The conditions for wild orangutan invention and the persistent scientist had not intersected before in the forest. By staying sufficiently detached and returning again and again, van Schaik and his research team proved something profoundly important to students of evolution.

Of course, everyone who works with orangutans in captive settings knows that they are tool makers. The capacity is exhibited daily in zoos and rehabilitation centers. Some discount this as mere mimicry of humans. Others rebut—mimicry is something else orangutans and humans have in common. In science, one person's epiphany is another person's target.

When Randy Harwood returned to shore to tell his friends about the close encounter with squid, some were envious, others were skeptical, and others laughed. If Dr. Harwood were a marine biologist, he might never have retold his story. But he's an adventurer, willing to accept the possibility that the world holds mysteries we cannot explain but can know only through empathy and intuition.

Why are we excited to find that wild orangutans make tools or that squid confer among themselves about floating humans? Other animals are not likely to teach us much we don't already know about tool use or about language. Those are human specialties. But they can show us the depth of fascination and affinity every living being has for its environment and the animals in it, including the human interlopers. Other animals have biophilia too. That makes us feel akin to them—and kinship is profoundly satisfying.

The Near-Life Experience

The longer a scientist stays in the wild, the harder it is to remain separated from the individual animals he or she sees every day. It's one thing to advance scientific knowledge or to experience the wonders of nature with aplomb. It's another to watch orphaned apes suffer the loss of their mothers and homeland to poachers and woodcutters. Biruté Galdikas has watched many such events and has had to respond. Twenty-seven years ago Galdikas, like Dian Fossey and Jane Goodall, took the Louis Leakey challenge to study great apes in their rain forest habitat. Before that she had only seen orangutans in photos.

Galdikas's first contact was with macaques housed in the basement of the UCLA psychology department. As an undergraduate, she groomed and talked to the curious animals when the scientist who was working with them wasn't there. She didn't know then that I was that scientist. We met three decades later at an international conference on orangutans: that's when we discovered our earlier connection and common interests.

Biruté was immediately taken by my observation that the profound moments in human-animal interaction follow measurable and predictable patterns. When I suggested that the most powerful natural epiphanies seemed similar to the mysterious Near-Death Experience (NDE)—a kind of "crossing over" from one world to another, Biruté became animated and enthralled.

"Yes, you are right—I believe you have done what every scientist longs to do—identified an important phenomenon and given it a label. I am sure what you call the Profound Interspecies Event (PIE) is real, and you definitely must study it." A year later, after tracking in the Borneo rain forest where Biruté had done her early research, we met again in Los Angeles. This time I turned on a tape recorder, and we spent an afternoon talking about our major moments observing and interacting with orangutans and other wildlife. From that interview I have selected an excerpt which is especially revealing of the power of these interspecies epiphanies.

Biruté and I had been talking about the Dyak concept of "ghost" as it applies to the orangutan. I asked her if the time that her wild orangutan

daughter Akmad brought a newborn baby ape to Camp Leakey after being unseen in some far-off forest for a year was like a ghost coming through the barrier between two worlds. This led to a series of remarkable insights into the profound interspecies event. Here's the verbatim interview:

Galdikas: As I understand the Dyak cosmology . . . the ghost is something totally unpredictable because it's not of this world. This creates a huge barrier.

Rose: Then we might seem like ghosts to other species?

Galdikas: Of course, I operate in a different world, and the orangutan, the chimp, the zebra, or giraffe has to get past that barrier, too.

Rose: Then would you say Akmad came through that barrier to visit mama . . . did you think of yourself fully as mama then?

Galdikas: Oh, absolutely. I had this relationship where she was very close, stayed with me, touched me, clung to me. She obviously wanted that closeness once. But that all disappeared with adolescence. This distancing had occurred, and suddenly, with this experience . . . I was allowed through. It must be like physicists talk about these wormholes that allow for time travel but they're the size of one electron . . . a wormhole from one universe to the other . . . and that's what it was.

Rose: Who had traveled through?

Galdikas: In this case I traveled through, but she had allowed me to travel through. . . . she allowed me to pass into her world.

Rose: Can you describe what it felt like? Was it fast, or did it happen slowly?

Galdikas: It was more like a freefall down the wormhole. You know the Doors' song—*Break on Through to the Other Side*? All those images come to mind and came to mind at that time. I'd been studying orangutans for fifteen years. I had actually been there, I already was there, but that incident . . .

Rose: It took the last bit of you in and said you are there...

Galdikas: Right. But she allowed it. She was the one who did it. It wasn't me.

Rose: Can you describe what she did that allowed it?

Galdikas: She wouldn't allow Mr. Achyar to touch her baby. It was when she attacked him, that's when it occurred. I had never seen Akmad like that ... she's basically a wild orangutan who entered the human life for a short while and then left. When she attacked Mr. Achyar, that's when the pie occurred.... *She told me I was in her world and Mr. Achyar wasn't.* Mr. Achyar was astute enough to know what had happened—he's had those PIEs. If we could access the depths of his soul...

Rose: You'd get plenty of them.

Galdikas: Yes ... his whole life has been shaped by them....

Rose: And yours... and Akmad's... when she came back?

Galdikas: Yes ... it was mutual ...

Rose: You were both in a mutual place ... and zap ...

Galdikas: ... that's really true, that moment was truly profound, that moment was one of those moments—the nanoseconds when you see the eyes of God, you're one with nature.... It's so intense that it must have physical or physiological correlates ... and you're experiencing God!

Rose: Akmad let you know that you were God?

Galdikas: That she was God ... it came through her.

Rose: Through her?

Galdikas: That she was the wormhole to God.

It is instructive to examine this report carefully. At first I interpreted the published story of Akmad's return from the wild with her baby as a

powerful *humanistic* event, like mine with the macaque or Harwood's with the squid, in which an animal seeks a friendly encounter with a human. That seems a fair reading of the incident from the orangutan point of view. But focusing on the spiritual power of the report, I began to see the event as akin to my experience with the death of our mama tortoise—an awe-inspiring *naturalistic* event in which I was *Shown an Extraordinary Element of Nature* (the SEEN scenario).

Of course Biruté's experience was awesome and spiritual. But what was most profound for her was the contrasting hostile reaction of Akmad to Mr. Achyar—an empirical detail that informed a moment of profound *scientific enlightenment*. Biruté's humanistic response to her orangutan daughter's return with a newborn grandchild was catapulted to an epiphany when Akmad demonstrated that it was Biruté, and no one else, that she had come to share her baby with. That is when Biruté felt herself being taken through the tunnel to face suddenly a proven Truth—that she and this orangutan were in one world, pure kindred spirits in union within the original and evolving Creation.

What is important to all of us here is the fact that a wild animal, cared for during a difficult time in childhood, may return to live in the wilderness yet retain affinity for particular members of its foster family. So much affinity that when the ape has her own child, she brings it to show to one foster human parent while enforcing the distance of others. Again, those epiphanies that are characterized as scientific and naturalistic by their reporters have a central humanistic component. The discoveries and realizations that move us most, that we never forget, always seem to tell us something personally important about ourselves and our kinship with the other animals.

THE ULTIMATE EPIPHANY

Early in this journey Jane Goodall sent me to see Marc Cusano. Marc worked for seven years as caretaker of more than thirty chimpanzees living on five moated islands in the Lion Country Safari wildlife park in West Palm Beach, Florida. Cusano's fame among primate caretakers is earned. With heroic effort he managed to befriend chimpanzees that

were exceedingly hostile to all other humans. Powerful apes that once chased or threw him off their islands came to accept him. The occasion when the ostensibly mean alpha male named Old Man ran to rescue his human friend, threw off four other chimps who had Marc pinned down and were biting him fiercely, and helped Marc get back to his boat and off the island, is often told as the ultimate interspecies event.

In his home in Florida, Marc told me that this event, which Jane Goodall has described in two books, while incredibly profound, was just one of many peak experiences in his career working with chimps. As I listened to Cusano I realized that he may be the only human alive who has become an integral part of chimpanzee society. Sunrise to sunset, and often into the night, Marc Cusano worked and played, fought and reconciled, ate and slept with these different bands of apes.

From teaching the apes how to scare hippos and cattle off their islands to convincing them that his skin was too thin and they had to pull their punches to play with him, Marc Cusano has as much to tell about our own primate nature as anyone I've met. At the end of six hours of stories I was hard-pressed to decide what was his greatest natural epiphany. He wouldn't say.

I think Marc's most wonderful experiences happened later, after all the animals had accepted him, during the years when interspecies conflict had subsided and enduring friendship emerged. Marc remembered countless afternoons when he had fed all the chimps, cleaned up trash, repaired structures, and had a couple of hours left to play with the guys. He describes how they wrestled, raced, and climbed, his keeping up as best he could, their helping as best they could. If it was hot, they tired faster.

The alpha male climbed into the shade of a culvert in the center of the island. Two other males were already there grooming. Marc, who was second in the hierarchy, secured his boat, then walked over, sat down, and began grooming his friend. As usual, the others made space for him. Then one chimp lay over and fell asleep, leaning against Marc. Marc lay down by him, and another animal came to join them. Marc dozed, and soon there were five chimps with him, all asleep. Perhaps a half hour later he woke up—the others had gone, save one who slumbered beside him in perfect peace.

Marc talks about "a kind of tranquillity I never felt anywhere else, certainly not with human friends." I imagine the deep peace he must have experienced, heavy with the contentment of unquestioned brotherhood, smooth skin and coarse hair pressed together, the smells, the heat of bodies, the soft breathing—his absolutely wordless ape mind in total communion with the beings around him. Marc had worked day after day, sunup to sundown, and beyond into dark nights, to reach this point that no other human has ever experienced—all chimpanzees, all brothers under the sun and stars.

These animals did not want to be with Marc merely to play, to groom, or to eat. They truly valued his presence—who he was mattered to them. They loved him, and they could affirm their love of him by lying down beside his sleeping body and slumbering with him—communing serene in their common home. Twelve years ago Marc had to leave his chimpanzee friends. He hasn't seen them since, but they still haunt his dreams. If he ever goes back, I want to be there. It will be a reunion!

ACTS OF REUNION

Albert Einstein wrote that the enlightened person "looks upon individual existence as a sort of prison and wants . . . to feel the sublimity and marvelous order which reveal themselves both in nature and in the world of thought." Natural scientists like van Schaik, Galdikas, and Goodall, adventurers like Harwood, animal caretakers like Cusano, have felt that sublimity and marvelous order. They have risked total immersion in their corners of wilderness and have experienced the reunion of humanity and nature. George Schaller speaks from deep experience when he says, "The recent decades have been a turning point, indeed a revolution in our relationship with animals. Humans have begun to overcome cross-species barriers, achieving intimacy with humpback whales, chimpanzees, lions, mountain sheep, wolves . . . the gorilla, of course, is more than an animal. These apes are part of human heritage. Our kin." In this essay and this volume, we struggle to bring that kinship experience to the world of thought.

These worlds in which we evolve, that primordial ooze, the sea, the beachhead, the swamp, and the savanna, are home to us and to all

our common ancestors. We commit countless acts of reunion. From the fleshy tunnels and watery caves where we are conceived to the mudholes and mouths where we die, all forms of glory on this planet blend in mysterious ballets and symphonies, all minds and voices contribute, all eyes and ears are tuned to the numinous interplay of life. The biota of earth is interwoven in an ever-changing *biosynergy*, like threads on a multi-dimensional loom, the tapestry of nirvana. Tortoises, monkeys, and men—we are all strands of blood and bone, spirit and feeling, informing the dance of many, calling out in the voice of all.

For Further Reading

Kellert, Stephen R. 1996. *The Value of Life: Biological Diversity and Human Society*. Washington, D.C.: Island Press.

Montgomery, Sy. 1991. *Walking with the Great Apes*. Boston: Houghton-Mifflin.

Rose, Anthony L. 1996. "Orangutan, Science and Collective Reality." In *The Neglected Ape*. Ed. Nadler, Galdikas et al. 29–40. New York: Plenum Press.

Schaller, George. 1995. "Gentle Gorillas, Turbulent Times." In *National Geographic*, October: 65–83.

DEEP ETHOLOGY

MARC BEKOFF

WHAT ANIMALS HAVE TAUGHT ME

After reading one of my papers on animal welfare, a colleague asked, "Hey, are you trying to put us out of business?" While some of my colleagues may conclude that I am trying as hard as I can to end my career as a scientist and also to hamper their own work, I would like to assure them that this is not the case.

I consider myself lucky and privileged to have been able to have made the intimate acquaintance of many and diverse animals—to be touched by their essence and by their presence. However, in some instances, they were not as lucky or as privileged to make my acquaintance, as I certainly had a negative influence on their lives.

The animals' collective influence, which has resulted from their unselfish and intimate sharing of their lives with me—I am sure that in some instances they were watching, smelling, hearing, and studying me as closely as I was observing them—is clearly reflected in my views on the nature of animal minds, on animal well-being, and on the business of science.

These include: (1) taking the animals' points of view; (2) putting respect, compassion, and admiration for other animals first and foremost; (3) erring on the animals' side when uncertain about their feeling pain or suffering; (4) recognizing that almost all of the methods that are used to study animals, even in the field, are intrusions on their lives—much research is fundamentally exploitive; (5) recognizing how misguided are speciesistic views concerning vague notions, such as intelligence and cognitive or mental complexity, for informing assessments of well-being;

(6) focusing on the importance of individuals; (7) appreciating individual variation and the diversity of the lives of different individuals in the worlds within which they live; (8) using broadly based rules of fidelity and nonintervention as guiding principles; and (9) appealing to what some call questionable practices that have no place in the conduct of science, such as the use of common sense and empathy.

Although I have always been concerned with animal well-being, I have not always applied the same standards of conduct to my own research. I have done experiments on predatory behavior in infant coyotes in which mice and chickens were provided as bait in staged encounters that I would never do again.

What I mean by the phrase "I am sure that in some instances they were watching, smelling, hearing, and studying me as closely as I was observing them" is simply, but surely *not* trivially, that while observing these wonderful and amazing carnivores, I can recall feeling their presence and curiosity about who I and my field team were and what we were doing.

When we encountered our first wild coyote, I remember having the same feeling that I had when I saw my first Adélie penguin in Antarctica—"What in the world am I doing here and what am I doing to these animals who never asked for me to come here in the first place?" With the coyotes, their eyes were open wide and piercing, their noses were held upright, and clearly they were taking in our odors, and their ears were erect and moving around—they wanted to vacuum us up into their different and well-developed senses and learn about us. They were keenly curious. I often thought then, as I do now, that, if these animals could record their findings, knowledge about human behavior would be markedly increased!

I also want to stress how important are broad, comparative, and evolutionary studies of animal behavior. These types of endeavors will help us to learn more about individual animal's worlds and allow us to apply standards of conduct more in line with the needs of the individual members of the diverse taxa that are studied—for example, how they live and use modalities other than vision. Humans are strongly visual animals, and perhaps we need to pay more attention to the fact that animals can

be both helped and harmed by exposure to, for example, auditory or olfactory stimuli.

I also reject the notion of *speciesism*, in which animals are treated according to the biological species to which they are assigned. I prefer the view that the moral consideration of *individuals* is of paramount importance in any debate about how humans view and treat their animal counterparts (as well as other humans). Human activities that result in the loss of individual lives must be given serious attention, for there seems to be little (but in my view there should be no) question that animals are a vulnerable class of individuals deserving protection.

HAVING IT BOTH WAYS AND GIVING ANIMALS THE BENEFIT OF THE DOUBT

If some of what I write seems naive or "unscientific," this is how I really feel when I let my hair down and allow myself to become detached from the strong constraints of supposedly objective, value-free science. Scientists rarely expose publicly their deep thoughts about human-nonhuman relationships and the world in general. Perhaps the business of science would be more respected nowadays if more people who did science also showed that they thought deeply about what they are doing and claiming. I like collecting anecdotes and numbers, doing statistics, making tables, and drawing graphs, but I also greatly enjoy being intimately connected to the animals I study.

However "schizophrenic" it may seem, I have no doubt that one can have it both ways—you can do "good science" and also respect and form intimate relationships with the animals with whom you work. But I also assert that it is wrong for humans intentionally to cause harm to any human or nonhuman animal or purposely to kill any human or non-human animal, whether sea horses, ants, bees, worms, rats, mice, birds, cats, dogs, chickens, cows, or primates. While this may seem somewhat "radical," I believe that if it is used as a guiding principle, then it will force those who are in the position to use and to abuse animals to think deeply about what they are doing *every time* they make a decision to use an individual.

When in doubt about the negative effects of intentional human action directed toward nonhumans, whether for purposes of research, education, amusement, or food, *we should err on the side of animals.*

Similar suggestions have been offered for humans. For example, with respect to pain in infants, Fitzgerald claims that the question "Do infants feel pain?" is unanswerable and unhelpful when taken at face value. She notes that it is "better to assume that they do, take a step sideways, and ask the question, 'Can we measure pain responses in infants, and are these measures sensitive to analgesics?'"[1] The study of facial expression in infants seems to be one of the most promising measures of their pain responses.

THE JOYS OF ANTHROPOMORPHISM

In my own studies I am freely anthropomorphic and wonder why some of my colleagues view anthropomorphism as a disease. For example, John S. Kennedy writes that we can be confident that anthropomorphism will be "brought under control, even if it cannot be cured completely. Although it is probably programmed into us genetically as well as being inoculated culturally, that does not mean the disease is untreatable."[2] Kennedy is typical of critics who write as if the only alternatives are an unconstrained, fuzzy-minded use of anthropomorphism on the one hand and the total elimination of anthropomorphism on the other.

But there is a middle position which they ignore. Anthropomorphism can be useful if it serves to focus attention on questions about animal behavior that might otherwise be ignored. I recall knowing that the remaining members in a pack of coyotes missed the female who was both a mother and wife when she voluntarily left the group. When she left for forays of increasing duration, various individuals would look at her curiously, and some would follow her. When she returned, they would greet her effusively and lick her muzzle—they had missed her when she was gone. One day she left the pack and never again returned. The pack waited for days and days. They traveled in the direction she had gone, sniffed where she might have been, and howled as if calling her home. For more than a week, some spark seemed to have gone out of them.

They missed her. I know that this sounds anthropomorphic, but that doesn't bother me. I know that coyotes have deep and complicated feelings.

MINDING ANIMALS AND BREAKING LOOSE FROM TRADITIONAL MIND-SETS

Ruth Hubbard writes, "At that point I was working with squid, and I think squid are the most beautiful animals in the world. And it just began to bother me. I began to have the feeling that nothing I could find out was worth killing another squid."[3]

According to my parents, I have always "minded animals," respecting them, caring for them, feeling for them, and attributing minds (mental states and content) to individuals. I used to ask about what animals might be thinking or feeling as they went about their daily activities. Since I began working with animals, I have always spent a lot of time pondering nonhuman-human relationships. Now I often find myself obsessed with the terrible things that humans do to other animals with whom they share this planet. I recognize fully that most people who harm nonhumans for purposes of research, education, or amusement also might bring some joy to some animals at other times. No rational humans, I hope, would ever want to curtail activities that benefit animals, whereas, many, I fear, do not see the necessity for curtailing activities that produce pain, suffering, and death—wanton disrespect for animals.

As time goes on, I find myself growing more and more "radical." I place the word *radical* in scare quotes because it also strikes me as perverse that to some, "radical" means giving animals the benefit of the doubt with respect to their capacities to suffer and experience pain rather than referring to more permissive attitudes concerning the use of nonhumans by humans.

My early scientific training as an undergraduate and a beginning graduate student was grounded in what Bernard Rollin calls the "common sense of science," in which science is viewed as a fact-gathering, value-free activity. Of course, science is not value-free, but it took some time for me to come to this realization because of the heavy indoctrination and arrogance concerning the need for scientific objectivity. I am thrilled

to have been given the opportunity to break the reins of unemotional austerity and to form close partnerships with the animals who have entered my life and have allowed me to enter their lives.

With respect to the plight of the nonhumans who were used in classes or for research, there was little or no overt expression of concern for their well-being. Questions concerning morals and ethics rarely arose. When they did, they were invariably dismissed either by invoking what I have come to call "vulgar" or "facile" utilitarianism, in which suspected costs and benefits were offered from the human's point of view with no concern for the nonhuman's perspective, or by simply asserting that the animal really didn't know, care, or mind (or whatever word could be used to communicate the animal's supposed indifference to) what was going on. Only once do I remember someone vaguely implying that something beneficial for the animal might come out of a research project.

One afternoon one of my professors calmly strutted into class announcing, while sporting a wide grin, that he was going to kill a rabbit for us to use in an experiment by using a method named after the rabbit himself, namely, a "rabbit punch." He proceeded to kill the rabbit, breaking his neck by chopping him with the side of the hand. I was astonished and sickened by the entire spectacle. I refused to partake in the laboratory exercise and also decided that what I was doing at the time was simply wrong for me. I began to think seriously about alternatives. I enjoyed science, but I suspected that there were other ways for doing science that centered on incorporating respect for animals and allowing for individual differences among scientists concerning how science is done in the first place.

My laboratory and field experience has shown me that all behavioral research is interventive, even that which appears merely to be simple observation. This fact must be taken seriously by all researchers. Increasingly I recognize the crucial links between evolutionary biology, cognitive ethology, moral philosophy, philosophy of mind, and animal rights. Many prominent scientists have recently attacked those who are interested in animal protection. In one essay concerning how scientists are supposedly being selectively targeted by proponents of animal rights,

it is interesting to note the combative tone of the subtitle ("Ammunition for counter-offensive for scientists")—you'd think they were fighting a world war. Well, maybe they think they are, and this is too bad, for they are not. I am not (and have never been) anti-science, nor a Luddite, and I certainly do not want to halt all animal research, at least not right now.

One can do science, question scientific practices, yet respect animals. When I think about ethical and moral issues and how humans and non-humans ought to interact, I find it difficult to come up with a consistent train of thought. Sometimes I find myself concluding that all animal research should be terminated, along with the use of animals in education and for amusement and food. At other moments, when, for example, I think about research that can benefit animals as well as humans, I retreat back to my principled and highly restrictive moderate stance, which centers on (1) accepting that it is almost always wrong to harm other animals; (2) assuming that all individuals, regardless of species, suffer to some degree; (3) using as few animals as possible only when there are no alternatives; (4) using the most humane methods known; (5) being certain that the well-being of all animals is given serious attention after they have been used; (6) telling all potential readers of scientific papers how animals were negatively affected by the research so that others could avoid making the same mistakes; and (7) recognizing that humans are necessarily anthropocentric and that the animal's point of view can never be totally understood and appreciated regardless of how right-minded are individual people.

In the best of all possible worlds, animals would not be used at all. Limited time, money, energy, and motivation are not excuses for using animals when alternatives are available or can be developed.

Toward a Deep Ethology:
Naming and Bonding with Animals

Lawrence Johnson writes, "Certainly it seems like a dirty double-cross to enter into a relationship of trust and affection with any creature that can enter into such a relationship, and then to be a party to its premeditated and premature destruction."[4]

Let me emphasize once again that *studying nonhuman animals is a privilege that must not be abused*. We must take this privilege seriously. Many principles have been proposed that perhaps could guide us in our treatment of animals: utilitarian ones, rights-based ones, interests-based ones, and so forth. Scientists often operate on the basis of implicit principles and guidelines that are often not discussed. All of these principles need to be brought out into the open and explicitly debated.

First and foremost in any deliberations about other animals must be deep concern and respect for their lives and the worlds within which they live—respect for who they are in their worlds, and not respect motivated by who we want them to be in our anthropocentric scheme of things. As Paul Taylor notes, a switch away from anthropocentrism to biocentrism, in which human superiority comes under critical scrutiny, "may require a profound moral reorientation."[5] Can we really believe that we are the only species with feelings, beliefs, desires, goals, expectations, the ability to think, the ability to think about things, the ability to feel pain, or the capacity to suffer?

We need to talk to the animals and let them talk to us. Surprises are always forthcoming concerning the cognitive skills of nonhumans, and it is essential that people who write about animal issues be cognizant of these findings. I do not see how any coherent thoughts about moral and ethical aspects of animal use could be put forth without using biological/evolutionary, ethological, and philosophical information. Ethologists must read philosophy and philosophers must not only read ethology but also watch animals.

I believe that a deep reflective ethology is needed to make people more aware of what they do to nonhumans and to make them aware of their moral and ethical obligations to animals. I use the term *deep reflective ethology* to convey some of the same general ideas that underlie the "deep ecology" movement in which it is asked that people recognize that not only are they an integral part of nature but also that they have unique responsibilities to nature.

Most people who think deeply about the troubling issues surrounding animal welfare would agree that the use of animals in research and education and for amusement and food needs to be severely restricted,

and in some cases simply stopped. Our unique responsibilities to the world mandate, in my view, that a noninterventionist policy should be our goal in the future. Accepting that most nonhuman animals experience pain and do suffer, even if it is not necessarily the same sort of pain and suffering that is experienced by humans or even other nonhumans, and rigorously determining just how invasive most animal studies are, is essential. Many books in the popular press also are helpful in communicating messages concerned with animal rights to a wide audience.

Adopting a commonsense approach to many of the issues, especially how we view not only the cognitive skills of nonhumans but also their pain and suffering, will make this a better world in which humans and nonhumans can live compatibly. What one believes about the cognitive capacities of nonhumans informs how he or she thinks about animal rights—different views dispose a person to look at animals in particular ways. Ascribing intentionality and other cognitive abilities to animals is not moot if there are moral consequences, and there are.

We and the animals who we use should be viewed as partners in a joint venture. As Nobel laureate Barbara McClintock notes, we must have a feeling for the organisms with whom we are privileged to work. Thus, bonding with animals and calling animals by name are steps in the right direction. It seems unnatural for humans to continue to resist developing bonds with the animals whom they study. By bonding with animals, one should not fear that the animals' points of view will be dismissed. In fact, bonding will result in a deeper examination and understanding of the animals' points of view, and this knowledge will inform further studies on the nature of human-animal interactions.

If we forget that humans and other animals are all part of the same world, and if we forget that humans and animals are deeply connected at many levels of interaction, when things go amiss in our interactions with animals, as they surely will, and animals are set apart from and inevitably below humans, I feel certain that we will miss the animals more than the animal survivors will miss us. The interconnectivity and spirit of the world will be lost forever, and these losses will make for a severely impoverished universe.

For Further Reading

Allen, C., and M. Bekoff. 1997. *Species of Mind: The Philosophy and Biology of Cognitive Ethology*. Cambridge, Mass.: MIT Press.

Bekoff, M. 1997. "'Do Dogs Ape' or 'Do Apes Dog?' Broadening and Deepening Cognitive Ethology." *Animal Law* 3:13–23.

Bekoff, M. (ed.) 1998. *Encyclopedia of Animal Rights and Animal Welfare*. Westport, Conn.: Greenwood Publishing Group, Inc.

Bekoff, M. 1998. "Deep Ethology." *AV Magazine* (a publication of the American Anti-Vivisection Society), 106(1):10–18 (Winter).

Bekoff, M. 1999. "Deep Ethology, Cognitive Ethology, and the Great Ape/Animal Project: Expanding the Community of Equals." In *Applied Ethics in Animal Research*. Ed. J. Gluck and B. Orlans. West Lafayette, Ind.: Purdue University Press.

References

1. Fitzgerald, M. 1987. "Pain and Analgesia in Neonates." *Trends in Neurosciences* 10:346.

2. Kennedy, J. S. 1992. *The New Anthropomorphism*. 167. New York: Cambridge University Press.

3. Quoted in Holloway, M. 1995. "Profile: Ruth Hubbard—Turning the Inside Out." *Scientific American*, 272:49–50.

4. Johnson, L. E. 1991. *A Morally Deep World: An Essay on Moral Significance and Environmental Ethics*. 122. New York: Cambridge University Press.

5. Taylor, P. W. 1986. *Respect for Nature: A Theory of Environmental Ethics*. 313. Princeton, N.J.: Princeton University Press.

OTHER NATIONS

KELLY STEWART

For the animal shall not be measured by man. In a world older and more complete than ours they move finished and complete, gifted with extensions of the senses we have lost or never attained, living by voices we shall never hear. They are not brethren, they are not underlings, they are other Nations, caught with ourselves in the net of life and time, fellow prisoners of the splendour and travail of the earth.

—*Henry Beston, 1928*

Charismatic megafauna. This is what gorillas are called in current conservation jargon. In plain English, it means they are big, beautiful animals that capture our imaginations and break our hearts. Perhaps it has something to do with the slow and dignified way in which they move. Whatever the reason, to be close to a wild gorilla for the first time is a transcendental experience that will change your soul; you will never forget the awe and reverence they stir in your breast, the feeling that you have just looked into the face of Nature.

But what if you are someone who spends hours and hours, day in and day out, in the presence of gorillas? What if you are a researcher studying behavior and ecology? What kind of emotional responses do scientists experience toward their subjects, and what do the animals feel about the scientists?

Science is commonly viewed as being a desensitizing, anesthetic discipline. Just the other day I read this statement in a respected literary magazine: "Science is taking away our capacity for wonder." As part of this picture, researchers who study animals are seen as emotionally distanced

from their subjects, regarding them as data points for graphs and fodder for theories. Scientific understanding is not actually believed to be "true" or "deep" understanding.

The general public embraces pioneering researchers like Jane Goodall and Dian Fossey, not as scientists but as heroic figures whose love for their animals led to unique insights and understanding of them. Indeed, many regard these heroines as having accomplished their goals despite science. Basically, research is seen as incompatible with an emotional attachment toward one's animals. Scientific knowledge kills empathy. This stereotype is close to being the opposite of the truth. I don't know any good biologists who are not driven by a love for and wonder at the natural world. And I can't think of a better candidate than scientific understanding for instilling this love and wonder in others.

I studied wild mountain gorillas for several years while based at Dian Fossey's research camp in Rwanda. For months at a time I'd spend every day following a gorilla group through the forest, clipboard, pen, and stopwatch in hand. I had check sheets divided into columns for different behaviors, and rows for time intervals. Into the grids, I would record in detail, timed in seconds, the behavior of my study subjects, identified by initials: "Ef approaches Pu within 5 meters; Pu makes no response; Pu feeds on wild celery; Ef grunts and Pu responds with grunt; Bv approaches Pu within 2 meters, Pu leaves"—the entries for half a minute. I recorded page after page, hour after hour.

This plodding activity may seem a far cry from anything that might be called "communing with Nature." Yet such dispassionate, detailed methodology provided a special looking glass into the gorillas' lives, bringing the animals into sharp focus while blurring my own reality. When I moved into the midst of a gorilla group, I moved into their world, checking most of my human baggage at the gate. What mattered was appreciating them for what they were, not for how they made me feel. This is the beauty and strength of objective, scientific observation. It enables us to seek Nature on its own terms, as Thoreau wrote, "to conceive of a region not inhabited by man."

Gorillas evolved a social order that does not include humans, and this is the system we seek to understand. Science does not ban insights based

on personal intuition (known as "anthropomorphism"), but it demands a distinction between "it is" (bad anthropomorphism) and "it is as if" (good anthropomorphism). A scientific perspective does not kill emotional reactions to animals; rather, it allows an understanding that is separate from these reactions. It fosters interpretations of their behavior that are relatively free from our human longings, values, and judgments.

Take, for instance, the killing of infants. Adult male gorillas, called silverbacks for the saddle of gray-white hair they develop at maturity, are extremely tolerant and protective of infants who are likely to be their own, or at least close relatives. These will be infants born to the females in their group. It is not unusual to see a silverback during a rest period surrounded by playing youngsters, while the mothers are nowhere in sight—off for a bit of uninterrupted feeding or just peace and quiet. Infants chase each other around and around the big male while he rests, climbing up the front of his head and sliding down his sloping silver back. If a mother dies, her infant turns to the silverback for solace, and he pays special attention to it, in a sense, "adopting" the orphan.

In striking contrast, if a male encounters infants that are unrelated to him, in other words, infants of unfamiliar females, he turns into a killer. When would this situation arise? Imagine that the silverback of a group dies and there is no other adult male in the group to assume leadership. In this case, all females, including mothers with infants, will scatter and join other groups or lone males. The new silverbacks will welcome the incoming females but will deliberately kill any infant who is less than about two years of age.

Many people cannot see infanticide as anything other than pathological behavior with no function, as if the killing male had suddenly gone mad or been temporarily possessed by evil. But mightn't this attitude simply be a reflection of our own emotional responses to baby-killing? Doesn't it pass judgment on gorillas? What if we step out of the ethical framework we apply to humans and objectively examine infanticide? We arrive at an explanation, one that has emerged after years of observation, that does not invoke the vision of psychopathic silverbacks.

When a male kills a young infant, the mother comes back into reproductive condition, which is suspended as long as that female is nursing a

baby. A gorilla mother does not normally wean her offspring until sometime during its third year. But if she loses the baby, she will be ready to mate again within two weeks. By killing the infants of unfamiliar females, a silverback is increasing his chances of mating and producing his own progeny sooner rather than later. This is an evolutionary explanation that sees infanticide in terms of animals' struggle to pass on their genes to the next generation.

The behavior has evolved in many other species of animals, from lions to mice, and occurs in similar situations, with similar outcomes as in gorillas. Viewed in this way, the strategy no longer seems senseless. We can predict when infanticide will occur, which males will commit it, and which infants will be killed. If infanticide were pathological, it would be more random and unpredictable.

While it is a terrible, heart-wrenching thing to see a baby gorilla that has been brutally bitten and killed by a silverback, there is a logic about infanticide that is beautiful, as Nature's logic often is. It is an important part of being a gorilla, and one cannot fully understand their social system without understanding this phenomenon, detached from human sentiment and moral judgment.

By "detached" I do not mean distant. I find it hard to imagine anyone who could observe gorillas and not feel a psychological and emotional bond with them. In addition to their "megafauna" mystique, they are so closely related to us that there exists a natural affinity between our species. Almost everything they do has a reminiscent look—the way they move their hands, the expressions in their eyes. We shared much of the same world. I used the same footholds and handholds they did to climb in and out of steep ravines. When the river swelled in the rainy season, we all crossed it at the same few fordable spots.

My sense of camaraderie with gorillas was heightened when we suffered the same adversity. When I was in their midst, I felt surrounded by kindred spirits, a feeling that was heightened when we suffered the same adversity. Imagine this: It's near the end of a long rest period and the gorillas are shifting and grumbling, getting ready to move off and feed again. Suddenly the sky darkens, a cold wind blows, and the heavens open, pelting us with hail. The gorillas and I hunker down against the

onslaught. We use the same movements to settle into the same position: legs tucked underneath us, arms folded across our chests, shoulders hunched and heads bowed. Sitting down, I am about the same height as the adult females. White hailstones accumulate in the crooks of our arms, and we are all hungry and cold. Comrades in misery.

At times like this I felt deep affection for the gorillas, as if they were my good friends, as if they had admitted me to their inner circle. I was tempted to feel flattered, but this would have supposed that my sentiments were reciprocated. Our species has always been seduced by the idea of being loved and honored by wild animals. It's the allure behind Tarzan and Mowgli. It's like a state of grace. Sometimes people ask me if the gorillas were glad to see me when I returned after a period of absence from the forest. There is disappointment when I say "no." It's a paradox: We love them for their wildness and freedom, and yet we want them to miss us when we're gone.

Wild animals do not need our companionship. They are not brethren. I imagine that the gorillas saw me as another animal, with familiar actions and reactions, but I'm quite sure they didn't consider me or any other observer as one of them. They didn't "like" us or seek relationships with us. On the sporadic occasions when they did interact with us, it was often to convey the message *Get out of my way*. If, for instance, we were sitting next to a plant they wanted to eat, then they might get us to move with the rough grunts that indicate mild aggression. Or if we were in the path of a young male's chest-beating display, he might give us a thump or knock us over. Sometimes youngsters would test us out to see if we were fun to play with as they did with other objects, from shrubs to silverbacks' feet. But the adults seemed to disapprove of such fraternizing and often put an end to it with a rough grunt.

They "accepted" us into their groups only in the sense that they tolerated our proximity. In the beginning, when they were not used to seeing humans regularly, they were wary of us. This gave way to curiosity, which enabled them to find out whether or not we were dangerous. It's important for wild animals to know what to expect. Since we always dressed in the same drab clothes and always behaved in the same deferent manner,

they gradually came to see us as safe and predictable. Once they had learned that we were not a threat, they largely ignored us.

Not to be feared. This is probably as close to Eden as our species is going to get. I was never so touched by the gorillas as when they turned their backs on me. Certainly the most moving photograph I've ever seen of a gorilla is the one taken by Bob Campbell, displayed on the dust jacket of Dian Fossey's book, *Gorillas in the Mist*. It is a close-up shot of a seated male, his head and shoulders sparkling with raindrops. We see him from the back because he is facing away from the camera. The silverback in the photo, Uncle Bert, was killed by poachers many years later.

The trust of wild animals is the ultimate privilege, but it comes with a terrible burden. If I had to put a name on the most intense emotion I experienced toward gorillas, it would be compassion: the heart-rending sort of compassion that comes from loving a vulnerable creature. When the gorillas were injured or died in the natural course of events—including infanticide—it was always sad but acceptable because this was the way of the gorilla world. But when the animals suffered at human hands, it was devastating. I felt as if I had betrayed them when they needed my protection, and the only thing they needed protecting from was humanity. In return for their trust, I had assumed responsibility, not just for my own behavior but for that of my entire species.

We humans have many different ways of harming gorillas. We drag them into our wars; we hunt them for meat or profit; we destroy their habitat by using it for ourselves. This last is the most pervasive and long-term damage we inflict, and as for other threatened species, it will be what pushes them into extinction.

Whenever a human-caused calamity befell the gorillas, the people who worked closely with them felt a burden of guilt. Perhaps this is why it became the practice at the Research Center to bury gorillas who had died at the hands of poachers in marked graves. Each had a cross bearing the animal's name. This Christian-style cemetery is a memorial. The graves hammer at our conscience, and I suppose this is fitting and proper, lest we forget, lest we relax our vigilance. But our duty to Nature should not be rooted in a sense of sin and a need for atonement.

It should be based on the acceptance of responsibility that goes, as part of the territory, with power.

We happen to be a species with a big brain that can invent ever more advanced technology, and this has led to power over other living creatures—the power to destroy or preserve. Because of this power, our species has a responsibility, not just to "charismatic megafauna" who have blessed us with their trust but to all of Nature. We will take this responsibility seriously only when we learn to value the existence and diversity of other life forms; this will come through understanding and appreciating these life forms on their own terms.

We cannot deny that our big brains have caused terrible destruction to this planet and the life that evolved on it. But remember also, these are the same big brains that can "...conceive of a region not inhabited by man." We must learn to hold that region sacred, to cherish and protect the "other Nations" of this earth.

TO LOVE LIKE A BIRD

LORIN LINDNER

As far back as I can remember, I've loved cows. Cow stories are part of my family's folklore along with stuffed cows, cow-design clothing, and cow-shaped furniture. Every year my parents would tote boxes of candies for the farm children along the way as we drove from New York to Florida. Very few families refused the request of a little three- or four-year-old girl to hold communion with their cows—and back then, plenty of cows were grazing along the road. We had to budget extra time into our trip for these cow stops.

No one else in my family shared the fascination I had for cows. Yet looking back, I think that their tolerance and even encouragement of this behavior—strange for a young girl born and raised in New York City—allowed my love for animals and the natural world to flourish. They did not understand it, and I frequently heard their musings to others: "Where could she have picked this up?" But there was no disapproval or ridicule, and I never got the idea that it had to stop.

The one place my family used caution, if not outright deception, was in getting me to eat my beloved creatures. Using euphemisms that would delude practically anyone, my family hid from me the fact that I was eating cow body parts (livers, tongues, flanks, rumps, etc.).

By the age of five, I developed a new passion—horses—and once again my family was curious but obliging. Soon, I also became devoted to birds. What my family could not or did not want to understand was the transition I made from having this uncanny attachment to animals to my being unwilling to eat them.

Trips to local pet shops soon became my favorite after-school treat. Holding scarlet macaws and cockatoos, I learned the contours of their

bodies—and they felt frighteningly similar to the chickens we would eat for dinner. When I was seven, my mother discovered me in the kitchen the night before Thanksgiving, cradling the defrosting Tom turkey in my arms. I was tall and gangly, and I remember my mother worrying over my "poor" eating habits. But I found it hard to eat anything that looked like it had once been an animal. As soon as I went away to college, I began making my own food choices—and they didn't include animals.

At college I thought that an emphasis in ethology would bring me closer to animals by helping me understand their behavior. When I think back, it was really a selfish motivation. I loved animals, but in a possessive, anthropocentric way. Although I told the chair of the biology department that I would not perform vivisection, I found it difficult not to be drawn into the world of scientific desensitization and objectification.

In the basement of the biology building, as at most universities, were the animal labs. The primates appeared so interesting to me because they are so much like us—ironic, isn't it? But there were also birds beckoning to me in this facility, so many birds. Many of them must have been former companion animals, as they would cling to the cage doors and call to be petted. Their eyes would follow me, and they would try so hard to get my attention it seemed their little hearts would break. I got some insight into one bird's former life by the words he would speak; the oft-repeated expression, "Bad bird, bad boy, stop that," made me imagine how this one guy may have ended up in the lab.

One female sulphur-crested cockatoo, a subspecies I never could resist, pleaded with me until, when all the other researchers were gone, I would tickle her through the bars. Many years later, I would rescue two salmon-crested cockatoos in need of a good home, and I would learn how closely attached these birds can become to humans and how much they thrive on physical contact. Thinking back on how that little sulphur-crest looked at me, how she once must have loved a human companion, how afraid she was and alone, why did I wait so long to comfort her, why did I do nothing else?

I could swear to you that I did not perform any of those egregious experiments, that I just wanted to be in the lab, as painful as it was for me, to try to change things. But all of those eyes, the way they watched

me, said that I was guilty, that by my silence I was giving assent to what was happening. I have still not completely come to terms with the collective trauma of all those lives. The little cockatoo, though, forgave me for her tribulations (the surgeries that wouldn't heal, the monotonous seed diet, the tiny cage, and more) in those few moments when she would bend her head into my hand and I would pull the feather casings from the places she couldn't reach.

But, of course, we budding scientists were reproached if we allowed emotion to interfere with "rational judgment." We were cautioned not to intrude on the "scientific method" by altering conditions that might confound the ongoing experiments. However, it was unclear to me how any study on animals in cages could be considered scientific, since there was no way to control for the numerous confounding variables that are endemic in the lab.

Of course the largest confounding factor is the very notion of making cross-species comparisons. In addition, experiments are confounded simply by isolation and confinement in unnatural settings; discomfort from electrodes, multiple surgeries, and healing wounds; lack of availability of native foods; inability to establish an appropriate hierarchy for feeding, grooming, and other social relatedness; and many other factors that can cause changes in brain chemistry and behavior and present extraneous variables to a study design.

The birds under our "care" were exempt from the federal Animal Welfare Act. Indeed, birds continue to be afforded no legal protection whatsoever—as an experimenter you can do essentially whatever you want to them. The Act offers only minimal protection anyway, mostly with regard to housing and exercise standards, for an increasingly smaller proportion of the animals used in research.

Ultimately, for those reasons and others, I switched to the study of human behavior and encountered a perpetually perplexing paradox—the premise behind psychological research on animals. That is, we start by saying that animals are similar to us in their need for conspecific affiliation, raising young, suckling, maternal-infant attachment, love, security, play, sleep, sensory stimulation, challenge, affection, tactile and gustatory gratification, grooming, sex, commitment; in their wish to

control their environment; in their avoidance of pain and seeking of pleasure; and in their emotional reactions such as anxiety, depression, jealousy, terror, and rage. And then we try to justify what is done to them in psychological research by saying that they don't experience suffering as we do.

Apart from this paradox, psychological research is often characterized by highly questionable methodology. Researchers may withhold anesthesia, claiming that it is procedurally necessary to do so and that this is allowed within the ethical guidelines of the American Psychological Association. For example, in pain research, the use of analgesic medication interferes with the study, so it does not have to be used.

In many other areas of psychological research, the suffering of animals is, itself, essential to the basic design of the experiment—for example, in learned helplessness studies of depression, often done in drowning tanks or with electric shocks; in studies of sleep and sensory deprivation that often go on until the animal goes insane; in starvation and water deprivation experiments, torture experiments, maternal-infant deprivation studies, self-mutilation studies, and drug-addiction studies.

What makes the situation even more distressing to me is that I have experienced the childlike innocence of these animals, the emotional intelligence, the benevolence, the benignity, the simple goodness, and I have seen all of that turned into a complete state of desolation.

If you dare to look at it and think about it, you start to realize that there are fundamental flaws in the use of animals in psychology research. Psychological experiments on animals are simply not based on human phenomena and cannot reveal the etiology of the disorders under study. The development of the symptomatology alone in nonhuman species does not tell us about what needs to be done to prevent and treat the pathology in humans. Clinical and epidemiological studies with humans have been shown to provide more reliable, more applicable, and more effective answers. For example, the psychological effects of most psychopharmacological agents have been discovered through human clinical investigation.

Why can someone so easily receive a grant to study maternal deprivation in monkeys when we are not funding day-care centers for children?

Why are we making cocaine addicts out of dogs and cats while people are being turned away from mental-health and drug-rehabilitation centers? For what reason are we doing head-injury experiments on pigs when we are closing down trauma-care centers? How can we fund experiments to make a pseudoscientific model of schizophrenia in primates while the mentally ill roam homeless down our streets? Something is terribly wrong.

In the training of a psychologist, another moral dilemma or paradox exists. How do you develop empathy for one species when you are trained to deny the pain of others? Where do you draw the line at compassion in your mind? How do you set limits with ethics?

Our quest for knowledge amounts to millions of dollars worth of basic research studies on millions of animals every year. While adherents of the scientific paradigm pat themselves on the back for their intellectual achievements, I am afraid they are omitting something critical—that we can learn more from animals by living peacefully with them on this planet than by studying them in the laboratory.

Salmon and Mango, my two "roommates," were kidnapped from their home—the Moluccan Islands of Indonesia. Salmon (called "Sam" for short) was taken about twenty years ago, and Mango ("Manny") approximately twelve. Collectively they have had at least ten homes, and I hope mine will be their last. But considering the longevity of this species—fifty to eighty years—I have made sure to provide for them in my will.

Both birds are light peach in color, with yellow and white on their underbodies and a deep salmon for their crests (thus the name, salmon-crested cockatoo). Quite beautiful. Because they are not sexually dimorphic, I am frequently asked how I tell them apart, but they are so distinct in their personalities and expressions that with just a little familiarity, I have no problem distinguishing them.

People seem to be more afraid of these birds, approximately two feet in length, than if they were two big growling dogs. There have been many misconceptions about birds being major disease carriers and unprovoked aggressors, as in the movie The Birds. But Mango, the male, lives, for the most part, to be petted. For this he will forego nearly

anything and ever so slowly rotate his entire body so that I have touched every possible surface.

Visitors to my home and people we meet on our adventures outside are amazed that "a bird can want to be petted just like a dog." He wants petting so much, in fact, that if passersby think they can get away without petting him, Mango calls to them with a "C'mere, I wuv you." When they approach, wondering, "What do I do with a bird?" Mango lets them know by placing his head in their hand. Very simple. When people seem too anxious to approach, Mango extends his neck as far as it will reach, even standing on "tippie toes" so that he can rest his head against their chest—and look up into their eyes. Unabashedly solicitous.

Lately Mango has taken to calling me to turn out the lights around his "bedtime." I have learned that he does not like much variation when it comes to this, and I must be prompt. Because I cannot always oblige his request with the immediacy that he'd like, he has discovered the light switch and turns off the lights himself. I never directly showed him this. He just associated the two. That's just his latest discovery.

Mango also uses tools in a creative fashion and loves to find the right key to unlock his special locks. He is also fond of matching his round and square blocks in their correct holes and gets quite proud of himself when he is accurate, laughing out loud. Mango also loves his big white teddy bear that hangs in his cage. (I keep large cages for both birds, which they use only to sleep.) He gets as close as possible to this "bear" and nibbles it gently with half-closed eyes until he falls asleep.

Sam, the female, is much more defiant and rambunctious than Mango. She is the self-appointed protector of our household, and all visitors come under direct scrutiny. However, once she finds you acceptable, Sam will bring you every one of her toys and place them in your lap. Gaining Sam's acceptance is something like an honor, and once won, she herself will come into your lap—beak down and "clicking" in a request for petting. Then, each wing is raised so that you are sure to scratch her favorite places.

Sam uses sarcasm sometimes in her communications with me. If she doesn't like what I have given her to eat, she will come right up to my face, moving her beak in an exaggerated fashion as though she is chew-

ing, to indicate she wants different food. However, she will forsake food at any moment, and petting, for that matter, if she thinks I will play with her instead. She initiates such game-playing as hide-and-go-seek and catch-me-if-you-can. This is one of the reasons I question the animal acts at zoos and amusement parks—those cockatoos have to be very, very hungry if they are performing for food alone. I usually resort to begging to get these two to eat.

Sam is remarkably inquisitive and investigates her environment with an obvious sense of delight. She can convey to me exactly where she wants to go by pointing, and she does so quite insistently. When I do not respond quickly enough to satisfy her, she stamps her foot and cries, "C'mere, c'mon c'mere."

She understands a surprising number of my communications and uses them herself—maybe not always with accurate words but with seemingly accurate intentions. When Mango grooms her she'll look up and say, "I love you, Manny." When birds fly on the balcony she runs to greet them with a, "Hello, pretty bird, how are you?" She potty-trained Mango by showing him where to go—she herself learned in a matter of hours. And she insists on regularly going outside to sit in trees. I know which type of tree she likes now—she doesn't have to show me anymore.

I must say that I do not believe either of these birds are extraordinary animals with special talents and attributes. Numerous other people who live with birds in their homes have comparable experiences with those animals. I have met many other birds who, when allowed to interact freely with their human companions, display similar curiosity, affection, play behavior, attachment, and love that seem intrinsic to these animals. It is the bird who is kept forever in a cage that makes very little meaningful contact with humans—simply existing in a state of hopelessness and helplessness.

I remember being at a planning meeting to help homeless war veterans held at the home of a woman known for her compassion and generosity. Off in the corner of a room where we placed our coats, I couldn't help but notice a small cage covered with an old blanket. Upon inquiring, I learned that the cockatiel inhabitant of that cage had lived that way for twenty years—with no toys and the same seed diet everyday. The woman

explained that the bird was not interested in coming out of his cage or in any different type of food because occasionally she would open the cage or offer him a grape. Birds, by and large, require quite some time to adjust to anything new, and this little fellow was unlikely to respond to change, good or bad, after years of the same routine. To her credit, the woman got him a companion not long after our meeting.

As part of my education by the cockatoos in my care, I have learned the difference between possessive, paternalistic, anthropocentric "love" and the liberating feeling of biocentric love. The biocentric view is that all living things have intrinsic value, an inherent worth outside of their value to humans. I began to see my part in the interdependence of Life—not at the apex of a hierarchy but as a peer in a larger community of interconnectedness. Awakened in me was a super-worldly experience that served to heal the alienation I have had with the natural environment. I felt my self-identity broaden by encompassing an enhanced sense of connection to all life on Earth and the accompanying responsibility that naturally follows.

Within professional literature, ecological awareness increasingly is referred to as a source of emotional well-being. Even Carl Jung spoke of how the human embryo, during ontogenetic development, passes through the phylogenetic stages of amphibian, reptilian, and other mammalian life. He claimed that just as the body has this evolutionary history, so does our psyche. All of this history becomes part of our self-identification if we listen to it. And the desire to preserve the natural world then comes as instinctively as the desire for our own self-preservation.

So I walk down the streets of Los Angeles with two large cockatoos on my shoulders and realize that they have no business being on this continent, in this hemisphere. I think about how they got here, how frightened they must have been when poached, stolen from the wild, their mothers probably killed to get access to the nest. The illegal transport to this country kills the vast majority of poached birds, and quarantine is simply a terrifying way station. I think about the fundamental values of our civilization and wonder, what is held sacred any longer? Economic success, material possessions, acquisitions—what has gone astray?

Once during a stroll with the birds, looking for the perfect tree for Sam, a woman excitedly stopped me and asked where I had purchased them—as if I would *buy* a bird. Why did she want to know? Because they so wonderfully matched her living room decor, she just needed to have some.

Sometimes I feel I need a disclaimer when the birds accompany me outside, making sure that people don't run to the pet shop because they look like such fun. I feel that I have to talk to people as though I am talking them out of taking a life, out of perpetuating a form of slavery. I have come to believe extra-individual relationships should be maintained only if they are mutually beneficial from a nonanthropocentric perspective.

Birds in captivity are beautiful to look at and listen to—they entertain us with their antics. But at such a cost. All birds living with humans are either captured or captive-bred. No bird was born to be a "cage-bird." Bird abuse is one of the most common types of animal abuse just by the simple nature of how we keep them—locked in cages usually for their entire lives. This for an animal who normally may travel hundreds of miles in one day. And ironically, we take away this crucial aspect of their identity—the ability to fly.

Birds are sold, given away, lost, or even set free at an average of every two to three years. Or worse, they are put in some way-off corner, garage, or basement to spend the rest of their lives in a cage alone. For a species accustomed to living in a flock, never out of the sight or touch of their flock-mates, this can be unbearable.

Many people pay a great deal for parrots and cockatoos, but I have found that just as many people are looking for good homes for birds that they no longer can care for. Bird rescue centers have been sprouting up across the country because of the large numbers of abandoned birds. Although some people see these animals as collectibles, disposable or exchangeable, many others are quite distraught at having to give up their "babies."

One of the reasons for the high turnover rate in the keeping of birds is that, admittedly, they are noisy, messy, and extremely "high maintenance"; cockatoos are like two-year-olds who never grow up. Parrots can chew through nearly anything, so it becomes difficult to leave them

out of their cages unsupervised without your facing some destruction. But chewing is natural for them and not something that can, or should, be unlearned. It takes the savvy bird lover to find suitable substitutes for phone cords, drapes, and furniture. Another reason for giving up birds is that many people, especially those susceptible to asthma and chronic lung disease, have developed respiratory diseases and allergies as a result of bird "dust," the powdery substance coming from the down feathers.

Ideally I would like to see contact with birds limited to observing them in their natural habitat. Not that we should release all the birds in our care. For Sam and Mango, I have tried to make them as comfortable as possible in their sacrifice of nearly everything that is natural to them. I researched how they normally live in the wild, what they would eat in their native habitat, suitable temperatures, mating needs, bathing habits, and more. (Of course, I have also learned that they love to be blow-dried, want cooked food that is steaming hot, and must ride on the vacuum whenever it's in operation—nothing I would have expected from my research.) I ended up adopting Mango two years after I rescued Sam because I realized that all animals, including humans, need to be with conspecifics. And salmon-crested cockatoos, unlike most people, mate for life.

These birds require an incredible amount of my time and energy, but they have given a great deal back. In particular, they have given me a different perspective in my practice of psychology. If I had to boil down all the cases I see, I would say that the root cause of many people's problems is a lack of empathetic understanding, usually due to early childhood experiences. This manifests as an enormous difficulty in asking for needs to be met in effective and appropriate ways—a critical feature of mature, healthy relationships.

At certain points in their lives, some people learn not to bother asking, believing they will not get what they need anyway. This can lead to a self-fulfilling prophecy of thinking they are undeserving and then choosing relationships that confirm this belief. Usually this results in a tremendous deficit in self-esteem. In addition, people who want to nurture them find it difficult to know how to do so.

Other people may learn from their early experiences to ask inappropriately for their needs to be met through demands, manipulations, or escape into fantasy wish-fulfillment. Overall, this behavior leaves us without the means to create healthy relationships that can be healing and reeducative.

There is no greater gift we can give to our self-esteem than to acknowledge that all life on Earth can help in the building of our self-identity. Sometimes I think that we can learn how to live more socially adaptively from a bird. If you have ever seen a bird lift up your hand with his or her head in order to get petted, you would know what I mean. Perhaps we should learn to ask for our needs to be met just like that—no pretense, no defensiveness. No more mind-reading, second-guessing, missed opportunities—just direct, honest relating. Yes, I think we can learn how to love all over again—just like a bird.

THE LANGUAGE OF PRAIRIE DOGS

CON SLOBODCHIKOFF

A coyote emerges from the forest early in the morning, hoping to catch an unwary prairie dog. He walks slowly toward the prairie-dog colony, crouching and trying to stay behind bushes. Suddenly, a chorus of high-pitched barks erupts. A prairie dog has spotted the coyote. Animals who have been eating grass moments before now run to the lips of their burrows and stand up on their hind legs, watching the progress of the predator and barking so that everyone in the colony will know that a coyote is nearby.

Other animals who have been asleep inside their burrows run up to the ground surface to see where the coyote might be walking. Within moments, the entire colony of prairie dogs is out, standing on the lips of their burrows, barking an alarm call. The coyote sullenly walks through the colony and leaves. Breakfast this morning will not be a prairie dog.

Prairie dogs are highly social animals who live in the grassland areas of North America. They are formally classified as ground squirrels; unlike the tree squirrels, they have short, stubby tails and thick bodies with powerful front legs for digging. While a young prairie dog can easily fit into the palm of your hand, an adult can be about a foot long and weigh almost two pounds.

There are five species of prairie dogs. The Gunnison's prairie dog lives in higher-elevation meadows of Arizona, New Mexico, Colorado, and Utah. The Utah prairie dog is confined to a few areas in southern Utah. The white-tailed prairie dog lives in the rolling hills and grasslands of Wyoming and Montana. The black-tailed prairie dog inhabits the plains areas of the Midwest, from the Dakotas to Texas and as far west as New Mexico and Colorado. The Mexican prairie dog lives in the grasslands

of northern Mexico. All these animals produce alarm barks when a predator appears.

A decade ago biologists thought that the alarm barks of prairie dogs were simply vocal expressions of fear. According to this view, the prairie dogs did not intend to communicate information. When predators appeared, the prairie dogs would become frightened and barked as a way of relieving the nervous tension associated with the frightening situation. The bark itself, according to such conventional wisdom, was merely a noise and nothing else. It conveyed no information beyond the simple fact that the animal was upset.

We now know that the alarm calls of prairie dogs are part of a sophisticated animal language rather than merely an expression of fear. Animal language is still a concept that many biologists have difficulty accepting. For human languages, linguists have proposed a number of design features that characterize a language. Most of these design features depend on knowing the grammar, i.e., the basic rules. No matter whether a person is speaking French or Farsi, a set of basic rules exists for the language. By following these rules—for example, putting an adjective before a noun in English or after it in Spanish—the speakers of the language can understand one another. Someone studying a human language can interview a native speaker and ask about these rules. With animals, this is much more difficult to do.

Still, we can identify the basic components of language, whether human or animal. Two major components are semantics and syntax. Semantics involves the meaning of words. If someone says "red," you can picture a certain color even though nothing red might be in sight. The word itself conveys information that you as a listener can understand. Syntax involves the order of words in a sentence. We can change the meaning of a sentence just by rearranging the words. We can say, for example, "The man robbed the bank." We can then rearrange the words to a new sentence: "The bank robbed the man." The same words are used in each case, but the meaning has changed. We can rearrange the words, however, in only a limited, organized way, because the syntax reflects the underlying grammar of the language. Prairie-dog vocalizations contain both of these basic design elements of a language.

My students, colleagues, and I have spent the last ten years trying to decode this language. As we have gained more and more information through field observations and experiments, we have found that our understanding of this language is only beginning to scratch the surface of what the prairie dogs are probably able to communicate to one another.

When I first started studying Gunnison's prairie dogs, I knew that they barked when predators appeared. The tendency to bark an alarm was well-known; in fact, their common name—prairie dogs—originated because the Anglo settlers on the plains of the Midwest thought that the alarm call sounded like the bark of a dog. Actually, when you hear it for the first time, the bark sounds more like the chee-chee-chee of a bird than the bark of a dog. Still, with a bit of poetic license, we can construe it as a bark. From a distance, it sounds faintly like a collection of Chihuahuas yapping.

Because prairie dogs are social animals and live in large colonies, usually a number of animals bark at the same time. Within a colony are several to many territories, each occupied and defended by a group of prairie dogs. A territory can encompass a variety of combinations of males, females, and juvenile animals.

An alarm bark from one animal can be heard across the entire colony up to a mile away. When I started studying these alarms, I thought there might be two different types of calls. At that time, experts knew that several species of ground squirrels related to prairie dogs had one alarm call for terrestrial predators, such as coyotes, and another alarm call for aerial predators, such as hawks. I thought that we could examine prairie-dog vocalizations and see if something similar could be found.

A student and I set up an experiment at a prairie-dog colony in a mountain meadow. We built a blind, a towerlike structure that hid us from both prairie dogs and predators, and sat in the blind with a tape recorder turned on, day after day. When different kinds of predators appeared—coyotes, domestic dogs, red-tailed hawks, human hunters—we recorded the alarm calls.

We took the recordings to my laboratory and transformed the sound on the tape into sonograms. The sonograms gave us a visual representation—a voiceprint—of how the frequency (i.e., the pitch) of the call

changes over the time in which the call is given. We then measured these changes in frequency and analyzed the measurements with a statistical program called Discriminant Function Analysis. The sonogram technology is similar to that used in human-voice stress analysis.

Analyzing our results, we found that we indeed had different calls for terrestrial and for aerial predators: coyotes, domestic dogs, human hunters, and red-tailed hawks. We were puzzled that the variation in the structure of the alarm calls for terrestrial predators—coyotes, domestic dogs, and human hunters—was much greater than that for aerial predators, such as red-tailed hawks.

What if the prairie dogs had different calls for each type of predator, instead of just one call for ones on the ground and another call for ones in the air? If true, this could mean several things. One is that prairie dogs could tell the difference between a coyote, dog, and human. Another is that they could formulate abstract labels, similar to nouns in human language, and correctly label the species of predator. A third is that they could use these semantic, abstract concepts to communicate information to other prairie dogs. While the initial response to a predator might come from fear, the prairie dogs could translate this fear into a language that would have some specific information for other animals that might not have seen the predator.

The data that we collected confirmed this hypothesis and more. I noticed that there was considerable variation within the calls for a predator species. Some of my students and I set up a new experiment. In this one, we used a single human, dressed in a blue shirt and jeans, who walked through each of six different prairie-dog colonies, all at the same speed and route of travel. We also used a domestic dog, a Queensland heeler, who traversed each of these colonies. Within each colony, we recorded the alarm calls of a number of different prairie dogs. By using exactly the same human and exactly the same dog in each colony, we expected to see little variation among the prairie dogs in their alarm calls for each category, e.g., the calls for the human, if the prairie dogs were describing the individual features of the predator. On the other hand, if the variation in the calls came primarily from differences in the prairie-dog voices, we would still see a significant amount of variation in the calls.

Much to my surprise, the variation we saw before within a colony practically disappeared. We still had two distinct alarm calls, one for the human and one for the domestic dog. But within a colony, we saw almost no variation in the calls for the human among the different prairie dogs, and similarly we saw almost no variation in the calls for the dog. The experiment clearly suggested that the prairie dogs were incorporating descriptive information into their calls about the physical features of the human and the domestic dog.

The experiment also gave me an unexpected bonus. It showed that prairie dogs from different colonies differ in how they pronounce "human" and "dog." The two colonies that were the farthest apart, separated by twelve miles, had strong differences in pronunciation, analogous to human regional dialects. Colonies that were relatively close together, within a mile apart, had fairly similar pronunciations. This suggested that the calls might be learned by juvenile animals from their parents, just like human dialects, rather than being determined by some genetically controlled instinct for calling in a precise way.

All of this was interesting, but we still had to do a key experiment. We still needed to show that the prairie dogs really communicated actual information to other prairie dogs about the different predators that they saw. So far, we had shown that the prairie dogs could tell the difference between a hawk, a human, a coyote, and a domestic dog, and that they could produce different alarm calls in response to these different predators. But what if these different calls were not understood by other prairie dogs? We needed to show that each alarm call contained enough specific information about each predator that prairie dogs hearing it would take appropriate evasive measures.

To test this, we first recorded on videotape the escape responses of prairie dogs to naturally occurring predators on a colony. We found that each type of predator elicited a different escape response. When a human appeared near a colony, the prairie dogs would all run to their burrows, jump inside, and then would come partway up so that they could watch where the human was going. When a hawk swooped down on the colony, all the prairie dogs in the immediate flight path would run to their burrows and jump inside without partially emerging. Prairie dogs

who were not in the flight path of the swooping hawk would stand up on their hind legs and gawk, like onlookers at an accident scene, to see if the hawk had caught anyone. When a coyote appeared, the prairie dogs would all run to the lips of their burrows, stand on their hind legs, and would carefully watch the coyote. When a domestic dog appeared, the prairie dogs would stand up on their hind legs wherever they were foraging and would watch the dog. They would not bother to run to the lips of their burrows unless the dog came within thirty feet of them.

The differences in escape behaviors allowed us to do playback experiments. We hid a speaker in the grass in the middle of a colony. On the edge of the colony in a blind, hidden from the prairie dogs' view, we set up our videocamera and tape recorder. Through the speaker we broadcast prerecorded alarm calls for different types of predators and filmed the responses of the prairie dogs to these calls.

As we had expected, the prairie dogs used the appropriate escape responses for each different type of alarm call. Even though no predator could be seen, the prairie dogs ran to the lips of their burrows when we played a coyote alarm call and ran to their burrows and dove inside when we played a human alarm call. When we played a domestic-dog alarm call, the prairie dogs stood up wherever they were foraging but did not run. This showed us that indeed the prairie dogs were not only producing different calls for different predators but also were communicating these differences to other prairie dogs.

So far, we had found a fairly sophisticated system of communication. The only other species of animal that has a similar system of vocal communication is the vervet monkey. These monkeys live in the savanna woodlands of East Africa, where they are preyed upon by eagles, leopards, and pythons. Like our prairie dogs, these monkeys can signal the approach of different predators by producing different alarm calls. Also like our prairie dogs, the monkeys have different escape behaviors for each predator. This kind of sophistication seems reasonable for a monkey. We did not expect that kind of sophistication for a rodent, the prairie dog, considered by many Westerners as a stupid "varmint," a pest species.

We quickly found, however, that the sophistication of our prairie dog was even greater than that of the monkey. I was curious what sort of

specific details about a predator the prairie dogs conveyed to one another, so we did some more experiments to try to find out. In one experiment, we used four humans, two males and two females, who separately walked through a prairie-dog colony. They wore different colored T-shirts— we knew from an earlier study that prairie dogs have reasonably good color vision. Otherwise, all the people were dressed the same. Everyone wore jeans and dark glasses.

Now, much to our surprise, the prairie dogs could tell the individual humans apart—although all the humans elicited human alarm calls, the structure of the call varied depending on the color of shirt each person was wearing. In a third experiment, we used two of the same people and had them wear at different times one or the other of the same two shirts, an orange one and a gray one. Once again, the prairie dogs could tell the difference between the two people. We could even identify the part of the alarm call that coded for the shirt color.

These results led us to try an experiment using several domestic dogs that differed in size and coat color. As in the experiments with humans wearing different shirts, we had the dogs walk through a colony separately and recorded the alarm calls elicited by each of these different dogs. The results were the same as for the humans. The prairie dogs could differentiate each dog and could incorporate descriptive information about each dog into their alarm calls. We found that for the domestic dogs, the prairie dogs conveyed information about the general size and shape of each dog and also conveyed information about the coat color of each dog. That prairie dogs could incorporate information about colors, as well as about size and shape, into their alarm calls was indeed a surprise.

From an evolutionary and ecological standpoint, describing individual predators makes perfect sense for prairie dogs. For their entire lives, prairie dogs are tied to one piece of land. Day after day, month after month, the same individual predators come by—several coyotes, for example, whose home range includes the colony. These predators have different individual hunting styles.

Some coyotes walk through a colony, pretending not to notice any of the prairie dogs that are standing up at the lips of their burrows. Then,

if they spot an animal that looks away for even a second, they charge toward that animal, hoping to grab it before it has a chance to disappear into its burrow. Other coyotes walk up to a burrow, lie down next to it, and wait for up to an hour by that burrow. If a prairie dog gets bored with being below ground and pops up to see if the coast is clear, the coyote leaps up and snatches the animal out of the burrow lip.

By describing the predator's individual features, the prairie dogs can convey information about individual hunting styles: this one is the coyote that sits and waits, and that one is the coyote that charges. Other differences between individual predators might involve whether they are adults or juveniles, residents or visitors. All this information can be incorporated in the form of a physical description into the alarm calls.

In addition to the alarm calls, prairie dogs have a series of vocalizations that we call social chatters. One prairie dog might pause in the middle of foraging, stand up on its hind legs, and produce a string of rapid, staccato sounds, often with variations in pitch. Another prairie dog somewhere else in the colony might respond with a slightly different series of chatters. Do these chatters contain any meaningful information that one prairie dog conveys to another? We don't know. We don't have a key, a Rosetta stone to decipher these calls. They could be simply expressions of the internal mood of each prairie dog, communicating no meaningful information. Or they could be comments on how beautiful the day is.

One thing we do know is that these chatters have a definite syntax. They are not given in random order but have a pattern, just like words in a human sentence. In prairie-dog social chatters, we have found nine "words" that we can identify and describe. These words are used in a nonrandom way, just as the words of a human sentence. Some of these words are always used at the beginning of a chatter. Other words are always used at the end of the chatter. Still other words are always used in the middle. We are currently studying the behavioral contexts in which these chatters are given to try to get more clues to their meaning.

These rodents have much to tell us about the capacity of animals for vocal languages. However, it is becoming increasingly difficult for us to

find colonies that are undisturbed by human activity. Existing colonies are rapidly disappearing through a triumvirate of ecological disasters: poisoning, hunting, and habitat destruction. Colony after colony that we have attempted to study are systematically poisoned or destroyed for subdivisions or shopping centers. Even the colonies that are on federal land protected from poisoning or habitat destruction are often exterminated by hunters.

In this respect, the fate of our colonies is not much different from the fate of all the species of prairie dogs in North America. In the past, the prairie dogs lived wherever the great buffalo herds once roamed—hundreds of thousands of square miles of open grasslands were populated by huge prairie-dog colonies. Today, the once-sprawling colonies are reduced to tiny pockets of land here and there. Eradication programs run by federal and state agencies have reduced the amount of land occupied by prairie dogs by some 98 percent since the beginning of this century. These eradication programs are usually conducted under the mistaken belief that prairie dogs compete with cows for food. Recent research has shown that the diet of prairie dogs and cows overlaps by only some 4 to 7 percent and that cows actually prefer to graze on prairie-dog colonies because the prairie dogs clip the vegetation and cause it to resprout with tender, nutritious shoots that cows like to eat. Despite this, the livestock industry mounts a powerful lobby for eradication programs, usually at taxpayer expense.

Another source of prairie-dog mortality is through hunting. Hunters apparently find great delight in shooting these animals. Organized hunts such as those in Colorado slaughter thousands of animals. And since prairie dogs are generally considered to be vermin by state and federal agencies, they can be hunted at any time of the year with a hunting license. One hunter told us that he kills prairie dogs for practice so that he could cleanly and humanely kill larger animals such as deer and elk. Many hunters who supposedly shoot for humanitarian reasons do not even bother to go out into the colony to see the effects of their efforts— wounded prairie dogs are left to die slowly where they fall. Another hunter told me that shooting prairie dogs is a pleasant way to spend a Saturday afternoon.

Habitat destruction represents another source of mortality. In the West, as towns expand, more subdivisions and shopping centers are built, usually on flat meadows that are colonized by prairie dogs. In areas where the prairie dogs hibernate through the winter, construction often seems to begin when the prairie dogs are hibernating so that they and their colony are plowed under the ground by earthmoving equipment and encased in the concrete tombs of shopping-center parking lots.

Yet prairie dogs are a keystone species in the ecology of Western grasslands. In addition to providing food for predators, prairie-dog colonies provide shelter for some 170 species of vertebrate animals. Grasslands inhabited by prairie dogs have a higher biodiversity of both vertebrate and invertebrate animals than comparable grasslands without prairie dogs; these areas also have higher densities of birds.

Prairie dogs prefer to eat native species of plants, so they practice a kind of "farming" by destroying the less-preferred non-native weeds and letting the native species of plant grow. Grazing by cattle, on the other hand, encourages the growth of weedy, non-native species of plants, particularly when grasslands are overgrazed by having more cattle feed than the land can support. Such activities of prairie dogs promote the growth of native grasses and native plants, helping to restore overgrazed land to the kind of native vegetative diversity that existed prior to the introduction of cattle.

An irony is that various federal and state agencies are spending millions of dollars to recover the black-footed ferret from extinction while at the same time other federal and state agencies are mounting extensive eradication programs to exterminate the black-footed ferret's principal food source, the prairie dog. In 1991 the captive breeding and reintroduction program for the black-footed ferret was estimated as costing about $1.5 million, with only one projected reintroduction site for that year. Subsequent costs are likely to rise annually. The black-footed ferret, however, feeds almost exclusively on prairie dogs. Recently the U.S. Fish and Wildlife Service, Region 6, has refused to list the black-tailed prairie dog as a candidate species under the Endangered Species Act. Such listing would have stopped the eradication programs and might have given prairie-dog populations a chance to recover to viable levels.

Therefore, while we have much to learn about animal language from the prairie dog, we might not have much time in which to learn anything. We humans are killing and eradicating prairie dogs at a fast and furious pace. An animal that has one of the most sophisticated vocal languages known to science and that is an important component of grassland ecosystems might soon go the way of the passenger pigeon—extinct.

TO KISS SALAMANDERS
AND STONES

MICHAEL W. FOX

Animal powers are profound and real. Yet they are not appreciated or even recognized by modern technological society as having value or significance. Indeed, they are dismissed as mere superstition. Those who claim empowerment and ask respect for these inherent qualities (which some call the animals' gifts and blessings) are labeled variously as primitives, heathens (dwellers of the uncivilized heath), pagans, witches, mad shamans, social deviants, and perverts—sexually and spiritually—if not outright insane.

But if sanity lies in mental hygiene or purity, i.e., sanitation, then sanitization and sanctification are unifying processes. Taking a dog to bed and loving it like a human child—or any other nonhuman being, for that matter—is not insane or unsanitary.

People who appreciate, too often subliminally, animal powers not only sleep and dream with certain animals, they also revere them. They revere these animals because they are part of the divine wholeness and holiness of creation. That some creatures are domesticated and seen as human creations matters nought because their holiness remains, except to those who continue to perceive them otherwise.

Thirty years ago in an English pub an Irishman told me about a Celtic myth that stated, "One who has kissed a salamander will not be hurt by fire." The inebriated storyteller then embellished the tale by heating a poker in the fire and placing its red-hot end close to his tongue. If he had kissed a salamander, he said, his tongue would not be burned.

This folkloric fragment is from a time when humans lived much closer to nature, like the farming and gatherer-hunter communities of Old Ireland and most of Old Europe. Kissing a salamander is not done for power but out of reverence and awe.

In summer 1990 after a visit to the hollowed interior of an ancient oak, I told my six-year-old daughter, Mara, that if we were lucky and quiet, we might find a harmless garter snake on the trail through the woods close to our home.

I found the snake closer than I expected and hoped it would not move. I picked up Snake gently and reverently. Snake coiled slowly around my hand, staring at me unblinkingly, flicking her forked tongue as she probed my presence and intentions. I quietly told Mara that this snake was not poisonous, that she ate insects and lizards, and that she was not slimy but shiny and very beautiful. I pointed out her unblinking but consciousness-reflecting eyes and told Mara that the snake's tongue enabled her to smell and taste without touching us.

I then asked Mara if she would like to hold Ms. Snake. Mara did. I turned away and left them alone for a moment. In that moment Mara closed her eyes and kissed the woodland serpent on the mouth. Then she was ready, I knew, to say goodbye, and I stepped forward, took the snake in my hands, kissed her, too, and let her go free with thanks and our best wishes for her life in the woods.

Next to these woods, there's a street of homes with chemically treated lawns. The stream that runs through the woods, like the acid rain that falls upon it, is contaminated with pesticides and herbicides and the waste of heavy, toxic metals that drain from the urban streets of automobile- and people-infested Washington, D.C.

We haven't found a salamander in these woods yet. A friend recently came upon a box turtle and a cat-torn baby opossum that my veterinary training could not bring back to life. And I found, by sense of smell first, a homeless man living on the stinking heap of his own garbage. He had wrapped himself in a sort of shawl fashioned from a long green army blanket. When I asked him, he replied that he did not know if there were salamanders where he lived—or snakes or turtles. Perhaps he needed others to kiss him, but I had no time because of the dying woods and the

thought that soon no child will have a chance to kiss a wild snake, or the Irish to live their truth, free from the yoke of colonialism and industrial empirism that loves only the kiss of immortal gold.

Only those whom it concerns will care if the kiss of the salamander is disproved scientifically or medically. The difference between material, physical reality and spiritual, metaphysical reality is one of degree, not of kind or rationality. But such linkage—which is intuitive and empathic—is rejected as illusory, the dualistic world of Cartesian science and mechanistic medicine.

Science does not confirm that those who lick a cane-toad might see God, angels, and demons just because science has shown that the toad secretes a potent hallucinogen in its skin slime. There is a world of difference between licking a toad to get high (or taking a toad-slime enema as the Aztecs purportedly did in order to have visions) and kissing a salamander for spiritual power or a garter snake out of love and reverence.

It was in summer 1960 that I kissed the renowned Blarney Stone in Ireland. I was on vacation with my parents "cramming" for final examinations that fall at the Royal Veterinary College, London, while my father drove his secondhand Austin sedan and my mother pointed out the beauty along the quiet roads.

Irish legend has it that those who kiss the Blarney Stone have the power of convincing speech (hence, a zealot is often dubbed as being "full of the Blarney"). When I kissed the Blarney Stone, I wished that I might be blessed with the power of the stone to help alleviate the sufferings of the animal kingdom. Perhaps I'm just full of Blarney after all.

Many myths in Old Europe involve stones. The stone from which King Arthur pulled Merlin's sword tells a story. Many noblemen and warlords from far afield tried to pull the sword of Dominion, magically embedded in the stone. Only one succeeded because the power of the stone yielded and gave only to him who would use power—the power of Excalibur— to bring peace, justice, and unity to the ravaged late Iron Age fiefdoms and rival kingdoms of Avalon and its hinterlands and not to make war for retribution and self-aggrandizement.

The powers of Nature—of rocks, trees, and animals—were long celebrated by our ancestors who were surely wiser but not more primitive

than we because they did not crave the power to control and exploit life and its processes and elements to the degree we, the purportedly more "civilized" descendants, do. Why? Because perhaps they were less insecure, far fewer in number than we, and had not yet exhausted their natural environs of its resources or become dependent upon technology to rapaciously and desperately exploit such resources.

Some call this age of our forefathers and foremothers the Golden Age. It was during this epoch, when humans were primarily gatherer-hunters, that we first recognized the power of animals and Nature—blessings and gifts handed down from one generation to the next in myth and legend and which have been variously romanticized, analyzed objectively, and described as pagan, superstitious animism, primitive totemism, and irrational nonsense.

To return to this ancestral world view of respect and reverence for animal powers, blessings, and gifts is to be judged a heretic, a follower of pagan ideology and idolatry, and therefore a worshipper of the devil. But the devil, ex-Catholica, is Pan, the horned pagan deity who cared for creatures wild and tame and who panicked those who were separate from and who therefore feared all that is wild (uncivilized), beastly (subhuman), and seemingly nonrational.

Animal behavior exemplifies what in the vernacular we call doing what comes naturally. Animals embody the quality of authenticity, their kingdom mirroring our own lack thereof, and our artifice, contrivances, and selfish delusions.

To begin to understand and accept snakes and spiders and to see their inherent divinity and their place within the whole is to begin to accept one's self. But some children are taught to fear, scorn, and destroy such creatures. Rarely do they learn to revere and deeply understand. Consequently their place within the whole cannot be realized.

Wild and domestic animals express certain emotions in ways very similar to our own feelings and modes of expression. They may cry and squirm when hurt, curl up when afraid, strut and puff when being assertive, and close their eyes with deep satisfaction and even groan in contentment. So do we, and sharing such subjective states and modes of expression, animals mirror our own animal nature.

The clearer we see into this mirror, wiped clean of the dust of ages, of the karmic ashes of human egotism, the greater is our access to animal gifts and powers. If we were to go to a zoo and look at the animals reflected in that mirror, what would we see? As they stand naked, we see the power and Arctic aura of the polar bear; the will and wisdom of the wolf; the agility and awareness of the deer. But when we look at our- selves, naked, before such a mirror, what do we see?

By using animal powers, we can learn to let go and to be ourselves, authentic and natural. When we compare the grace, perfection, and dig- nity of animals with our own image, we see the dissonance and contem- plate the reality of our inferiority: that is, until we shed our fears and pretensions and stand and walk and talk in ways that the fully human being would choose, and approve, and enjoy.

THE SNOW LEOPARD: HIDDEN SPIRIT OF THE HIMALAYA

RODNEY JACKSON

Distinguished by their luxuriant misty-gray, yellowish pelage dotted with large, open rosettes, and a tail nearly as long as its body, the snow leopard inhabits mountains across twelve countries in Central Asia. These include the three-thousand-mile-long Himalayan chain of Nepal, India, Bhutan, and China, as well as the windswept ranges of Mongolia and the precipitous slopes of the Tien Shan of the former Soviet republics. Despite weighing less than one hundred pounds, snow leopards can kill wild sheep three times their weight. They have enormous forepaws, a short "heraldic head," and a reputation as skillful hunters and masters of maneuvering along narrow cliff-ledges.

Undertaking this study was like looking for a ghost that repeatedly prowled past our tents during the frigid Himalayan night yet rarely allowed us more than a fleeting glimpse. During all the months we spent in the uninhabited Langu Valley, we only saw the cats eighteen times.

Animals have a way of surprising you: the more information you gather on their behavior and natural history, the more you realize how meager your understanding of their reality is. The more elusive the creature, the more challenged you find yourself. Frustration gives way to immense admiration, combining perseverance and cunning.

The German biologist Peter Pallas formally introduced science to *Uncia uncia*, as the snow leopard is known scientifically, in 1779. But it evaded attention until George B. Schaller, among the world's leading field naturalists, ventured to Pakistan to study Himalayan wildlife. He

wrote, "I ventured into the mountains in the hope of studying snow leopard but my attempts failed, as almost perversely the animals eluded my efforts to observe them." He blamed poachers for hunting the population down to a few survivors and lamented man's greed and ignorance for turning the mountains into "Stones of Silence."

When I became interested in this mysterious creature of the Himalaya, its spectacular habitat and scenery captured my imagination and enthusiasm for exploration. George Schaller, I argued, had been unsuccessful simply because he had the bad fortune of picking the wrong place to study the cat; all I had to do was find a "blank place on the map," as far from human activity—poaching—as possible. A snow leopard pelt not only brings a windfall to the poor hunter but supports a lucrative black market for high-quality fur coats. As a recent university graduate, I believed the snow leopard could be dissected through the careful application of radio-collars, habitat mapping, and direct and indirect field observations, if imbued with a fair measure of time and patience. Although preying upon blue sheep endemic to the Tibetan plateau and bordering regions, the snow leopard resembled the mountain lion of the American West, whose intimate life had been recently exposed by intensive research.

All I had to do was raise some money, buy radio-tracking equipment, a warm down sleeping bag, and parka, and set out with the woman I had recently met. Now, nearly fifteen years later, as I look back I realize how much differently things were to be, but equally, how little I or the world continue to know of this mythical elusive creature. The five years Darla Hillard and I spent in the Himalayan wilderness studying this "ghost of the Himalayan night" strengthened my respect and awe for snow leopards and laid the foundation for my continuing efforts to conserve Asia's splendid high-mountain wildlife and natural biodiversity.

We were successful in providing the first detailed information on the behavior and ecology of the species, a vital utilitarian mission for effective management and conservation. In retrospect, I realize we learned substantially more of ourselves from studying those snow leopards than the facts we published in papers or a doctoral dissertation.

It took almost five years to find financial support. For a study area, I had settled on the Langu Gorge in the far wild west of Nepal, along the

slopes of Kanjiroba Himal, a modest 23,000-foot peak. Darla and I set off in October, on the assumption that snow leopards are best seen during winter when their tracks could be easily traced in the snow. We reached the remote mountain village of Dalphu after trekking for six weeks and surmounting what seemed to be endless bureaucratic and logistical obstacles.

The harshest winter in living memory kept us tent-bound for nearly two months. But finally we were able to trek into the core study area to set our traps. The cliff-side way, barely visible, penetrated the steeply precipitous Langu Gorge, following centuries-old wildlife trails used by blue sheep and Himalayan tahr, unique ungulates associated with snow leopard habitat. Here and there, the local Bhotia people had leaned a hewn log against a seemingly smooth rock face, enabling one to ascend. Periodically, football-sized rocks plummeted from above.

Darla and I, tied together by rope, lacked the mountaineering skills of the Bhotia porters who carried our gear and who laughed at our bow-kneed, rock-clinging postures and wide eyes. Fourteen-year-olds and grandmothers carrying sixty- to one-hundred-pound loads passed us as we lay like torpid lizards, anxiously wondering what we had gotten ourselves into. How, I ventured, could any creature live and hunt in such a difficult place? Had human poaching pressure driven snow leopards to the very brink of existence just for their fur? Or are snow leopards simply well-adapted to a life among rocks and cliffs rather than more gentle alpine valleys prone to being snowbound in winter? How do individual snow leopards find mates in such a maze of broken mountain slopes? And just what makes a snow leopard physically and socially secure?

We made camp at Dhukyell, where a side stream enters the Langu River at about 9,500 feet. Aptly named "the difficult place," it was also frigidly cold during winter—little wonder, for shafts of sunlight reached camp near noon only, lasting as little as fifteen minutes! I was elated to find snow leopard scrapes adorning the edge of the river bluff and a short time later set about placing live-traps and preparing the immobilization equipment and drugs for what we hoped would be the first capture, radio-collaring, and release of a snow leopard. We were

prepared to wait for several months if necessary, as the cat would have to walk within a few meters to see the bait, an old goat purchased from the villagers.

Remarkably, a large male snow leopard visited the trap site the very first night and became entrapped as it stalked the tied-up goat. Unseen by us and helped by a frantic surge of adrenaline, the goat broke free and raced down the hillside to a safer place.

With our Nepalese associates, Darla and I spent the next four years tracking five radio-collared snow leopards across the broken crags and high grassy slopes of the Langu Valley, gathering the detailed information about their movements, food requirements, social habits, home-range use, and land-tenure characteristics. We intended that our study would serve as the baseline against which all future studies will be measured and as the foundation for conservation action aimed at preserving this spectacular creature along with the other rich biodiversity of the high Himalaya. We would provide scientific counterpart to balance the international awareness generated by numerous popular articles and the impact of the best-seller *The Snow Leopard* by Peter Matthiessen. The book chronicles Matthiessen's pilgrimage with George Schaller to the holy Crystal Mountain located almost within a stone's throw of our own camp. Although Matthiessen considered that "the hope of glimpsing this near-mythic beast in the snow mountains was reason enough for the entire journey," his real mission was inward, an attempt to make sense of life in the wake of his wife's unexpected death. The images evoked by his poetic writing coupled with Schaller's ethereal photographs in *National Geographic* have motivated other Americans to embark on their own mid-life treks to remote Himalayan valleys, spurning along the way much of the modern-day mythology surrounding the mysterious snow leopard.

Many centuries ago, the Buddhist saint Milarepa resorted to black Nyingma-pa Tantra and transformed himself into a snow leopard to confound his disciples (not enemies, as Matthiessen suggests). The Song of the Snow Ranges tells the story of Jetsun Milarepa's reputed ability to conquer malignant demons and ghosts during his period of meditation in the Lapchi valley, a site now protected within the Qomolangma Nature Preserve along the flanks of Mount Everest.

One October, Milarepa set out in the company of six disciples for the "Great Cave of Conquering Demons," where he proposed to meditate in virtual isolation for several months. On their way home, his disciples encountered a terrible storm and were barely able to get back safely. The snow fell without respite for eighteen days and nights, cutting off all communication between the cave and the village for nearly six months, thus preventing any opportunity for them to provide their guru with periodic provisions of food and other essentials of life. Assuming he could not possibly have survived, his disciples held a sacramental feast but were not able to search for his corpse until the Tibetan month of Saga (late March).

Just short of the cave where they had left Milarepa, they sat down for a long rest. Suddenly, in the distance they saw a snow leopard yawning and stretching as it climbed up a large rock. They watched it for a long time until it finally disappeared. Venturing forward, they expected not even to find Milarepa's corpse, convinced his remains had been eaten by the snow leopard. Murmuring in anguish, they wondered if they still might obtain some remnants of his clothes or hair.

On reaching the entrance to the cave, they noticed many human footprints beside the leopard's pugmarks. They were mystified, asking themselves if this was a conjuration of a deva or a ghost. Then they heard Milarepa singing and chiding them by saying, "You laggards, you reached the other side of the mountain quite a while ago. Why did it take you so long to get here? The food has been prepared for a long time and must be cold. Hasten yourselves and enter!"

Overjoyed, the disciples cried and danced. Looking around the cave, they observed that the little flour they had given him six months earlier was still not used up. In fact, there was enough barley, rice, and meat to feed six persons. A disciple exclaimed, "Indeed, it is dinnertime for us, but surely you must have known we were coming." Milarepa replied, "When I was sitting on the rock, I saw you all resting on the other side of the pass." One of his disciples replied, "We saw a leopard sitting there, but we did not see you." "I was the leopard," Milarepa replied—as a master of the Four Elements, he had no trouble in achieving perfect control, transforming himself into whatever bodily form he chose.

How I wished I could have taken the form of a snow leopard, watching in the shadows as they moved about their home range in search of food and mates. It would have been so much more productive than setting traps and hoping for some hapless leopard to become entangled so that we could immobilize it and fit it with a radio transmitter. No matter, with its *beep . . . beep . . . beep* to us, or *tok . . tok . . tok* to a Tibetan boy who has just seen his first camera, one is able only to grapple at slender fragments of fact and reality. What the cats are really doing is supposition, perhaps even imagination.

While snow leopards are essentially solitary creatures, they are not asocial. In fact, they have a remarkably complex repertoire of scent and sign marking for informing others about their presence and intenseness. They do not have to see one another to know whether to encourage or avoid further contact. Their olfactory senses reach dimensions we cannot possibly imagine, let alone experience. So much of our social contact involves direct contact, aggression, or at least overt physical symbolism. We lack the subtle senses of the snow leopard, at perfect harmony with its harsh surroundings. The snow leopard stands apart as the quintessential invisible life form, the soul of the mountains.

If we can attach emotions and values to wildlife, I would have to call the snow leopard nonviolent; it is certainly not aggressive like its common cousin, the forest leopard. No documented case of a man-eating snow leopard exists. In Ladakh, India, man and snow leopard coexist remarkably amicably, despite the strong tendency of the snow leopard to kill domestic stock. Retribution is far more likely in cases where a dozen or more sheep or goats are killed in a single attack—there are quite a few instances of angry livestock owners attacking the snow leopard responsible and stoning or beating it to death with stocks. Yet the cornered cat makes little or no attempt to defend itself or to attack humans. Usually, herders drive the predator away rather than kill it in order to retrieve the remains of their sheep or goat. Indeed, snow leopards show great reluctance to abandon their kill and will often remain for days on a carcass, even when disturbed by humans. Could it be that human and animal have evolved mutual respect, an avoidance of one another, and in so doing, lost their fear of one another?

Now, ten years later, I realize that I have learned as much about myself and human values as I have of *Uncia uncia*. In concert with the Buddhist religion, the snow leopard has imbued in me a deep reverence for life and the urgency for conserving both cultural and natural heritages. Even in the face of loss or damage to valuable crops and livestock, poor Himalayan and Tibetan villagers revere and protect the local wildlife. The world would do well to embrace Buddhist precepts concerning the sanctity of all living creatures, no matter their status in the complex web of life.

All is not well in the high mountains of Asia. Wild areas are vanishing, taking with them a myriad of species and genetic diversity. Cultures are failing under the axe of consumerism and free-market forces, and we all will be immensely poorer as a result.

Imagine the peaks without snow leopard? I for one cannot. I am deeply concerned about the path we humans are taking in progressing to the future. We must learn from nature and animals like the snow leopard—before it is too late.

BE YOUR PURPOSE, MY FRIEND

CHRISTINE JURZYKOWSKI

Returning from a night outside under the stars, I noticed you wet and panting on the quilt. No doubt the work of one of my cats. Not a gash anywhere, a heart beating very fast. Internal injuries? Shock? You liked it on my arm, the warmth of another's summer skin. A body's smell. Are you young enough to have been clutched from your mother's care or just one of the species of field mice who never grow more than half the length of a finger? Either way, I don't know much about you.

Somehow this morning, I trust I will know what to do. Water and rescue remedy. At least you seem to ingest part of a few drops. The lightest touch circles seem to be too much on your soft, gray fur. I carry you on my arm as I feed the dogs and cats; everyone seems to accept you as the newest member of the family. The one who might have pounced earlier looks and acts bored at the sight of you; strange, as she probably was the one who brought you in.

"So, little one, what is the purpose of your visit today?" I ask. "To show you that you can love and care for all forms of life equally," came the faint reply. "Whether understood, known, or invited, you humans may all do so with ease and grace. You know these things. We share the same intelligence. It is in our cellular structure. You have it all in you as I have it in me. It is an act of willful remembrance. I accept your offer to nurse me back to health."

I have not cared for such a small, fragile being for a long, long time. Memories of my childhood wave in front of me like long blades of grass blowing in the wind. Spaces open to reveal pictures of the past. A distant

call beckons me to set these pictures free. Memories abound of humming-birds with broken wings, bees almost drowned in pools of water, two macaws, dogs, butterflies, and a motherless anteater. The sweet fragrances of the mimosa and bottlebrush trees match the vivid pictures as a reminder of times past.

As the shy, seven-year-old that I was, all these marvelous beings were my friends. At least for as long as I was able to stay in Brazil. We lived an hour and a half west of São Paulo. The area beyond our house was a jungle then. Full of life, full of a world that understood me. It was so simple and easy there.

And, without knowing really how or why, I felt connected and loved by the world of nature in a way that I never experienced with my family. I found solace, companionship, and an element of respectful surprise at every turn. When I think back on it, I indeed faced many unknowns beyond both thresholds to the jungle and the garden of my father's house. Although as a youngster I feared people, I somehow knew that I needn't be scared among the plants and the animals. The world of people signaled confrontation. The world of my plant and animal friends was simply a playground for cooperation. It was a place full of stories, full of meaning, full of seemingly silent instruction. I wish I could remember those conversations today.

Those times, however, were at best haphazard due to both family and national politics. Mother decided it was time to return to the United States when the junta government began to sound too frighteningly close to the tones of Hitler from whom she had already fled many years past. We moved sooner than I would have ever wanted. New York City: per-haps just a jungle of another kind. I now can laugh at the comparison. It was no laughing matter then. Three countries in eight years, and I had felt transplanted often enough.

I realize now just how important my times within that dark canopy of cover have been for me. My forest companions of all shapes, sizes, and forms have not only been my friends, they have also been my teachers. Once transferred into the concrete of city walls, this shy young girl became even more introverted. To mask the pain of this loss, I did a good job of closing myself down to the natural world for many years after the move.

If you had told me twenty years ago that I would find myself within the geological boundary between the Great Plains and what is known as the Texas hill country, I would have laughed off the prediction. Today I am blessed to live on three thousand acres of rolling juniper and oak hills and grassland savannas two hours southwest of Dallas.

Near the town of Glen Rose in north central Texas is dinosaur country. Footprints cut across river beds that run the same direction as they have for many millennia. Fossils tell of a time long ago that was very different: the rich marine ancestry of today's terrestrial residents. There is a long, long history here, and one feels it strongly and sees it in the strata of the land. Valleys, once the sea, lie between the elevated rims from which miles of vistas can be seen: a view that will bring any homesick African to smile or cry and feel "at home."

Home. This land is just that to more than 1,100 animals, many of whom are endangered, threatened, or at risk in the wild. These animals' ancestors come from faraway places across the world—Africa, Asia, South America, and as near as the Southwest of the United States. Species like the Grevy zebra; white and black rhino; addax antelope; cheetah; Mexican, red, and maned wolf; giraffe; and Attwater's prairie birds, to name just a few. "A modern-day Jurassic Park?" people chuckle and ask sometimes. Hardly so. I marvel at the animals, the land, and the people who have come together to form the place now known as Fossil Rim Wildlife Center—my home, school, and community for the past seven years.

Obviously, on the surface, Fossil Rim is a wildlife preserve, a living laboratory, an experiment in learning. We mirror and match many of the "islands" of protected habitat in countries such as South Africa and Zimbabwe. Here, like over there, are large areas of fenced land with semi-free-ranging herds of animals.

Fossil Rim also has a public side. Visitors of all ages come to visit for one-day or multi-night adventures, staying close to nature or in accommodations ranging from wilderness campsites to a five-star lodge. The associated activities and their related services provide an opportunity to educate visitors and create a source of revenue for our programs on site and around the world.

What started as a simple bridge loan in January 1987 to a small, private refuge in north central Texas suddenly ended six months later with our taking possession of its fourteen hundred acres of land and five hundred animals. We started modestly with the trusted guidance of a few who helped us move toward what we felt possible. Knowing little made us willing to experiment. By 1990, after much trial and error and study of existing systems of thinking, we found the courage to set out on a fairly radical path of mixing business with science, philosophy with ecology, and mainstream with alternative.

Just below the surface, we have been dedicated to the propagation, management, and study of endangered species; the training of students and professionals from around the world; the education of the public; and the support of conservation programs worldwide. Fossil Rim is a business with a traditionally philanthropic mission; a place for study, observation, and exploration; a developing process in mindful business—entrepreneurial conservation and community building; a vision in finding ways of bringing support to life and its ecosystems through cooperative learning.

Underneath it all, our actions will continue to be measured on an integrated foundation which values nature's intrinsic worth; which believes that both business and doing good can be mutually inclusive of the other; which understands that conservation can pay for itself; which holds that the process of systemic change occurs individually with the realization that we, the human species, are part of an interrelated system much larger than ourselves; which realizes that each one of us can (and must) choose to take responsibility for all our actions and for making a difference; and which recognizes that connecting with nature moves us from a dominating position to one of reciprocal and participatory livelihood in the larger community of planet earth.

The feelings of peace within me when I am on this land begin to take shape among the translations of the different languages of my life into form. The call to truth and action begins to stir in me. I am witness to the inner intelligence of and within species. I see the unspoken connection between the animals and our animal-care staff. Obviously they are "in sync" with the animals in their care. I begin to feel there is another

way beyond that which I am living. When I first notice the animals speaking to me, subtly or directly, the walls of my earlier city life, of well-incorporated patterns, bid me to run away.

He was six years old. From birth, he had never really enjoyed good health. It was not as if anything was specifically wrong, yet nothing was quite right either. Swollen joints, less active than the rest, thinner too. We found him fully horizontal one afternoon. "Quick, prop his head up," someone said. A giraffe must have its head elevated or else the buildup of unused pressure causes an aneurysm of the brain. We spend the next forty-eight hours with this gentle giant on our laps.

After twelve hours, I begin to get into a matched rhythm with his breathing. I find myself supporting his strength or doubling my energy when his inability to fight dominates. His head alone feels like a fifty-pound weight on my knees. The other giraffes form a circle on the other side of the barn. Slowly they walk, in formation, in silence, heads arching forward and back, as they move in one continuous circle, stopping from time to time for a minute or two. Their pace seems in harmonious synchronicity to his own ability to fight or surrender.

Ceremony, ritual, a death dance, a communion of higher understanding? The bull becomes nervous. The females follow. We move the bull out in order to regain some quiet. Something tells us to watch them all at the same time. The memory is clear: whatever the bull did, the females followed both in body position and movements, all matching the energy level of the dying giraffe, all in silence, all in loyal reverence and support to his deteriorating condition.

His eyes would catch mine, and I would hear, "We are here to teach, we are here to learn. We have come by choice just as you; we *know* what we are doing. Do you?" His head would lean stronger on my lap when I acknowledged his questions. "Are you willing to do what it takes to serve the possibility of true partnership? Are you willing to engage in the mystery of the language of spoken silence?"

His gaze would turn away when my own fear surfaced. The circle, my affirmations, the questions, my cycles of hope and despair lasted another twenty-four hours. Moments after his death, a group of professors from

Texas A&M University arrived for their scheduled site visit. I met them with tears streaming down my face.

Allowing my emotions to flow honors the collective wisdom of the natural world. I am deeply grateful to have been brought to the sanctuary of the wilderness for "alone time" as a way to expand beyond the daily challenges of my own evolution and change. The loud silences of nature's call reflect for me the truth within each living being. To see myself simply as a reflection of the patterns of nature has increased my ability to embrace change as a natural state. I am reminded of T. S. Eliot's words: "In order to arrive at what you do not know, you must go by a way which is the way of ignorance. . . . What we call the beginning is often the end and to make an end is to make a beginning."

Fossil Rim has been in a preparation mode, weaving beginnings and endings. Now we must position and envision ourselves into what we are becoming. I am finally willing to surrender to "ignorance" and be the experiment. Where are we going? Are we willing to listen to inspiration? Are we shaping ourselves as a transformative incubator: a center where all living forms, the seen and unseen, can come, experience, study, understand, relate, acknowledge, and love each other and themselves fully? To this possibility, I fashion myself as a bridge, a willing communicator among species to celebrate and acknowledge the pleasure and pain of it all.

This brings me to the core of my questions, the questions I want to pose, to ask of all of us. And do I dare? Questions like these: What happens when all living things create their own destiny? What happens when we increase the survival of a species simply by our attitudes and acknowledgment of their own chosen destiny? What happens when we let go of control and domination to embrace cooperative partnership among all living beings? What happens when we honor all living things as we used to honor our own elders? What happens when we dare to engage in a process of total equanimity with and within the natural world? What happens when human intelligence is not considered universal intelligence but only a part thereof? What happens when we choose to share fully the surface of the earth with all living things? What

happens when the communication of individual will is accepted and honored by all and for all?

When we envision ourselves as a continuing evolution, we can create a place like Fossil Rim Wildlife Center that rejoices at being recognized. The animals (human and other), land, plants, elements, and minerals gather for a common purpose. The purpose is to return to a balanced and compassionate relationship among all living and sentient beings. Individual and collective refinement is accepted as the norm with balanced evolution its outcome. Taking ourselves out of the field of individuality to become one among many, we can examine what is relationship, relating, open communication, partnership, respect, reverence, livelihood, and connectedness.

What is it to live in the question rather than always look for the comfort of an answer? Let's have this place to speak of possibility, while considering that this is a planet of choice. What if we lived from that essence within ourselves toward every living being? We are part of a true partnership with each and every living thing; we are not their managers, their stewards, or their keepers in the stewardship of life.

For a long time, the little mouse remains in the folds of my clothes next to my skin. This tiny fragile being has as much free will and divine guidance as I. Is he aware more than I? Is his expression of trust and dependence a function of my attitude, his attitude, or ours combined? "Tell me what more, little one, is there for me to listen to, learn from, and translate?" I know you must return to the fields from which you came. As I place you gently on the earth in your natural habitat, I know the dream of Fossil Rim is coming closer to reality with each heartbeat.

UNDERSTANDING ANIMALS

STEPHEN R. L. CLARK

SEEING THE POINT OF WHAT THEY DO

"If a lion could talk," the Wittgensteinian aphorism runs, "we could not understand him."[1] No sounds that a lion could utter would be interpretable as human speech because we would not know from the start what he was doing in uttering them.

Some recent philosophers have used this thought to argue that a lion (and any other nonhuman animal) cannot express, and therefore cannot think, any of the thoughts that in another moment we unthinkingly attribute to them. Lions, we are to suppose, are not really hunting, lying in wait, fighting off intruders, or just playing, because they cannot communicate any such intentions to us or to each other. Living without language, they must also live without an inner life, without a way of representing anything to their own thought, and so without a thought or feeling.

Those who say all this rarely have offered any serious account of how our hominid ancestors began to talk—or even how an ordinary human infant does here and now. Even people who suppose that animals (nonhuman animals) are rather stupid entities solely designed to be of use to "us" will probably reject this theory.

For many millennia, we have had to "understand" what animals are doing and want to do: how else can we have hunted them successfully, or tamed them, or trained them? Even creatures of a radically different kind, divided from us since our respective ancestors first crawled from the sea, are not entirely alien. Most of an insect's life is thoroughly

opaque to us (and ours, no doubt, to them), but we can still cooperate with bees and understand a lot of what they do. We need to learn their "language" by mere observation, whereas most mammalian "languages" involve some shared conventions, shared responses.[2]

I enclosed the word *languages* in quotations, not wishing to beg important questions about grammar, truth, or reflexivity. It is enough that mammals (and many others) express themselves and communicate with their companions, and to us, because we share enough of common observation and desire to make good sense of what they mean. Of course, we get things wrong sometimes, yet that establishes, not that we're always wrong, but, on the contrary, that we are sometimes right.

What is even stranger about post-Wittgensteinian Cartesians is that Wittgenstein's own arguments go quite the other way.[3] Cartesians, following a suggestion of the great French philosopher René Descartes, believe that nonhuman animals have no "point of view," no thoughts or feelings—a doctrine that has been convenient for those who wished to disregard such feelings.

Wittgensteinians, following another great philosopher, Ludwig Wittgenstein, are usually scornful of Cartesian convictions: it is pointless, and even meaningless, to practice the sort of "Cartesian doubt" that Descartes advocated. We do not need to prove everything we ordinarily and unalterably believe (that we have heads, that we were born of human stock, that the world is not a grand charade), and we could not even speak about our private feelings if we were not unalterably convinced of our presence in a genuinely public world, shared with all manner of other creatures.

The "Wittgensteinian revolution" (and the reason Wittgenstein was a great and profoundly important philosopher despite his casual approach to argument and his negative effect on later philosophers' style) was that the public world was restored to us. We do not, after all, begin as solitary intelligences who need to be convinced that there are people, cats, and trees "out there." On the contrary, our own grip upon our own identity and feelings depends on our ability to navigate the public realm of physical objects, social meanings, and the like. Those who deny that

"animals" can feel because they cannot "talk" take a more extreme position than Descartes himself, who said only that we lack the evidence to say that they do or don't, not that they can't.

But the position is absurd. If we cannot tell that something is in pain until it says, "Hey, I'm in pain" (or some equivalent sentence in another human language), then we could not teach our children those locutions, nor could they learn. We have to recognize pain in others before we can tell them that they are "in pain." They have to have been in pain before they can learn that "pain" is what they're in. Expression of pain is a human (even a mammalian or vertebrate or animal) given; we do not need to learn it, nor do we need to learn to recognize it, even though it comes with many variations and even though we can be taught to respond to "it" in many ways. We cannot be taught everything because we cannot learn anything unless we already know enough to learn.

A newborn human whose eyes are tightly closed against bright light, whose mouth is open in a piercing yell, whose hands are stretching out and then withdrawn, "raised to the head in the classic gesture of despair," is undoubtedly in deep distress; those who do question this condition are infected by a false philosophy which says that "neonates aren't capable of feeling."[4] A slightly older child who gazes at her parent, hugs her, chatters nonsense, bounces up and down, and points at what it is she wants, is excited and affectionate long before she can say why.

The same is true for creatures not of our own species. Another remark of Wittgenstein's is more apposite: "What is the natural expression of an intention? Look at a cat when it stalks a bird, or a beast when it wants to escape."[5] If Wittgenstein could not understand that cat, how could he interpret it as "stalking"?

Other commentators see no reason to deny that, for example, chimpanzees show the "full picture of human anger in its three main forms: anger (i.e., aggressive action), sulking, and the temper tantrum."[6] Similarly, "Anyone would surely judge (Harlow's monkeys) as looking severely depressed and regressed (in a clinical sense). The parallel behaviors observed in children and in monkeys exposed to somewhat similar deprivations strongly suggest that the same emotional system, grief or depression, has been activated."[7]

Even if a somewhat different physical structure or process is involved (and there seems no reason, *a priori*, to suppose this here), we need not shrink from labeling it "depression" any more than we refuse to call a cephalopod's light-receptors "eyes" merely because they have a different evolutionary ancestry from vertebrate "eyes."[8]

Similarly, the *wings* of bird, bat, and butterfly. In all these cases we recognize what the organ or the behavior is about and could understand a talking beast as well as any talking person. Ethologists schooled to avoid "anthropomorphism" resort to scare-quotation-marks when writing for their peers but rarely explain, for example, how "rape" by an orangutan or by a drake is different from "rape."[9] Nor do they usually (as in principle they should) place words like "see" or "seek" within such markers. Rhetorical tropes like this are ways of saving face, while the researchers still rely on their empathetic identification of what the animals are doing.[10]

Common sense may add that infants and animals are more securely judged to be in pain precisely because they are in no position to "pretend." Actually, the Wittgensteinian claim that "dogs cannot simulate pain"[11] provides some evidence that Wittgenstein knew as little about dogs as about lions, but the connection between the possibility of truth-speaking and sincerity and the possibility of play-acting is a real one. Only those who can "pretend" to be in pain can know what they are doing (though it by no means follows that those who can't are never in pain). We reach the stage of "telling truths" only when we could tell a lie instead.

Language, indeed, begins with lies. "No one in the world knew what truth was till someone had told a story."[12] Kipling identifies the "pride, the awestruck admiration of himself" that the First Liar experienced "when he saw that, by mere word of mouth, he could send his simpler companions shinnying up trees in search of fruit that he knew was not there."[13] But the birth of truthfulness (and fiction) precedes the birth of humankind. Bateson points out that game-playing (and pretense) is a skill more widely spread than our own species. Many social mammals signal that what comes next, pretend attack or fury, is play. Some can use those very signals to distract their companions from a real attack or fraud.[14]

Why should anyone think otherwise? We teach our children from infancy that it is wise to notice that the family cat is getting cross or that the dog wants a walk. We teach our pets to understand commands and are not unduly startled if they sometimes understand intelligently. Of course, we don't believe that they will "literally" talk to us (or to each other). The folk legend that on Christmas Eve the animals can speak expresses a fond hope but not one that is realized here and now.

Nonhuman animals are not human, and we should no more expect them to use human language (characterized by rules of reference and predication, transformative grammar, and generalizable syntax) than we should expect people to catch flies with their tongues. Different capacities lurk within the distinct gene pools of different species.[15] It is even rather offensive to interpret nonhuman animals, of any kind, as if they were really people (rather stupid people) dressed up in fur or feather. Chimpanzees are not backward, language-impaired people (and neither are people with those disabilities much like apes). They are not, as the popular interpretation of Darwinian theory implies, earlier or more primitive versions of ourselves but radically *other* creatures with different criteria of health and happiness. It is, accordingly, a good idea to divest ourselves of Disneyesque delusions and to take those other creatures seriously as themselves. In doing so, we may begin to understand them and to converse in something other than a human language.

But the reaction against Disney, so to speak, can go too far—and often has. The fact that chimpanzees, dogs, whales, nightingales, lizards, squids, or honeybees are wildly different from us and are unlikely ever to learn a language we could teach does not establish that they are entirely different from us. Human language is a species-specific trait (which not all humans, even intelligent humans, have) that is grounded in capacities common to most mammals, or most vertebrates, or most animals. Species are not distinct natural kinds but evolving populations working from a genetic heritage, far more of which is common than is different.

Certainly, we get things wrong (and therefore, for good reason, sometimes try to describe what's going on as calmly and objectively as possible). It does not follow that we should always trust "objective researchers"

(deliberately self-blinded) more than those who actually love the creatures they are talking to. Sometimes it takes a degree of empathy, of love, to see what infants, and nonhumans, are about.

Jane Goodall is a far better witness to what chimpanzees may mean than someone whose only interest in them is to prove them fit for use. Loving parents know far more about their children than those philosophers who doubt—on the basis of a foolish theory—that an infant is a person (and so deny her the rights that, without good arguments, they restrict to persons).

OPENING THE EYES

All that I have said so far would probably be acceptable to anyone who works halfway efficiently with animals, whether they are pet owners, farmers, trainers, or laboratory technicians. One other species-specific trait is that we have been working with nonhumans for millennia. Only the hunters and farmers who could understand those creatures (and ensure their understanding too) left many progeny. We have been selecting ourselves *to understand* and must now begin to pay the price for this: that we see too clearly what we cost the creatures and must begin to disentangle and reform a way of life profoundly based upon injustice.

Understanding need not be an occult or peculiar process. It rests straightforwardly upon shared forms of life, shared appetites, a common range of gesture and expression (exactly as it does for understanding members of our own species). Language opens up new possibilities—of incomprehension and misunderstanding as well. It can do so only by relying on pre-verbal understandings that are not confined to a single species. Even our understanding of bee-language (roughly so called), which rests upon a careful analysis of what, objectively, bees do, relies upon a prior grasp of what they are about (foraging, returning, dancing). Conversely, our untutored grasp of what a cow or cat or budgerigar is doing had better be informed by attentive, careful, and unbiased observation.

But there are other possibilities worth entertaining for a while, if only because not everyone is wholly convinced that scientific empiricism and

evolutionary theory have together given a full account of who and what we are. Some people are indeed convinced that both are largely false. The usual inference they draw is that "we," after all, are of another kind than "animals": chimpanzees are more like worms or amoebas than they are like people, despite the near genetic identity of chimpanzees and people. We, they say, are spiritual beings, and our capacities are not to be judged from any apparent similarity to "beasts." This position, even if it is, as I suppose, in partial error, is at least more reasonable than that of scientists who say that we are merely natural beings and yet that "animals" are wholly other, and fair game for any use "we" please. Natural beings as closely related as we are cannot be so completely different as to license wildly different treatment. If we were of distinct kinds "morally" it could only be because we were distinct kinds "ontologically."

The post-Cartesian version of this metaphysical divide insists that "animals" are mere automata and that people are thinking beings as well as bodies. Any attempt to "think along with animals" is as fruitless, as self-projective, as thinking along with stones or railway engines. Wittgenstein again: "Only remember that the spirit of the snake, of the lion, is *your* spirit."[16] To which I can offer here no answer but a straight rebuttal.

Most people who deny our consanguinity are not Cartesians nor even Wittgensteinians. The more traditional view was that "we" differed from "beasts" by adding an intellectual or rational soul to the animal soul we shared with them. Correspondingly, it was thought possible to find affinities between our own experience and theirs. That indeed was why, for some traditionalists, it was so wrong to sympathize with beasts: by doing so we pandered to our own beastly selves. "When [man] came to believe that the beasts were like himself, he straightway began to imitate their emotions and to lose his freedom, which the Patriarchs later regained under the guidance of the spirit of Christ, that is, the idea of God."[17] "The requirement to refrain from slaughtering beasts," so Spinoza insists, "is founded on groundless superstition and womanish compassion rather than on sound reason."[18]

One reply to all this is simply to reject it completely and to declare that all of us are merely natural creatures, without distinct natures that could ground so radical a division. But a partial rejection also has some merits.

Suppose that we are indeed not merely "natural" and that it is possible to locate, within our spiritual being, some affinities, by which no doubt we should not let ourselves be ruled, with beasts. "Man is a lumpe where all beasts kneaded be: Wisdom makes him an arke where all agree."[19] Perhaps if we are to rule ourselves, we need to acknowledge what it is we have to rule. And if we can rule "the beasts within," may we not thereby come to understand the beasts without? Not every form of rule is oppression. And nonoppressive rule depends on understanding.

So if we are spiritual beings, in addition to or instead of being "natural," we may expect to find it possible to open up our hearts or minds or spiritual eyes to "see" or feel what beasts are doing. We do not do so just by imagining what "we" would do in their place. Rather, the point is to locate a memory or present trace within ourselves, to tune ourselves into the right condition, rather as Olaf Stapledon's time-traveling Neptunian must tune himself into the distinctive forms of our own primitive thought. "I had now to select that mode of the primitive which is distinctive of your own species, a mode characterized by repressed sexuality, excessive self-regard, and an intelligence which is both rudimentary and in bondage to unruly cravings."[20] It was a thought not uncommon in the first half of this century. The poet W. B. Yeats records that he "once visited a Cabbalist who spent the day trying to look out of the eyes of his canary; he announced at nightfall that things had for it colour but no outline. His method of contemplation was probably in error."[21] Actually, the result is at least compatible with the results of more ordinary ethological research. Male robins, for example, respond to red objects, whatever their shape, as if to rival robins.

This visionary intelligence, to be distinguished from the insight of long experience, needs checking. So do insight and the laborious analysis of what the creature "does." Once again, the fact that all these can be wrong does not establish that we are always wrong but, on the contrary, that we are sometimes right. Sometimes we can see/hear/feel as others do, when that slice of the world itself is opened up to us. Even when we cannot see—or cannot recall—the details, we may be sure that those whose eyes we momentarily see through are not simple objects. Birds are not small brown fluttering things:

How do you know but ev'ry Bird that cuts the airy way,
Is an immense world of delight, clos'd by your senses five?[22]

Even our understanding of our fellow humans is, in part, by visionary intelligence: we do not know people only from the outside but by interpreting the motion of our own interior feeling, as well. Even ordinarily scientific understanding of the material world is founded on "the way of intuition, helped by a feeling for the order lying behind appearance."[23]

CHUANG TZU AND THE FISHES

Chuang Tzu, walking by the river, remarked to his companion, Hui Tzu, how happily the fish were swimming. Hui retorted that he was not a fish: how could he, Chuang Tzu, know how fishes felt? "You are not me," replied Chuang Tzu. "How can you know what I know?" Hui replied that, since he was not Chuang Tzu, he didn't (didn't, that is, experience things as Chuang did), but by the same token Chuang Tzu could not know how fishes felt. "Let us begin again," said Chuang Tzu. "You asked me how I knew how happily the fish were swimming, though you pretended not to know what it was I knew. I knew it along the river."[24]

That almost Wittgensteinian exchange could almost serve as coda to this chapter. Those who deny us the right to understand what a fellow creature feels cannot consistently debate the issue with us; by the same token, they do not understand our answers nor believe that we have understood their question. Debate, and doubt, are only possible within a larger framework of unquestioned sympathy.

Someone may retort—and some post-Wittgensteinian Cartesians have retorted—that *human beings* have an innate ability to understand each other, to grasp what each is doing, and hence to interpret sounds or signs as language. Creatures of "different kinds" have no such biological basis for mutual comprehension. But this reply rests on a failed theory: namely, that there are "distinct biological kinds." I have argued elsewhere that current biological theory gives us no reason to identify such radically divided "natural kinds."[25] Difficult as it is for all of us to imagine, we inhabit a world of individuals drawn from a common stock according to a shared pattern. "We are of one blood, you and I," so

Kipling caused his jungle animals to say. Even if they don't actually say it (as most probably they don't), the claim is true.

So Chuang Tzu was right to insist that he could, in principle, recognize the "joy of fishes" as he walked along the river. But was he right in fact? We inhabit one public world, perhaps, and have a common stock of feelings and desires to draw upon. But "a fool sees not the same tree that a wise man sees," so Blake declared, "with justice."[26] Of course it is possible for us to feel things as another does and so to understand that other, but it is also possible for us to misinterpret others because we take our own perceptions as the norm.

Whales may seem to freeze when assaulted by a killer whale. Is their feeling one of abject terror, or a willingness to give themselves for food? Are they frightened, stupefied, or saintly?[27] What we "see" in them may be only what we would feel ourselves (or choose to think that we would feel). Birds sing "joyfully" before the dawn—or is it only that they shout their loudest to put off their rivals?

Did Chuang Tzu's fishes recognize *his* feelings? Of course not: they were fishes, and lacked—we are strangely sure—the apparatus to identify what air-breathing, vocalizing bipeds do. But by the same token, we might wonder whether it is true, after all, that "man is a beast where all beasts kneaded be." Do we have the apparatus to understand all others? Even if we do, how can we tell if we are misusing it? How could we tell whether we lack the senses, lack the sympathies, to make sense of what some strange creature far beyond our nature does?

Briefly, because we still think ourselves "superior" to other creatures, we think that we can understand them while denying that they can understand us. If naturalistic evolutionary theory is all the truth we know, then it seems probable that, despite the many commonalities, each evolutionary line may pass outside the comprehension of all others. The worlds they see are ones we never could—and correspondingly can't know what it is they feel on many specialized occasions. "What, after all, is it like to be a bat?"[28] Can we be confident that we are not being "understood," in ways we can't imagine, by creatures far beyond our comprehension? Can we be confident that the worlds of cuttlefish, spider, and wasp are really "smaller" and more comprehensible than ours?

What we think we know of them is that small region where our senses, our capacities, coincide. If their worlds are larger than ours in one dimension or another, we shall not understand them nor even notice that we have not understood.

Only if these other worlds are, after all, contained within the one world to which we have given the name of the Divine Intellect, or the Perfect Human, can we, as servants of that intellect, realistically hope to understand. But even if they are, of course, it does not follow that we here and now are automatically saints and wholly at ease with the divine.

The chances are, whether we are "merely natural beings" or "images of the divine," that there is a great deal which we do not understand. The feelings of Chuang Tzu's fishes will probably not be ours. It does not follow that those feelings will be "simpler" ones than ours. They may just be different and not accessible to ordinarily rapacious humans.

One further analogy: It would be absurd to claim that male and female human beings have no point of contact and cannot comprehend each other; it would be equally absurd to deny the difficulties of comprehension. There may be—there must be—a point of view from which the experience and feelings of both men and women can be comprehended, shared, and acted on. It does not follow that every inquisitive male or female instantly understands what the other wants or dreams or says. "Understanding" others can often be an excuse for prurient or oppressive curiosity.[29] Cartesian doubt is, after all, a discipline as vital as that love "purged of concupiscence" that Augustine labels friendship: shed your preconceptions and the easy readings of another's acts and feelings, but only so as to reach a deeper understanding later on, guided by the realization that others may always understand us better than we do ourselves and that the world is always stranger, and more beautiful, than we supposed.

References

1. Ludwig Josef Johan Wittgenstein. 1958. *Philosophical Investigations*. Tr. G. E. M. Anscombe. 223g. Oxford: Blackwell.
2. See James L. Gould & Carol G. Gould. 1983. "Can a Bee Behave Intelligently?" *New Scientist*, 14 April, reprinted in *The Understanding of Animals*. 1984. Ed. Georgina Ferry. 272–83. Oxford: Blackwell.

3. For a more Wittgensteinian approach to understanding animals, see Vicki Hearne. 1986. *Adam's Task: Calling Animals by Name.* New York: Knopf.

4. See F. Leboyer. 1975. *Birth Without Violence.* 7ff. London: Wildwood House.

5. Wittgenstein. Op. cit. 647 (165e).

6. D. O. Hebb. 1972. *Textbook of Psychology.* 3rd ed. 202. Philadelphia: W. B. Saunders.

7. R. Plutchik. 1980. *Emotion: A Psychoevolutionary Synthesis.* 107. New York: Harper & Row.

8. K. Z. Lorenz. 1981. *The Foundations of Ethology.* 90. Tr. K. Z. Lorenz & R. W. Kickert. New York: Springer-Verlag.

9. There might well be a difference, namely that human rapists, but probably not drakes or orangutans, may be moved by hate as much as lust. But the act is still rape even if this is not so.

10. See D. R. Crocker. 1981. "Anthropomorphism: Bad Practice, Honest Prejudice?" *New Scientist*, 16 July. Reprinted in Georgina Ferry. Op. cit. 304–313.

11. Wittgenstein. Op. cit. 250.

12. Rudyard Kipling. 1928. *Fiction: A Book of Words.* 282. London: Macmillan.

13. Kipling. *Independence: A Book of Words.* 234.

14. G. Bateson. 1973. *Steps Towards an Ecology of Mind.* 150ff. London: Paladin. See also Barbara Noske. 1989. *Humans and Other Animals.* 146ff. London: Pluto Press.

15. See Stephen Pinker. 1994. *The Language Instinct.* 334ff. Harmandsworth: Allen Lane.

16. Wittgenstein. 1916. *Notebooks: 1914–1916.* 20 October 1916. Oxford: Blackwell.

17. Benedict de Spinoza. *Ethics.* 1982. Tr. S. Shirley, ed. S. Feldman. 193 (4p68s). Indianapolis: Hackett.

18. Spinoza. Op. cit. 175 (4p37s1). See my "Humans, Animals and 'Animal Behavior.'" 1983. 169ff. In *Ethics and Animals.* Ed. H. B. Miller & W. H. Williams. Humana Press. Also see my "The Description and Evaluation of Animal Emotion." 1987. 139–49. In *Mindwaves.* Ed. C. Blakemore & S. Greenwood. Oxford: Blackwell.

19. John Donne. 1929. *Complete Verse and Selected Prose.* 163. Ed. J. Hayward. London: Nonesuch Press.

20. Olaf Stapledon. 1972. *Last and First Men* and *Last Men in London.* 380. Harmondsworth: Penguin. (First published 1932.)

21. William Butler Yeats. 1961. *Essays and Introductions*. 411. London: Macmillan.

22. William Blake. 1966. *Complete Writings*. Ed. G. Keynes. 150. London: Oxford University Press.

23. Albert Einstein, cited by W. I. B. Beveridge. 1953. *The Art of Scientific Investigation*. 2nd ed. 57. London: Heinemann.

24. After Chuang Tzu. 1963. Ed. Wing-Tsit Chan. *Sourcebook in Chinese Philosophy*. Ch. 17: 209f. Princeton, N.J.: Princeton University Press.

25. "Apes and the Idea of Kindred." 1993. *The Great Ape Project: Equality Beyond Humanity*. Ed. P. Singer & P. Cavalieri. 113–25. London: Fourth Estate.

26. Blake. "Marriage of Heaven and Hell." *Complete Writings*. Ed. Keynes. Op. cit. 151.

27. See my "The Reality of Shared Emotion." In *Interpretation and Explanation in the Study of Behavior*. Ed. M. Bekoff & D. Jamieson. Vol. 1, 449–72. Westview Press. 1990.

28. See Thomas Nagel. 1979. "What Is It Like to Be a Bat?" *Mortal Questions*. 165–180. Oxford: Blackwell.

29. See my *A Parliament of Souls*. 1990. Oxford: Clarendon Press. 100ff. After J. Hillman. 1967. *Insearch: Psychology and Religion*. London: Hodder & Stoughton.

PART 2

TRADITIONAL RELATIONSHIPS

ONE EARTH, ONE SPIRIT

GARY KOWALSKI

People in every time and culture have found the living earth a source of awe and inspiration. The Greeks elevated her to the level of goddess, Gaia. Her miracles of chemistry and evolution have created life in its amazing variety and abundance. And the intricate balance of her ecology sustains our bodies and spirits.

The wonder we feel in the presence of nature is well-nigh universal. It may even extend beyond the realms of human thought. In December 1963, the zoologist Adriaan Kortland witnessed the following amazing tableau:

Sunset in an African rain forest. The splendor of these sunsets. A chimpanzee arrives on the scene, carrying a papaya, holding it with one hand against his loins as he walks along. This is his bedside snack. The chimp puts down the papaya. For a full fifteen minutes the animal remains as if spellbound by the spectacle of the changing colors of the dusk and watches without moving. Then he withdraws silently into the thicket, forgetting his papaya.

One can only guess what was going through the chimpanzee's mind as he stood musing on the fading light of day. Was it the soft blending of violets and magentas that stirred his imagination? Did the twilight awaken memories of other days or companions who had gone before, bringing on long, lonely thoughts of nightfall? Was it a moment of trance or daydream or reverie? No one can say, but this almost human cousin clearly was satisfying a hunger beyond his immediate needs for food or

sustenance. He was responding to an urge that transcended the imperatives of physical survival and that can only be called spiritual.

When we gaze enraptured at the setting sun; when we look up and marvel at the nighttime full of stars; when we are swept away by the roar of ocean surf or stand in meditation beneath a redwood older than any human bible, we participate in a religion as real and powerful as any on earth. What we experience at such a time—our feelings of kinship and reverence—is nothing less than the universe contemplating its own hidden depths.

We should not be surprised that nature worship—communion with the Holy present in bird, beast, and forest—may be the original and most elemental form of human spirituality. In the high mountain caves of Germany and Switzerland, Old Stone Age implements lie side by side with the skulls of cave bears that appear to have been arranged in symbolic patterns, remains which most scholars interpret as evidence of a cult of bear veneration that existed among the Neanderthals who inhabited the region 70,000 years ago.

Fifty thousand years later, the people of what is now Lascaux, France, created the world's first religious art as they decorated the ceilings of their caves with magnificent images of bison, black stag, ibex, and arctic pony. When the Canadian government recently sent a delegation of Eskimo hunters to see those caverns, a guide explained the carbon-14 dating of the site. But their antiquity appeared to escape the visitors, who only recognized the kindred spirit behind the paintings and expressed a desire to meet the artists.

While it is impossible to reconstruct the sacred cosmos of our human and protohuman ancestors, it may have shared aspects with the thought world of people such as Native Americans, who carried a similar hunting-and-gathering existence into modern times.

"In the beginning of all things," said the Pawnee Chief Letakots-Lesa at the turn of the century, "wisdom and knowledge were with the animals; for Tirawa, the One Above, did not speak directly to man. He sent certain animals to tell men that he showed himself through the beasts, and that from them, and from the stars and the sun and the moon, man should learn." For such people, the creatures of the earth naturally possessed a sacred significance.

I felt something primal last fall when I traveled to the Dead Creek management area in central Vermont to watch the snow geese touch down on their annual migration from the shores of Hudson Bay to their winter homes in the Chesapeake. Eight or nine thousand of the big birds rested and fed in the marshes and cornfields, while others circled the sky in numbers that filled the binoculars in every direction. The spectacle of so much swirling freedom and energy lit up my brain with pure elation, so that I could only stare. When a friend visited the area two days later to discover the geese had all gone, I felt blessed that I'd happened on this portion of their yearly pilgrimage.

The thrill we receive from seeing a thousand snow geese flying south and the more quiet enjoyment we feel watching a chickadee visit the feeder outside the kitchen window may both be part of our evolutionary inheritance. Harvard biologist E. O. Wilson suggests that human beings have an innate affinity with other creatures.

Over the millennia, our nervous systems evolved through interplay with a wild environment, so we naturally respond with fascination to the animals who are members of our own family tree. They awaken memories of our own origins and help us understand our own rootedness in nature. Wilson calls this drive *biophilia*, literally meaning the love of life, and more generally our tendency to be enthused and excited by the butterflies, blue whales, and other fabulous beasts who share the planet.

Biophilia would explain why children seem to have an almost automatic attraction to most animals. "From infancy," says Wilson, "we concentrate happily on ourselves and other organisms. We learn to distinguish life from the inanimate and move toward it like moths to a porch light." In much the same way a gosling imprints on its mother or any nearby ethologist, children seem predisposed to fixate on things that writhe or wriggle.

When a group of librarians recently surveyed over ten thousand schoolchildren to determine young people's likes and dislikes, they found that children's favorite books fell into two categories: "Animals" and "Here and Now." The top choices in "Here and Now" were tales like Carol Carrick's *The Accident* and *The Foundling*, realistic stories of the grief a young boy feels when losing his dog and the healing that takes

place when he adopts a new puppy. Animals seem to be a necessary part of the mental landscape for children as they grow. Without animals, our development would be emotionally stunted and morally impoverished.

Before they can be numbed and desensitized, children deeply empathize with the suffering of other species. Abundant evidence confirms this. Carl Sandburg tells us that when Abraham Lincoln was a boy, he shot a wild turkey with his father's rifle. It was his first encounter with hunting and also his last, for he never again felt like pulling the trigger.

Clara Barton tells us that as a young girl, she witnessed a cow being slaughtered on the family farm. At the precise moment the hired hand brought the heavy axe down on the cow's skull, Clara felt a blow to her own head and lost consciousness. When she woke up, she became a vegetarian and never willingly ate meat again. Such stories suggest that compassion is not a learned quality. Rather, cruelty must be cultivated and encouraged as tender feelings are slowly calloused and hardened.

Over time, however, most of us lose our innate sympathy. From parents and elders, from church and school, we learn the lesson that only one species on earth really matters and that people who care about animals are sentimental, irrational, or otherwise misinformed. Animals, we are told, have no feelings. They have no souls. They are nothing more than complex machines or collections of conditioned reflexes. They have no significance in and of themselves but exist only to serve and satisfy human wishes.

We deny the inner wisdom we possessed as children. We suppress our intuitive feelings of reverence and relatedness. And this denial is what enables us to use and exploit animals as research tools, commodities, and resources. It explains why so many people accept as "normal" a diet and lifestyle that demand the needless suffering of so many other creatures.

The time has come to break down those walls of denial and restore our birthright of sensitivity and respect for other living beings. This task is especially critical at this moment when the earth itself seems to be in danger, for the way we treat other animals is a vital indicator of our attitude toward the natural world in general. Unless we can open our hearts to the animals who are so much like ourselves, how can we hope to

respond with passion to problems like destruction of the rain forests or depletion of the ozone?

The concept of extinction, like the notion of "forever," is not one we easily understand. We know firsthand what it means for an individual to die. Indeed, human beings are not the only animals who grieve or suffer when a loved one leaves the world. Elephants mourn their dead, much like us, and sometimes even bury them. The mother seal sheds tears like ours when her pup is killed by hunters. Our biology guides us in how to feel and what to do when facing death, but the extermination of a species is something else entirely, since it means not just the demise of every living representative of the tribe but of all unborn generations as well.

Death is a part of life and the corollary of birth, whereas extinction means the annihilation of life and the end of birth. Imagining what that means when multiplied a million-fold is literally beyond our grasp. We lack the neural equipment to respond to threats that seem so imponderable and far removed from immediate experience.

At the same time, the story of one animal, like Keiko, the real-life killer whale who starred in the movie *Free Willy* and who was finally removed from the tiny tank where he spent his life and transported to a specially designed and constructed marine-mammal rehabilitation facility on the Oregon coast. From there he was moved back to his native Iceland and might eventually be reunited with the open ocean. His journey has grabbed the attention of the entire world.

One animal in pain—be it a whale, a dog, or a deer—is something we viscerally can understand. We respond with the urgency that's needed. This in itself seems to be part of our instinctive repertoire. As great apes, we have the capacity to care for the sick and injured, not only of our own species but of others as well.

When a young boy recently was knocked unconscious by falling into the gorilla enclosure in a city zoo, the animal's immediate response was to approach the child and stroke him gently until assistance arrived.

We primates exhibit our share of aggression, of course, but we can also be compassionate creatures under the right circumstances. In one experiment, monkeys could choose to receive food by delivering an electric jolt to another animal that could be seen in restraints through a

one-way mirror. Unless they pressed the button, the monkeys starved. Eighty-seven percent of the animals tested turned out to be conscientious objectors; they refused to shock and torment their helpless companions. One monkey went without food for two weeks rather than succumb to such deliberate cruelty.

Although humans are not always so kind, we too can be touched by the suffering of others. The outpouring of concern that moved hundreds of volunteers to hand-wash the oil-soaked birds who were victims of the *Exxon Valdez* is the kind of energy we need to harness permanently. The crusade for animal rights intersects the campaign to save the earth precisely at the point where we have the ability to care.

The environmental crisis is, above all, a spiritual crisis. And we can not resolve it until we can recapture the knowledge we seem to have lost—that we are not separate from the web of life but merely one strand in the design. Animals might be the teachers who will help us recover that sense of connection. If we let them, they can touch our hearts. If we look into their eyes, we can see the grief and joy that reflects our own humanity. If we expand the circle of our awareness, we realize that we are not the only species on this planet who dance, dream, or glory in the majesty of the sunset. "Until one has loved an animal, a part of one's soul remains unawakened," said Anatole France. Animals might be the agents who once again make us realize that all life is precious.

The unity of life is an immemorial teaching recorded in many times and places:

"Ask now the beasts and they shall teach thee," we read in the Bible, "and the fowls of the air, and they shall teach thee. Or speak to the earth, and it shall teach thee, and the fishes of the earth shall declare unto thee."

Says the Koran, holy book of the Moslems, "There is not an animal on the earth, nor a flying creature flying on two wings, but they are peoples like unto you."

In the famous inscription of Chang Tsai from eleventh-century China, we read: "Heaven is my father and earth is my mother and even such a small creature as I finds an intimate place in its midst. All people are my brothers and sisters and all things are my companions."

And from the Sioux holy man Black Elk: "We should understand well that all things are the work of the Great Spirit. We should know the Great Spirit is within all things: the trees, the grasses, the rivers, the mountains, and the four-legged and winged peoples. . . . When we do understand this deeply in hearts, then we will fear, and love, and know the Great Spirit, and then we will be and act and live as the Spirit intends."

"The greatness of a nation and its moral progress," said Mahatma Ghandi, "can be measured by the way in which its animals are treated." In recovering the primordial knowledge that all life is sacred, we may not only manage to save our world, we also just might save our own souls. In learning how to live nonviolently with other creatures, we just might find peace within.

TURTLE MAN

JOSEPH BRUCHAC

Every spring, when I was a small child, in those few weeks after the last hepatica blossoms had faded in the woods, my grandmother and my grandfather and I would go for evening rides. We'd usually head for Saratoga Lake or Schuylerville, and we'd go slower than most of the other cars on the road. Slower because we were looking for turtles.

Every year, just like clockwork, we'd find them in the same places crossing the roads. My job was to get out and pick the turtles up, rescuing them before they started across that strip of blacktop that could spell their doom or, making sure I looked both ways, picking up a turtle which had stranded itself in the very middle of the road and was waiting out the danger. Head and legs and tail pulled in might have made that wood turtle or red-eared slider safe from a fox or even a bear, but two tons of wheeled vehicle was too much for the thickest shell.

"Turtles is tough," my grandfather said, "but they needs a little help now and again."

My grandfather's people were Abenaki Indian, though he would always hunch up his shoulder and tell those who asked why he was so dark that it was because he was French-Canadian. In a way that was true, for his father had come down to Greenfield Center, New York, in the Adirondack mountain foothills from the village of St. Francis in Québec.

At Odanak, which means "The Village" and is the Abenaki name for St. Francis, Rogers Rangers staged that raid made immortal in the book and movie *Northwest Passage*, a raid that supposedly "wiped out" the Abenakis, though it was mostly women and children that the Rangers

killed that day—many as they sought shelter in the Catholic Church at St. Francis. The people of St. Francis, like the turtle who was one of their two main clan animals, have always been tough survivors.

My grandfather would hold up a turtle that had its head stuck in its shell and say something soft to it. Immediately that turtle would begin to poke its head out and open its eyes to look at him. That always made my grandfather smile.

"Now jes' look at him," my grandfather would say.

I noticed how the leathery flesh of that turtle's neck looked a lot like the tough, wrinkled skin of my grandfather's hands. Perhaps that was why I dreamed one night as a child that my grandfather was holding a turtle as big as he was and they looked so much alike that it was hard for me to figure out where the turtle ended and my grandfather began.

I remember those spring evenings. The weather was so warm and the smells in the air so sweet that it seemed as if everything in the natural world was awake and alive, celebrating. We would hear the calls of birds that had been gone from the forest through the long cold winter—from the sweet ululation of the Baltimore oriole to the small, high voices of the warblers, who'd fill the treetops with their songs and their many colors, like flowers that had miraculously sprung up and blossomed overnight.

Some evenings we'd find two or three turtles, and on the weekends we might rescue as many as half a dozen of them. I'd made a little enclosure with boards in our backyard around one of the blue spruce trees, and we'd sometimes keep a turtle or two in there for a while before taking them deep into the woods or to a pond far enough from the roads. We had a special relationship with turtles, and it went back farther than I knew when I was a child.

Don Bowman, a man in his late eighties who used to live not far from here, started writing letters to me seven years ago from his home in Delaware after he saw a review of one of my books. He saw that I was living on Splinterville Hill and asked me if I might have ever known a Jesse Bowman—no relation of his, he added—who used to run the little store there. I wrote back that Jesse was my grandfather.

It turned out that Don Bowman had known him in the '20s and '30s, long before I was born. A natural storyteller and a lifelong collector of

stories of all kinds, including local history and tall tales, Don began writing me letters that filled me in on what it was like here before my time.

"Did they still call your grandfather 'Mr. Turtle Man' when you were a child?" he asked me in one letter. And he explained how my grandfather got that name, a story that I had never heard before.

One spring day, Don said, he came by my grandfather's store and noticed that there were two old bathtubs set up there to the side of the building. He guessed those bathtubs had been there for some time but had never taken a close look at them. This time he did. One of them had dirt in it and there were two or three toads in there hopping about. The other one was partially filled with water, and there were a dozen or more turtles swimming around.

Just as he was about to ask my grandfather why he had bathtubs full of turtles and toads, a little girl came to the station on her bicycle. She had a turtle in her hand.

"Mr. Turtle Man," she said, "here's another turtle I found in the road. Can I have my penny?"

At that my grandfather gave her a penny—which she then used to buy a handful of licorice candy—and put the turtle in the bathtub with the others.

"What's this all about, Jess?" Don Bowman asked.

"Ever time a kid brings me a toad or a turtle I gives 'em a penny. Them toads goes into my garden," my grandfather said. "They does a real good job of eating the bugs."

"And the turtles?" Don Bowman said.

"Oh, I'll just take them over to the pond sometime. Turtles is tough, but they needs a little help now and again."

When Don looked at him as if that was not explanation enough, my grandfather shrugged his shoulders. "My father," he said, "always told me we ought to take care of turtles."

Because of the long understanding, the long tradition of recognizing animals as our relatives, of reinforcing our animal identity through the system of clan, the Native people of the Americas have a different starting place for their worldviews and the way they act out their lives in relation to the natural world.

My Mohawk friend Tom Porter recently wrote a book called *Clanology* about the clan system among the Iroquois people. Although Iroquois culture and language are much different from Abenaki, we share many things in common. At one point in his slender but powerful volume, he talks about the characteristics of the people of the principal Mohawk clans—Turtle, Wolf, and Bear.

"The Turtle Clan," Tom wrote, "is one of the principal clans of the Mohawk. The turtle is the symbol of the entire earth. We walk upon the turtle's back. The people of the Turtle Clan are the foundation of our Nation. Because of this fact, the Turtle Clan people are very consistent, determined, and humbly stubborn."

Two decades ago, late on a summer day in the Adirondack town of Old Forge, I stood in the backyard of my friend and teacher Maurice Dennis. A small fire, the fire that he always kept burning, threw fragrant smoke around us, smoke that scented the air and kept away the mosquitoes. Maurice, whose Abenaki name *Mdawelasis* meant "Little Loon," was carving a totem pole from a length of cedar. Pausing, he pointed out the turtle at its base.

"The Turtle," he said, "is always there at the bottom, holding the weight on its back."

He put his hand on the carved shape of its shell and had me count with him the plates on the turtle's back.

"Thirteen," I said.

"Every turtle has thirteen scales on its back," he said. 'Those thirteen stand for the thirteen moons in every year. They stand for the thirteen Abenaki nations. There were thirteen of our nations before there were ever thirteen colonies."

There was a moment of silence, and then I heard a soft whistling sound overhead. I looked up and saw a loon. The whistling sound was made by its great wings as it cut through the air above us. Maurice raised a hand, as if in greeting to the bird which was his namesake. I thought, then, how that bird, *Mdawela* had also given its name to our old ones who were the deep-seers, the shamans. We call them *mdeowlinno*, those who dive down under the surface to see the things that others cannot recognize, those who dive down to another world just as the loon does.

"It's going to the Moose River," Maurice said. Then he put his hand back onto the carved shape of the ancient turtle. "Turtle remembers our thirteen nations," he said. "Turtle will never forget us."

Even longer ago, the earth was covered with water. There was no firm place to stand and if the people were going to live on this earth they needed such a place. The birds and animals that lived in the water talked this over, knowing that human beings would soon be created. One of them—some say it was the duck—remembered that there was something firm deep under the water. So they began to dive to bring up earth.

There are many versions of this story, a story that some call "The Earth-diver Myth," but which I have always thought of as the story of Turtle's gift.

In the Iroquois version of that great tale of creation, all of them fail except for the muskrat. In the Shawnee version, many of the water animals bring up earth together. In all of them there are basic understandings that are the underpinning of those Native cultures which have tried—for thousands of years—to live lightly on this land, to show respect for all life. One of those understandings is that the animals make it possible for us to survive. Teachers and elders, they made this world. They are wiser and stronger than we are, and thus we must always respect them and be mindful of them. Another understanding is that this earth itself is as alive as that great turtle which supports us on its back. It does not do so out of self-interest but because the nature of life (the ancient nature of life that the animals can teach us) is to give, to cooperate, and to share. Those are only some of the lessons to be found in that story of the turtle's gift.

In one Abenaki version of that story, a story that it seems I have dreamed more often than I have heard it, it is the great loon who flies beneath the water and reaches the bottom, bringing up earth in its beak.

When it breaks the surface, the loon looks for a place for that earth, for it will fall back down to the bottom without a place to put it. That is when the great turtle floats to the surface. The great turtle lifts up its head and speaks.

"I will carry the earth on my back," it says.

Then loon places that small bit of earth on the back of the turtle. That bit of earth grows and grows until it becomes the world which supports us today. This world balanced on the patient back of the great turtle, the turtle that has never forgotten us.

"We ought to take care of turtles," my great-grandfather told my grandfather—the turtles whose shells carry the memory of thirteen Abenaki nations: Micmac, Maliseet, Penobscot, Passmaquoddy, Penacook, Cowasuck, Pocumtuck, Nipmuck, Pigwacket, Kennebec, Sokoki, Missisquoi, Arosaguntacook. And so, each spring, I too have gone seeking the turtles to rescue them from the roads.

But that is not the end of this circle. This spring my wife, Carol, was looking out from our camp across the lawn of the piece of land we just purchased in the Kaydeross Range. Bucket Pond—the same pond my grandfather fished in when he was a boy—is just below that camp. As she was standing there our little fox terrier came up to her with something in her mouth. It was a turtle. It was a female red-eared slider. You could tell its sex by the shortness of her tail and her claws—the males have claws and tails that are much longer.

"Did she catch this turtle in the pond?" my wife and I asked each other before I carried the turtle back down to Bucket Pond and watched it swim away underwater. It had plenty of company. For the past three weeks we had been going down to the pond to watch the heads of dozens of turtles, from big snappers to delicate red-eared sliders, poke above the water. It was mating season.

"What they're saying to each other right now," I said to Carol, "is something like—'Hey, hey, are you a guy or a girl?'" I looked out over the pond. No turtle heads were visible today. "Do you think that turtle was going somewhere to lay its eggs?" I said.

The next day, when it rained, I got my answer. I walked outside and saw not one or two but four turtles, all of them females, all of them digging holes in the thin sandy soil around our camp. I came close and knelt and watched as one of them dug with her hind legs, scooping out the dirt. Then, wedging the end of her shell down into that hole, she laid four perfect eggs. An oriole was singing in the chestnut tree overhead as the

rain fell harder. But the turtle and the bird and I didn't mind that warm spring rain.

Finally, though, I went in to leave her and her sisters to their work, noticing that yet another turtle was coming up the wooded path from the pond fifty yards down the hill. After two generations of bringing turtles to our home to rescue them, we were now caring for a place where the turtles came to bring new generations of turtles into the world. Our lawn was a nesting ground for turtles. And I could feel my grandfather with me. I knew that the next time I saw him in my dreams, cradling a turtle in his rough leathery hands, he would be smiling.

Reference

Porter, Tom. 1993. *Clanology: Clan System of the Iroquois*. North American Indian Travelling College, P.O. Box 73, Hogansburg, N.Y. 13655.

FIERCE CONSCIOUSNESS

TREBBE JOHNSON

Two barred owls peer down from an Astroturf-covered perch as Wendy Thomlinson, an intern at the Raptor Center in Woodstock, Vermont, enters the cage and latches the door behind her. The owls' plumage is buff, cinnamon, soot, white, and gray, the colors of winter woods. They move no muscle except their eyes. Their expression is both wary and flirtatious, the latter impression conveyed by the nictating membranes, inner eyelids that protect the birds from twigs and long grasses as they glide low toward prey and that wink over their pupils every few seconds. The wariness is that of two old friends who suspect that afternoon tea is about to be interrupted by some nuisance involving a maintenance crew.

Wendy swings in the direction of the owls with a net and, suspicions confirmed, they rise lazily from the perch and head instinctively for the end of the cage, where I wait outside. Finding it impassable, they turn and fly in the opposite direction toward a doorway just below the ceiling that offers passage into a second cage. A moment later, two more owls zoom in, talons extended, from a third cage, where they have been urged up by another net-bearing intern. They hit the vinyl-coated mesh above me with their feet and spin back again, like swimmers flipping themselves around at the end of the pool so as not to break their momentum.

Like all the birds at the Raptor Center, these owls were brought here because they were sick or injured. Now they have recuperated and are almost well enough to be returned to the wild. First, however, each bird has to pass two crucial tests: it must be able to fly and it must be able to catch prey.

The flight cage, actually three adjoining cages each thirty feet long, was built to satisfy the first requirement. Flying laps and negotiating the openings, which are set at angles to prevent it from taking the easy way out and simply flying in a straight line, the owl strengthens the wing muscles that have weakened during its captivity. When its flight is strong and easy, the bird proceeds to the second and final test. The recovery diet, a frozen mouse or rat injected with a little warm water and served in the food box in its cage, will be replaced by a live creature that the interns will turn loose under a covering of hay and twigs made a little denser and more challenging each day. Only after the staff is satisfied that the bird can, in the words of one local veterinarian, "100 percent earn its living in the wild," will they release it.

The flight cage is the transitional corridor the birds must pass through to return to health. It is the avian treadmill on which they exercise to regain mobility and self-sufficiency in their natural domain. What do the owls experience, I wonder, as they do their laps? Owls have very acute hearing. When an owl's ears pick up a sound—a vole, say, gnawing seeds under leaves—specialized neurons in the brain translate it to a precise three-dimensional map of the space the bird must maneuver to reach its prey. What happens to this sense when the owl is confined to a cage? Does it atrophy like the wing muscles, and is it then gradually reinvigorated with each lap, so the bird is mentally geared up, as well as physically fit to return to the wild? Or does the bird, confined to its perch, tune in to all kinds of sounds emanating from the woods, the Raptor Center infirmary, and the educational center at the foot of the hill, and does this sophisticated activity of their physiology ache for completion in a foot full of prey?

Physician and author Richard Selzer calls surgery "travel in a dangerous country." Indeed, any venture into the life-and-death processes of another is risky, no matter how skilled the healer. How can anyone truly know the contours of another's illness, or discern tracks, so faint as to be almost undetectable, that could lead to recovery? The difficulty is compounded when the treatment is being conducted by members of one species on behalf of another.

"We try to understand not just the physical but the psychological needs of the birds," Raptor Center director Julie Tracy tells me. "We try

to think like the birds. Barred owls are generally pretty mellow and easy to handle. An accipiter, like a goshawk, is a very high-strung bird. They move around a lot; they're very fast flyers in the woods. When you have an accipiter as a patient and the bird is holding still and letting you handle it without causing any problems, you know you have a very sick bird.

"We raise hamsters for prey-testing snowy owls because hamsters behave like lemmings, which these birds eat in the wild. They turn around and try to bite their predators when they're caught. So you've got to really know what the bird needs. What does the bird need for security and shelter? What is its behavior like? Does the bird normally stand on one leg all day long, or is there a problem? That kind of diagnostic work."

Like Julie, the rest of the staff—Raptor Rehabilitation Coordinator Charity Uman and four interns—tends to be pragmatic about what they do. But their diagnostic techniques are regularly supplemented by another, less teachable skill. Charity first dismisses it as "common sense" and gives what she considers an obvious example. When she is under stress, she makes it a habit to pause and do deep-breathing exercises before she approaches a bird. "A cat or a dog will snuggle up to you and comfort you if you've had a bad day," she says. "But a bird of prey will sense your tension and pick up on it."

Common sense, maybe, to those who work with wild animals, but this sensibility takes time to develop.

Charity describes the time she was struggling to treat a goshawk who happened to be a particularly nervous member of this characteristically skittish species. Julie came by, observed for a moment, and then, quite spontaneously, began to tweak at the bird's feathers with her fingers, as if she were another bird grooming it with a beak. The bird calmed down immediately. "It was amazing," Charity says. "This bird was so paranoid you couldn't get close to it, and it was letting Julie touch it! She just has this ability to tune in to what a bird needs."

There was no precedent for what Julie did, no textbook recommendation of feather-preening as an antidote to goshawk anxiety. Julie simply followed her intuition and stepped over the boundary that normally separates humans from animals, and because there was something calm and

confident and apparently noninvasive about what she was doing, the goshawk consented to move beyond its own customary boundaries. The two met in a metaphysical fringe territory, where an exchange of energies took place—one voluntarily given, the other welcomed.

"What do you want?" I ask a peregrine falcon the next morning.

The bird perches on a bough covered with Astroturf in a large cage that looks out over a ripple of high hills and a broad, overcast sky. Although a couple of perches in the cage are dry and protected, she has chosen to stand in an open area where misty rain falls onto her body. With her helmet of black feathers and her protruding brow, she looks like a warrior in contemplation.

Her wing web was damaged when she alit on a downed power line; her condition worsened when the people who found her, excited by the notion of possessing a wild creature as a pet, kept her in an old dog kennel for several weeks. There she developed a severe infection called bumble foot, caused when a normally active bird stands idly on a dirty perch. The bumble foot has nearly healed in the year she has been at the Raptor Center, but she can fly no more than eight or ten feet. Eventually she will be trained to become a "teaching bird," calm enough to stand on a perch before wide-eyed children while a lecturer describes her habits in the wild.

Once this bird was one of the fastest flyers in the world, able to dive toward her prey at speeds of up to 275 miles per hour. Her eyesight, eight times more acute than that of humans, enabled her to spot prey two miles off, and she could snatch a songbird in mid-flight. Biologists, not known for creative flair in the naming of wild things, have been inspired to call the moves the peregrine executes in flight "sky dancing," "parachuting," and "whirling." The poet Robinson Jeffers envisioned the peregrine falcon as an emblem of "fierce consciousness."

"What do you want?" I ask the peregrine, for I cannot believe that such a skilled being, a long-distance traveler and aerial acrobat, is not fully cognizant of her condition. I get no response, although I am aware of her awareness of me. Wildness radiates from her. She may be in captivity, but she has not submitted to a thing. Erect, focused, alert, she

seems to have consented, for now, to wait for what may happen next. I get these impressions not through words but through her presence, which reveals itself gradually as I stand in the rain outside her cage.

Still, I long for something more. I long to brush consciousness with her in that fringe territory that belongs neither to her nor to me but that is accessible to both of us if we are willing to go there.

Most birds who come to the Raptor Center have been the victims, deliberately or inadvertently, of humans. They have been shot by guns and hit by cars. They have flown into picture windows and been attacked by pet cats. They have lost their nests to chain saws and their habitats to bulldozers. (The interns in the flight cage wave nets at the birds not only to impel them to fly but also to remind them that humans tend not to have their best interests at heart.)

Once, it is said, when the ways of animals and humans were less disjunct, both species regularly crossed the line between them. Then the healing process worked both ways. Humans could heal animals, and animals could heal people. Many Native American legends tell of a person or even an entire community rescued from danger by an animal. Often, all the animal asked in return was protection for itself and its kind.

Shamans from Siberia to Peru have relied on animals to assist them in their work as intercessors between those who ail and the otherworldly beings that have caused the ailment. To the shaman, the whole cosmos is alive. All animals, waters, plants, rocks, diseases, and states of mind are not only cognizant but able to communicate with all other forms of life.

The more powerful the shaman, the more skillfully he can mediate among them. But he never ventures forth alone, for like the modern surgeon, he knows that the country of sickness is perilous. He travels in the company of his spirit guides, the animals who come to meet him when he enters a trance state. They counsel him how to negotiate obstacles, what herbs to gather for medicine, how to find the sickness and coax or rout it out.

Sometimes the guide enables the shaman to assume its own animal form, so he can experience fleetness, a keen sense of smell, stealth, or sureness of aim that he could never attain merely by trying to pattern his

behavior that way. Diving deep into the realm where all living creatures are peers and paddling with the feet of his animal teacher, the shaman experiences the commonality and the complexity of all creatures and uses this knowledge on behalf of his patients.

A Navajo friend of mine says that when an animal comes into your life, it means to teach you something. She told me a story about her great-grandmother, who once heard a cry, almost like that of a child, coming from a redrock canyon near her home in Arizona. When she went to investigate, she found a porcupine trapped under a stone. She freed the animal, and it led her to a hidden freshwater spring, a precious gift in that arid land.

"Medicine" is the name many Native Americans use for a vision or counsel bestowed on them by an animal. The gift holds a special power, for it represents the animal's recognition and encouragement of a person's most valuable personal attributes, now enhanced by the attributes of the animal. A bonding occurs that lasts a lifetime. This power must never be wielded over others, for it is sacred. The recipient uses it for the benefit of her community, always acknowledging that it came to her by the grace of the animal.

I thought about the mysterious power of animals and medicine on the occasion when I first heard about the Raptor Center. My brother, who lives about seventy miles north of Woodstock, was driving home one day when he saw a barred owl standing in the road. He stopped beside it, but it didn't move, so he wrapped it in his jacket and took it to the Raptor Center. The staff examined the bird and found it had a fractured wing. They told Frederick they expected the bird to recover fully and invited him to be present for its release.

When my brother told me this story, I began to nurse the wild hope that the owl had deliberately placed itself in his path. For years, Frederick has suffered from debilitating bouts of depression. He has been a patient in many hospitals, tried a pharmacopoeia of medications, consulted numerous psychologists. Nothing works for long. Nobody can figure out what's wrong. But when an animal comes into your life, it means to teach you something. Maybe, I thought, the physical act of saving the owl's life, combined with the mental energy he was now devoting to its

recovery, would produce a tonic potent enough to cure him of his own illness. I didn't know about the flight cage at the time, but I did imagine that as the owl thrived and regained its ability to fly, my brother might regain the use of his emotional wings.

Things did not work out the way I'd hoped. Frederick was unable to attend the triumphant occasion of the owl's release because he was back in the hospital. And although the memory of its weeks in captivity is now presumably only a faint smudge on the owl's awareness, my brother becomes more and more a captive of his illness. He has not earned his own living in years. During the weeks of halcyon sanity, he tries valiantly to patch together a life for himself, but he is forgetting how to exist in days made up of ordinary chores, unpredictable frustrations, little riffs of joy.

The Navajos say that illness is caused by imbalance. In a healthy, natural state, the earth and all that exists upon it are composed of complementary pairs: for example, male/female, light/dark, dryness/moisture. When one of the pair overpowers the other, sickness results. By sickness they mean not just physical aches and pains but personal misfortune and social ills as well.

When I look at my brother's life, I see a world out of balance. What is frightening and unruly has subsumed the ordinary; nothing can be relied on. The raptors are the victims of imbalance of the opposite kind. Their habitats are under siege from all kinds of environmental "taming" seen as necessary to human comfort and convenience, and people have little idea how to behave in, and with, the wilderness that's left. If an animal did come forth to tell us what it needed or to advise us how we might use our truest aptitudes, who among us would be able to listen?

In conversations with Raptor Center staff and volunteers, I notice that a genuine respect for the birds' innate nature is mixed with an unstated hope that the feeling might be reciprocated. They often veer from the subject of birds who are recuperating and will be released to focus instead on their progress with the teaching birds.

"I can't believe how calm Aquila was with me today," Heather Hersh, a young volunteer, frequently exclaims about a one-winged red-tailed

hawk she's training. Even Raptor Center founder Sally Laughlin, when I ask for some memorable stories about her years in Woodstock, first recalls a great horned owl that was released only to return to her home the following winter to tap on her window with its beak, begging for food.

What made such moments memorable was not that the birds had become tame, for they had not, but that bird and human were able, briefly but fully, to perceive the otherness of the one in its company and to recognize that something could be shared precisely because of that otherness. "The birds know I don't want anything from them except to admire their beauty and wildness," Heather tells me by way of explaining the uncanny tendency most birds have to relax with her.

As I myself experienced in the peregrine falcon's presence, the qualities of beauty and wildness can radiate like light from a bird. To witness, perhaps even to absorb a bit of it, feels like a blessing. It seems likely that for these intuitive, highly sensitive birds of prey, appreciation unattached to fear, impatience, or the greed to possess is a gift as well.

Several contemporary thinkers, including anti-nuclear activist Hazel Henderson, Vice President Al Gore, and psychologist Anne Wilson Schaef, have compared the collective behavior of modern society, where the pace of burgeoning materialism is matched only by the despoliation of nature, to that of an addict who craves more and more of the substance that satisfies him less and less. "We consume the earth and its resources as a way to distract ourselves from the pain," Gore writes in *Earth in the Balance*, "and we search insatiably for artificial substitutes to replace the experience of communion with the world that has been taken from us."

According to evolutionary biologist E. O. Wilson, the sickness our species suffers from may actually be genetic rather than psychological. His "biophilia hypothesis" proposes that *homo sapiens* may have benefited in several ways from a deep emotional need to be close to nature. The trait may become so weakened after prolonged immersion in urban life that a person could become, first, indifferent to, later, even hostile to nature. However, the trend may not be irreversible. As the owls regain the power of their atrophied wing muscles through exercise, we might be

able to revitalize this critical part of our makeup just by renewing our contact with nature.

But where are the flight cages we might enter to work our way back to the natural world? What can we do to share the fierce consciousness of a peregrine falcon?

The vision quest is a deliberate withdrawal from one's community to a wilderness place, where a man or woman sits alone, fasting and praying for a vision, a message from the spirit world that will clarify his or her path in life. It was on such a retreat from the everyday that several great spiritual leaders, including Jesus, Mohammed, the Buddha, and the Lakota warrior Crazy Horse, received the enlightenment they needed to lead their people. On his vision fast, the twentieth-century Lakota medicine man Lame Deer was lifted high above the ground, up to the realm of the owls, hawks, and eagles. They told him that he henceforth would be part of their winged nation and that they would provide him with the skills he needed to be a medicine man.

I myself have gone on a vision quest and have led them as well, and I have seen how the experience can transform a person. The impact of a prolonged stay in the wilderness does not necessarily come from a single spectacular moment of truth, as it did for Lame Deer. Often it is a cumulative effect brought about as the quester permits herself to be weathered by the place where she's rooted herself. The sun and dust, wind and moonlight pass over her skin. Birds, animals, and insects accept her as a feature of the land and go about their business around her. As she notices her surroundings in ever finer detail, she sees reflections of herself in them; witnessing their slow and exquisite changes throughout the day, she, too, is changed.

A participant in a vision quest I assisted on in the Utah Canyonlands was a social worker. Her husband of twenty years had recently died, and she had just committed her mother, suffering from Alzheimer's, to a nursing home. She had not spent much time outside the large city where she had always lived, and she was nervous about the wildlife she might encounter.

On the second day of her vision quest, however, this woman found herself sitting on a sunny rock and telling her entire life story to a lizard,

which sat perfectly still, facing her, until she was finished. In all her relationships, she had assumed the role of caretaker and was unable to ask for comfort and counsel for herself. What she learned from the lizard was that nature is generous enough to bear witness to her sorrow and compassionate enough to weave it lightly into the fabric that is all life on earth.

Animals are also the agents for transformation in a psychotherapeutic technique called the Personal Totem Pole Process. In a state of deep relaxation, people focus on any of the infinite dimensions of themselves—memories, fears, illness, job problems—and allow that dimension to manifest itself as an image. What often emerges is an animal, probably, says psychologist Eligio Stephen Gallegos, who developed the practice in 1982, because animals were our distant forebears. Animals are lively, inventive, aware, supremely competent in their environment—and they are not burdened by personal foibles as we humans are.

Those who practice this deep imagery not only see the animals vividly but engage in dialogues with them and accompany them on journeys that are often mythic in tone and detail. Sometimes, like shamans, they see themselves taking the animal's form, experiencing the world through its eyes and paws and hungers. At times the animal is caged or wounded, indication that an aspect of the person is afflicted. A simple act of care may be enough to restore the animal to health and effect in the person a new outlook on that aspect of his life.

In both the vision quest and the Personal Totem Pole Process, the meeting between human and animal is generally more successful if the human follows a few simple guidelines. Humility is perhaps the most important quality to bring to the partnership. We humans are not in charge here, a circumstance that takes some getting used to. And so we cultivate a second ethic: unconditional patience. We do not rush toward the animal, smiling and effusive, eager to take control and leave a strong first impression, manners, we have been taught, that ensure success in business and society. We wait. We let the animal make the first move.

As Julie Tracy remarked when describing the qualities she looks for in interns, "People who don't have a natural respect for someone else's personal space tend not to do well with birds." In the fringe territory, we

must suspend disbelief. Familiar patterns of cause and effect often have little meaning, whereas intuition and flares of insight or emotion can be as genuine as they are inexplicable.

These tips on interspecies etiquette can be applied to any situation in which a human edges closer than usual to the fierce consciousness of animals, for it is not necessary to fast on a mountaintop or undertake psychotherapeutic journeys to cross to a place where gifts may be exchanged between species.

American conservationist Bert Schwarzschild had traveled to Italy for the express purpose of hiking on Mount Subasio, where St. Francis preached his famous sermon to the birds. As he walked, he grew increasingly distressed by the silence in the air and by the litter of shotgun shells on the ground, for songbirds in Italy are shot as game. That night, as he lay in his sleeping bag, a nightingale began to sing in a bush very close to him, and in a moment of absolute clarity, Schwarzschild heard the bird asking directly for his help. When he got back to the United States, he launched an international campaign that resulted in the designation of Mount Subasio as a wildlife refuge. Simply by paying attention and suspending disbelief long enough to receive the message his heart needed, he was able to benefit humans and animals alike.

Driving north from Woodstock to visit my brother before heading back home to northeastern Pennsylvania, I think about Charity's description of the release of birds that have been patients at the Raptor Center. "By that time, you've removed the jesses, the leather straps we keep on their legs while they're here. What happens a lot of times is that the bird doesn't know yet that it's free, so it just stands there in your hands. You lower your hands a little bit, just a couple of inches, and the bird feels the gravity and pulls against it, and that's when it realizes it can fly. And off it goes." So, in the end, it is the bird's natural proclivity to be airborne that sets her free. And the last act of assistance offered by the hand of the rehabilitator is simply to serve as a launching platform.

Of course, not every bird can be released. Those whose injuries would be severely crippling must be euthanized. Others, for example those who have lost the use of a wing or sight in one eye, often stay on to become

teaching birds and, when necessary, surrogate parents to orphaned babies of their species.

Sally Laughlin told me that many birds adjust well to captivity. "Owls are perfectly content as long as they have a solid wall at their backs, so they know no one can sneak up on them, and a perch that's high enough up so they can look down on everyone and feel superior." Ravens and hawks, who, Sally said, "fly for the joy of it," may adapt less successfully to life in a cage. "It all depends," Sally emphasized, "on the individual bird."

Sometimes, then, there's no way to get back to the wild, for even the fairly straightforward passages of the flight cage remain unattainable. In this case, the bird will come to terms with life in captivity or, failing that, simply give up and die, an acquiescence to fate known to every creature who has lived by the guidelines of predator-and-prey.

What, I wonder, as I speed along the highway, will become of the wild and beautiful peregrine? Then I think: maybe the same ultimatum is presented to humans as well. Maybe, after long periods of sickness, we too must choose between returning to our natural habitat and remaining in unnatural captivity. If so, what will become of my brother? What will become of us humans if we forget what is required to receive the medicine of animals?

INTIMATE RELATIONSHIPS

MICHAEL TOBIAS

For many years my wife and I have lived with several magnificent parrots. We share everything with these friends; we moon together, goose each other, run hysterically around the house, blow out our tandem ecstasies, shake out the water, stalk, shout, laugh, groan, and sleep together. These avians commune with us on a half acre of indoor and outdoor tropics, and I have oriented my life to be able to spend most of my time with them, sharing to the extent possible the exquisite wonders of the world that we all perceive in different ways.

Secretly, I feel incredibly lucky, for there are no greater wonders than these avians. They rival the sunlight, are tantamount to every wild scent and vision. They embody the extraterrestrial, the Earth Goddess, and all those unknowables about which philosophers have rhapsodized nostalgically for millennia.

At times I have struggled to "know" them. But, more frequently, I am content to bask in the mystery of their friendship and to be refreshed by the unknown, which, in most spheres of our lives, we have denuded.

"Every act of communication is an act of translation," said the literary critic George Steiner. This is as true among members of the same species as of different ones. All relationships require systematic effort. The goal, as I have long discovered with my own mate, is companionship-in-mystery, not an artificial regularity. My intense time with the birds, and with many, many other creatures, has taught me that the relationships I most admire and nurture are those from which I should expect the least.

Having renounced desire, as most Buddhists will explain, one's likelihood of experiencing an in-depth encounter is greatly improved. Usually,

as the following encounters suggest, most "friendship" with other creatures happens unexpectedly and in totally fleeting instances but leaves lifelong impressions and can instill images and feelings and insights that are important to the well-being of oneself and the world. They are the messages, in fact, that define our own humanity. Without them, without these unexpected gifts, these wild ephemera, I am certain my life would be as cold, inorganic, and meaningless as an empty bathtub.

Permit me to describe some of those fleeting encounters in the wild.

I was ascending a steep ravine in the Colorado Rockies one spring morning many years ago when a wild Canadian gray jay landed on my shoulder. I stopped, remained motionless, and then began speaking to the newcomer. He (or she) chirped inquisitively. I sat down, and the bird hopped onto my lap and partook of my granola bar, which I crumbled and/or regurgitated into beak-sized swallows for him, concerns about transbacterial infections aside. This was the prelude to a day's journey in the company of two birds, the first, and, shortly thereafter, its mate. I climbed a 14,000-foot peak that day, and they rode for much of the journey on my shoulders. They lent nearly continuous commentary on the route I'd chosen, and when I reached the highest ramparts, they flew off, apparently uninterested in the summit.

On my descent by twilight, they were there, waiting for me. Now there were a half-dozen of the birds, though I could easily pick out the two I had spent most of the day with. All of the birds alighted on a rock where I sat down my pack and ate some apple and more granola. They all helped themselves, hopping on and off the rock, my lap, my shoulders, even my head. There was no hesitancy on their part, no fear. I reached the trail at the base of the mountain that would lead me eventually to a parking lot. By that time, it was dark and the birds had flown off.

Another mountain, the Eiger, around six o'clock one Swiss summer morning. I was sleeping in deep grass near the base of the north face when I opened my eyes and observed two foraging chamois not twenty feet away. I sat up in my sleeping bag, began whistling in harmony, and the two goatlike antelopes sat down to listen. For twenty minutes I

performed pieces by Handel and Mozart and Barber, and they thoroughly enjoyed the concert.

I was snorkeling alone in the Red Sea down near Nweiba, a deserted spot on the map. This was years before it was to become a resort. An enormous cowfish swept by, circled, and came back around to look at me. It must have weighed three hundred pounds, a giant amid a riot of other coral-flocking creatures as well as the sharks that preyed upon some of them. The cowfish bumped into me and quite hovered so that our flesh remained in contact. Our eyes connected. I took hold of its fins, and it pulled me several hundred meters through its world before I let go and returned to the surface. It followed me up toward the surface and then disappeared down into the depths.

One evening I found myself pinioned on a ledge ten feet above an Alaskan grizzly bear and her newborn cub. The stars were egregious, the breeze off the Tar Inlet scented with the sweetness of wet grass, dogwood, wild strawberry, and the distinct odor of glacier nearby. The arrangement was an accident: I would never have positioned myself in that spot deliberately.

In trying to retrace my footsteps across the steep slope, I inadvertently dislodged a rock that tore loose, smacking the sow on her shoulder. She reared up, all nine feet of her, and roared at me. I ran across the slope, plunging off a precipice some one hundred feet, smashing into a steep slope of detritus that fortunately cushioned my fall. Instead of a severed spine, I had gashes in my hip but nothing to worry about. I continued running along the shoreline of the fjord. The sow and her cub were in pursuit for nearly a mile. By the time I reached my campsite, where a half-dozen others were making dinner beside their tents, the bears had stopped, warily eyeing this strange congeries of human beings. That sow focused on me. She seemed to tell me that I had been out of bounds, and she was correct, though it was an accident. Then, the mother and her cub rummaged ever so silently through the boulder field above camp and disappeared.

For six weeks we lived on that inlet with the bears, who grew accustomed to our presence but never once exhibited unfriendliness. We left

all food outside the tents at night. There seemed to be a dozen or so grizzly living along that ten-mile inlet, but they never once went for our food, content with their own. At times I met that sow along a side creek, crossing a sandbar, or hiking up a ridge. We had plenty of moments to watch one another at fantastically close range. She traveled with her cub. But after that first encounter, she knew I was OK.

At the end of my six weeks' stay in Glacier Bay, I happened to catch the footprints of a bear in the black mud heading out into the inlet, where the griz frequently swim. These paw prints were 50 percent larger than the sow's, the size of a large pizza. I assumed it was the phantom mate that I never saw.

John Muir once stated that the sight of a grizzly bear, loping or moseying, rummaging or frolicking, was the greatest experience one could obtain of the American wilderness. I know that for a month and a half I was welcomed by a community of grizzly bears. When I think back to those days and nights, I realize that I felt protected by them at night and gently monitored by day. In a sense, they exerted parental control, and it felt right.

An Antarctic summer, my first sustained date with the woman who was to become my mate, Jane. For three days at Base Esperanza we wallowed in Adélie penguin guano, on our elbows, bellies and butts, communing with a colony that must have numbered in the tens of thousands. The weather changed rapidly during those seventy-two hours, four seasons coalescing with a flourish at times ferocious but never mean-spirited. At moments it was hot, and we took off our parkas, sweaters, and shirts. But these are trivialities: what mattered was the fact of our acceptance by thousands of pedestrians who were, it must be alleged, terribly busy with the maintenance of their penguin civilization.

For two newcomers of our enormity to wander nearby would best be likened to a brontosaurus couple stopping by the local mall for a look-see. But our leisurely visit invoked no Japanese B-movie equivalent. We were, if anything, welcomed, asked to sit down and stay awhile. Inquiries flooded our way, posed with characteristically adroit, bipedal

effrontery that unloaded multiples of queries, eyes flat, wide, huge, and gaping, beaks and head positions thrusting upward to accent the meaning of their thrusts, all in all, a genuinely earnest succession of interactions that left us filled with news of goings-on beneath the nearby icebergs and talk of the town.

The rumor mill in a penguin colony is fast and furious, filled with empathy and altruism, mad gab and hilarious sport. We found ourselves in the thick of it and after three days and three nights were "craaacking" ourselves silly with penguin philosophy, penguin art, penguin literature, and penguin spirituality. We had been initiated and would never be human again, or not entirely.

Needless to say, it was a successful first date.

Recalling close encounters and first contact in the wild is not merely an exercise in reverie. They are, or can be, life transforming if one is sufficiently attuned and open to them. To come close to an Australian sea dragon, or sea horse, or dragonfly, is as provocative and far-fetched a séance as if it were occurring on another planet.

Joy and dizziness—the momentary transcendence of one's own finite, human ego—are not the only lessons, however. Messages of every conceivable kind are encoded in the fragile intersection of different species. While all organisms share the same essential planetary models at the cellular and molecular levels, it is in the richer neurological, cognitive, and behavioral centers that differences become arresting. As gregarious humans who have never been good at keeping secrets, we are likely to interpret such encounters in ways that relate to our own species-specific environment.

Hence, the sensation of true friendship one midnight in Young, Arizona, where two white mares, feeding on the wild grasses, came up to me, shyly, excitedly, astonished to see a human that late at night out and about.

The truth of fragility, as witnessed in a minute sand crab hiding in a tiny shell that my wife had picked up one afternoon on a remote island in the Maldives. The shell was the size of a bead, the crab, barely visible, hiding inside. It poked out its head and, with two keenly intelligent eyes,

stared at us, who stared back, demanded calm, then returned to its hiding place, safe and forever secure.

The fact of joyous abandon, when Roses, a malamute I once lived in Big Sur with, rolled for hours on the carcass of a beached seal. The unremitting, uncleansible stench was all the evidence I needed of a hierarchy of joys in the world.

The sense of majesty, as I sat in a blind watching two California condors fly to their nest, not ten feet away, and court one another.

The fallacy of fear. I lay all afternoon in a hammock in Khao Yai National Park in Thailand waiting for a tiger to visit. I was eight miles out, well off any trail, four feet above the ground, reading Don Quixote. All around me was the fresh scent of tiger urine. I was frightened, yes. But after a few hours, the fear was gone. And at that moment I heard a tiger nearby. Eventually, the sound went away, replaced by the heavy flapping of wings as two nesting giant hornbills flew overhead.

Later, a hornbill that stood three feet tall landed on my shoulder, and we preened one another. And then an orphaned hoolock gibbon jumped into my arms, while I stroked the back of a wild guar. The tiger had just become part of the overall merging with the forest.

We filmed a mahout in Corbett National Park in India who had been attacked by a tiger and his scalp lacerated. The tiger had dragged him forty feet, then sat on him, presumably in preparation for a leisurely dinner. The mahout begged the tiger to go away, and the tiger acceded to his supplication. It is very, very rare that a tiger will attack a human. The instances occur when the tiger is starving, or its habitat has been eliminated, which is the case for most of the world's few remaining big cats. Fear has nothing to do with it. I learned that, about tigers, about myself.

Devotional matrimony. I scrambled up the mossy rocks beneath Mount Cook, on New Zealand's South Island, following at a distance as two Kea parrots foraged side by side. In the period of an hour, I observed that they preened one another, kissed, and fondled over fifty times, or nearly once per minute.

The wisdom of precision. My parents and I were out canoeing in the large lake at the Myaka River Preserve near Sarasota, Florida, during the time when female alligators lay their eggs. They do so inside a nest of

deep mud; the temperature rises, and the alligators can virtually determine whether they will hatch males or females. Population control seems to be inherent to their gender manipulations.

The universality of curiosity. I awoke with a coyote resting on my sleeping bag in a Yosemite morning. As I opened my eyes (it was about 5:15 A.M., the valley ensconced in mist), the coyote, who was two feet from my face, just sat peacefully. For a good thirty seconds, our eyes stared at each other. Then, sedately, he got up and strolled away, but not before I was able to extend my hand and receive a lick from his tongue across my wrist.

The importance of play was conveyed to me one late summer night. I had hidden myself at a Swiss zoo. The guards had gone, the gates were locked, but the tigers were still out in their cage. I walked up to the enclosure that had an entire family of cats. I did a backbend so that my upside-down face was facing into the cage. At once the cubs raced to me. I then sang for them. The parents relaxed, in the rear.

Then I started running back and forth. Now all of the cats joined in, running with me. For five minutes we exercised. Then the cats reclined on their backsides, and, sticking my hand through the cage (stupid, in most circumstances), I stroked their bellies. The adults came down to see what was going on. I continued stroking the cubs, and the parents just watched, curious but unperturbed. It was the playfulness that had convinced them of my benign nature. The same experience occurred some years later at the zoo in Seattle, where I was able to fondle wild snow leopards without the slightest doubt or hesitation. Other related patterns of human acceptance by large felines occur regularly in East Africa, where certain tribal elders and novitiates practice *pride walking*. In a state of total calm, naked or nearly so, they wander up to and past a resting pride of lions. With absolute unconcern they keep walking, just a few feet away from where a half-dozen big cats are reclining. Stories about such pride walking abound, but none (that I've heard) ever involving the slightest hostility.

The merits of single-mindedness. I was trekking in British Columbia when I came across a large yellow banana slug slowly making its way through the damp forest duff toward some destination. I followed it for

an hour, and in that time moved nearly fifty feet. During that intense time together, I came to know British Columbia with an intimacy that had eluded me previously, despite countless trips there. Those fifty feet yielded up a plenum of details at the outer limits of the human visible spectrum that gave me to understand, however superficially, the life of that marvelous creature, the focus of its mission, the character of its tenacity, the very joy of its being.

This sensation was amplified one night while listening to a piece by Richard Strauss at the Santa Fe Opera. A rhinoceros beetle was ambling up the aisle during the performance. I removed it from harm's way—for the intermission was coming and a thousand people would have trampled that magnificent creature. I placed it in a green patch of forest alongside the building and stood, leaning against a wall watching the beetle's reaction to the opera. It could hear the music, I am quite sure, and seemed by my reckoning to enjoy it (though it was *Salome*, not ordinarily given to rapture). But after a short time, the beetle continued on its precise path, intent upon going somewhere that night. What amazed me was that the beetle moved back to the aisle, heavily carpeted, and then continued toward the front doors of the opera house. It was quite headstrong about that direction and the particular route. Of course, I helped it outside, avoiding the myriad throngs.

The true nature of society, as enumerated day after day for me among the ants of the French Alps. I lived with them on a cliffside above Argentière for a summer, following their every move, noting how in their back-and-forth processions—each set of antennae connected with the neighbors passing by, how everyone was perpetually stopping to inquire, to greet, to move on in assured friendship. Community unlike any known to human beings. I do think, however, such gregariousness would be intolerable.

Living by one's poetry. On a large old farm in Vermont, where once I dwelt, I had twenty semi-wild cows who used to sit around with me on the highest rocky hillock in the pasture, and I would often lose my writing to their appetites. I tried to prevent it (on account of the oil from my writing pen), but they were sneaky. They would distract me by sucking on my toes, or trying to eat my jeans, then grab the paper from my hand

and start chewing happily. I used this information to prove to my parents that one could eat one's words, that is to say, live by one's literary efforts, an important lesson for a writer.

The importance of unresolved mystery. In Ladakh, in July 1976, thirty miles from the nearest village, high on a glacier, I encountered at 17,000 feet, approximately, a yeti. There were four of us who saw it, standing together. As we each scrambled to remove cameras from our large backpacks, the yeti raced away. We soon reached the point where we had seen it running bipedally, appearing to be perhaps seven feet tall, dark, enormous, incredibly strong. But its footprints had become fragmentary in the deep snow, the heat, and the wind. We never saw it again, and to this day have not been able to reconcile the impression of that noble creature. We were all agreed that it was the so-called yeti. It could be nothing else. I am certain, and I pray, the yeti is never verified, or found out.

In northern Kenya I learned the lesson of overpopulation. Six chickens were for sale on the side of the road. Two boys were holding them upside down, swinging them in circles, the chickens' legs tied. The animals were quickly expiring. I purchased them, put them in the back of my van, drove frantically in search of a place without humans where I could leave them—a riverbank with thick brush. It was nearly dark. But there was no place that was not inhabited. Every creek had herders nearby who would capture the chickens and stew them.

Kenya, with nearly thirty million people, is a rural country. The people are everywhere. In the end, I found a marginal sanctuary. But as I was driving away, several young boys with their dogs came running to check out what was going on. There was no place in that country for a chicken to live out its natural life.

The lesson of insanity. On a street in Bamako (meaning "crocodile," though none are left), the capital of West African Mali, over two hundred rare parrots were being kept in despicable cages in the broad daylight of 110 degrees, without water or food or shade. I purchased the birds, while a crowd gathered and people laughed at me and called me insane. I got all of the birds safely in the back of a truck, covered them, and my associate drove two hours to one of three national parks in the

country, while I sat in the back of the truck trying to keep the dust from the dirt roads out of the cages.

Then, far from anyone or anything, I released them along a river in the park. The Senegalese parrots, with their long graceful tail feathers, were the first to fly out of the opened cages. They immediately started preening themselves and finding logs and holes in the mud where they could perch and, presumably, mate.

Sometimes at night I think about the varying definitions of "insanity" throughout the world. People are truly different from place to place. But I'm not sure education can break through certain barriers. I once encountered a group of people observing a single little goldfish in a bowl of water. A man held up the small bowl before the loud, polluted brawl of traffic that infests the market area known as Chadni Chowk in Old Delhi. I tried to explain to the man that they had absolutely nothing to gain by torturing that little fish, which had waited millions of years to be an individual goldfish, proud, colorful, benign, only to find itself marooned in a few inches of water, in a bowl. But people thought I was just stupid.

The idea of integrity. In southern Bhutan I came upon a family of golden langurs. The minute they saw me, they leapt into the jungle and disappeared. I had all of ten seconds to watch them. But in that time my eyes connected with theirs, I think I gleaned something of the exquisite, critical compact by which they lived, and it necessarily excluded primates like *Homo sapien sapiens*. I was grateful for their skittishness and was consequently made ever more aware of my own ungainliness in nature, the fact I am a beast, dangerous, unpredictable, lacking integrity. What would such integrity mean for my species? Total nonviolence.

The sheer beauty of nature and its critical role in evolution. Jane and I climbed a tree on Mount San Jicento one early April, upon meeting face-to-face an enormous mountain lion high on a slope. We had cleared a new trail on four miles of mountain when the contact occurred. It watched us for ten minutes. My wife, unfearful, insisted on going up to the big cat, which was the size of an African lion. I begged her to join me in the tree, which she finally did. I am convinced, however, that she and the lion would have gotten on famously.

Watching that cat move put every ballet into a humble perspective. Along the reefs of Bora Bora that unprecedented choreography of movement and color and living, breathing meaning was again played out all around me, where I snorkeled for days in a state of total dream time.

I once swam twelve miles of the Napali Coast of Kauai, from before sunrise to late night, and during that time was joined by several giant sea turtles and a few sharks. All that remains of those moments in my mind is the beauty of the world. A black bear that licked my nose as I awoke in a tube tent; Antarctic fur seals that let me stroke them in the wild; a white ermine and countless marmots high in the Rockies that have fed from my hand, talking with me, discussing the day; two Tennessee walkers with whom I crossed Arizona, furthering that discussion and furthering the astounding, cumulative impression of the glory, the unspeakable elegance, the heartbreaking beauty of this world. That moose in the Rockies who chased me into a lake when I was kid—the thrill of play! And those hippos beside whom I stayed out naked all night beneath Kilimanjaro. A herd of elephants in Amboseli that I moved with at sunset, the baby among them eyeing me with an astounding sense of delight and curiosity I shall never forget, and a baby Cape buffalo that talked to me, its wet flanks quivering amid a swarm of flies and the sun and dust striking its reddish hide, eyes gigantic and loving; eyes that I have seen in Kyoto dragonflies on a bright morning, dallying about my face, squirrels, hundreds of birds, a baby scorpion, a nest of rattlers, rats in our kitchen, a Cambodian black-necklaced laughing thrush who for three months had an ongoing discussion with me about things I cannot relate, a gigantic coral snake in the Sinai that took to me, as did mountain sheep near the Napiqua Valley of the North Cascades, the largest mosquito I have ever witnessed, in southern Bangladesh, even the lichens of the Cordillera Darwin, in southern Chile, the rain forests of Java, up along the volcanos over Bandung, the wild sheep of Santa Cruz Island out in the Pacific (which the National Park Service would prefer to exterminate), the dolphins and kelp forests, the great white sharks and prancing whales that course the "fertile crescent" of the Channel Islands, and those all-forgiving giant redwoods up in northern California and southern Oregon.

I took to all these creatures instantly, but they also took to me, I believe. In those reciprocities is all that I know about myself, and the nature of beauty.

I am overwhelmed by so many fortunate encounters, with hindsight, from childhood until the present. The beauty is no museum stroll, no aesthetic province of isolated delectation, but an integrated whole, that big bang of loveliness, which has its biological method—the survival of the ecosystem, both the outer world, with its biodiversity miracles, and the inner, what my old college prof Gregory Bateson terms "an ecology of mind." Beauty, I have learned from all my passing animal friends, is at the heart of evolution. Our ability to celebrate and revere beauty must be the key to our survival.

These aforementioned encounters are representative of just some of the blessings that have been conferred upon me in my brief life. They, and many others like them, have formed the basis for an orientation that is singularly fulfilled because of its dependency on other life forms. My earliest two memories are biological: I recall vividly my mother singing to me, "So hush, little baby . . . please don't cry," while I reclined like a pasha in my ornate San Francisco crib; and, two years later, encountering a caged wolf at the San Francisco zoo that paced forlornly and conveyed every synapse of its misery to my pounding, unprepared heart. We stared at one another, I looked up to my father who had escorted me that day, and the spate of questions overwhelmed my limited ability to articulate a colossal shriek that had risen up in my chest and throat like one unbearable avalanche of inexpressible grief.

Those two experiences—of being human and loved and of perceiving the evidently human habit of wreaking mayhem in the natural world—were so inconceivably opposite as to leave me stricken for the rest of my life, lodged between a misanthropic pang that eschewed my fellow kind and a delirious summons to explore, embrace, and make amends on behalf of the billions of other humans who had ignored or deliberately harmed animals other than humans.

True conscience is the by-product of a paradox whose animal origins and finale are central to its expressions: that our humanity should cause

us pain; that what we believe and would like to be generally regarded as a first principle, namely, that love and empathy permeate the biological world, should so fervently be contradicted by the indifference, greed, and laziness of our own homocentrism.

We cast our anchor in the harbors of humankind, converse, obtain necessities of one form or another, then set sail again into the life of the world that is other than human. Whether we hear it, see it, know it, or not, it exists. No silly anthropomorphic logic or equation can undo the truth of the far greater surroundings in which *Homo sapiens* are tenuously and temporarily upright. All the ludicrous debates in the world regarding "nonhumans"—their ability, or not, to reason, love, create, desire, build, work, have, have not, do, undo, aspire, invent, speak, reason, reason not, let go, abandon, restrain, inhibit, consider, ponder, pray, provide, allow, elaborate, chat, rummage, laugh, play, intellectualize, analyze, speculate, commiserate, describe, wonder, imagine, ascertain, delight, develop, evolve, empathize, give, design, domesticate, socialize, engineer, extrapolate, work every tool, renounce violence, make music, get drunk, commit suicide, carry on despite the worst adversity, and— most importantly, suffer—are insults to our own human strengths of observation and feeling.

If not by outright encounter, exchange, observation, and perception, then by inference, intuition, and subjective immersion in more than one hundred billion different settings, contexts, circumstances, and moments (for that is the approximate number of *Homo sapiens sapiens* that have been born on this planet, and each one has, inevitably, experienced a multitude of other-than-humans at all ages and phases of life), our species has made contact with other species. We are not alone on this earth, abundantly not. The more we deny this unambiguous truth, the more we clinically define the true terms of multiple-personality disorder, with its tragic consequences for Mother Earth.

It is one thing to ascribe feelings and thoughts, in which we have been steeped as specific organisms, to others, about whom we can only pretend to the most superficial knowledge. But it is quite another to come away from encounters with other life forms that leave an indelible

imprint on the learning center of our brains and the feeling center of our hearts.

Long-term acquaintance with plants and animals provides one rich source of assured impression, though there is absolutely no way to predict how such residual perceptions are likely to mold the capacity for human ethics. Based upon the data of slaughter, the dietary and animal-product consumerism of human beings, one must doubt the overall significance of such acquaintanceship. Hence, to acknowledge that the residents of a community encounter pigeons throughout their lives in their squares, along their sidewalks and gutters, in their parks, and resting on their power lines, has little or no bearing on the amount of fine-feathered friends who are slaughtered and consumed by those same residents continuously, not pigeons, necessarily—for they are frequently poisoned, or starved, and disposed of. In cities like Vienna, Austria, there is an implicit taboo against feeding pigeons. Do so and old women will scowl at you, and you might even get arrested. And while pets, and the culture of keeping and pampering pets, has long absorbed human beings, again, no evidence suggests that the experience of having a pet is more likely to induce vegetarianism. Dissociation of one intimate compact from a generalized compassion is at the root of humankind's evident tendency to spare those we know well and to think nothing of killing others.

Of course, even this tentative empathy is marred by the brutal fact of child and spousal abuse, of farming, and of violence toward pets. The farmer who raises pigs for slaughter, having given the semblance of love and trust to the animals, is doubly destroying them, whilst demolishing the last hope for a theory of human accountability under nearly any circumstance. And it comes as no surprise that pet hamsters are deliberately flushed down toilets or horses beaten by owners who, statistically, would engage in violent acts to their supposed loved ones with equal zeal. Countless scientists who might advocate some version of animal rights, in fact, keep their own animals used for research in abominable conditions, behind glass or bars.

Beleaguered by a desperation that the problem of violence cannot be altered, that I am overwhelmed by a species, of which I am said to be a part, which knows so little tolerance, is incapable of biological altruism,

and shows virtually no interest in other species, I can only fall back upon the consoling fact of my own soul, which exists only to the extent that it has been formed and extended, engendered, and refined during those many moments, hours, and days of love I have shared in company with other organisms, as with my own immediate human family.

I would like to call these myriad meetings "relationships." By that groping expression I hope to imply the yearning, on my part, to make it so. The human language-bearing gift is no more or less an advantage in the aspiration to partnership. In silence is great truth. In noise, often, languishes the obscured. To unearth anything that can be said to be mutual must require an effort to do so that is, equally, mutual. And so these so-called "relationships" are the result of either fantastic chance—a moment in the overall passing universe where the timing was perfect, the motivation somehow, by astronomical luck, on a par, the unencumbrances fitted in parity—or awesome patience and goodwill. Conservation biology, as practiced by people like the late Roger Tory Peterson, Rodney Jackson and Darla Hillard, Jane Goodall, and countless others, aspires to that parity and patience, often on all fours, through the thick of untoward topography, inclement weather, or whatever else goes into emulating and observing the life of another species.

A relationship, as we normally understand the word, implies trust, mutual pleasure in each other's company along many lines, loyalty, friendship, or just sheer fascination, as between lovers. Relationships with other-than-human plants and animals gain unlimited nuances; every conceivable characterization is plausible and necessary in attempting to understand the fullest possible potential for species interacting with each other. Anthropomorphism is just one of our important tools for understanding what's happening around us. That most science has eschewed human attributions in the wild is part and parcel of the scientific method that would also eschew human beings. My marriage to Jane embodies for me the closest approximation of that broadest-case scenario wherein two utterly different beings agree to be together out of sheer joy and desire in one another's presence.

Marriage is an intimate relationship that we can understand, even if at least half of all marriages end in breakup. That, too, embodies the power of intimacy and possibility for severance and moving away. One sees it constantly among other creatures, though it is not called divorce.

But marriage also harbors perhaps the best key to understanding the notion of imaginative projection between organisms. Jane and I live with countless other creatures, not merely the millions of follicle mites in our eyelashes or the approximately twenty-two billion bacteria we each carry around beneath our armpits. I am referring to the plants, rats, opossums, squirrels, hundreds of wild and semi-wild birds, and the several afore-mentioned parrots (Mac, Josey, and Feather, at present) that live in and around our home. We can see occasional whales from our windows and a constant stream—every minute of every day—of smaller creatures, ants, rats, midges, flies, spiders, and so on—that join in with us, live, and will die.

They have penetrated to the core of what we love about being together, a married couple, and being part of this Earth. They are what we talk about most of the time or relate to by way of analogy. Animals tend to make up the majority of our conversations. I dream about them at night, and Jane and I are always sharing those dreams and finding striking unisons.

Our metaphors and self-knowledge come from animals. Jane says she can relate to me because, at our first meeting, I scooped up some German shepherd poop that graced the brick path separating me from her and tossed it into the woods. She found that unselfconscious gesture (which it was) so noble and at home that—she tells me—she fell immediately in love with me. I'm not sure that a rancher scooping cow shit, a Masai herdsman moving jackal shit, a manure trundler, or a man with a broom cleaning up a rabbit warren would not have elicited a similar passion from my Swiftian wife. But no matter. It was the fact of getting one's hands close to the Earth, of encountering animal life in its primitive truth, that brought us together. And as I mentioned earlier, our first real date involved crawling through penguin guano, inches deep, where we kissed passionately amid those birds and felt as if we'd gone to heaven. We had. The intimate relationships of the penguins infected us with the

same passions and lusts and wants. That can happen to humans, clearly. It does every day.

I hope that with more and more discussion about it, sincere inner reflection, and the pursuit of respectful, loving trysts and outwardly modest romance in the wild—and the whole world's the wild—our vulnerability to the love of other creatures will rapidly increase. Then we, too, will soften, fully opening to the necessary joys of the Creation and the true relationships that are there to be initiated. There isn't much time left. Like all true loves, one has to be willing to experience it, to work at it, beyond the fleeting glances and too frequently repressed stirrings of the heart.

INTRODUCTION: THE WORD MADE PHYSICAL

GABRIEL HORN
(WHITE DEER OF AUTUMN)

For most of my remembered life, I have been closely connected to the word, to its sound, to its vibration, to its physical form. This particular path I am presently walking I have traveled already, even before I had the vision that would become the guiding force and influence of my life.

Even now, twenty-five years later, I can close my eyes, and . . . it is like a falling through. . . . I can remember that one summer long ago as I went on my first vision quest. I had been told by my elder Uncle Nippawanock that if I was to continue walking the path of heart and beauty, then it was time for me to seek a vision in the old way. So I had chosen a deserted beach on the shore of the Gulf of Mexico, not too far from my Florida home. This was the place where I would draw my circle in the sand and where I would remain for days and nights, fasting, meditating, and praying.

With my eyes still shut I can fall through . . . and in the space of my own mind I can still see the dolphins diving, breaching, and splashing, and I can still feel the joy for life that they brought to me even then as I cried for all that I had lost. . . . I remember watching a mother sea turtle one dawn, as I grew weak from not eating, and how she helped me become aware of all the love I had experienced in my life and of the gratitude I felt for the gifts of that love. . . . I remember the night when the cries of a cricket would become deafening sounds to my ears and how that tiny creature would humble me and teach me so much about my own fears.

And yet, the vision that became the guiding force of my life would come to me only after my older and wiser relatives, the dolphins, the sea turtle, and the cricket, had prepared me. The vision would come to me a year later on a wintry Minnesota night after a hard day of teaching kids and a long evening teaching adults.

It seems the night of my vision I had fallen exhausted onto my couch. . . . I can't recall falling asleep or even closing my eyes. I just remember how Time transcended and the how the Mystery of life suddenly unfolded. I fall through once again. . . .

And I can recall seeing people of different races lying about, dead and dying, but the kind of death I was seeing was not necessarily a physical one but rather a spirit death. . . . I remember how an Indian man struggled to breathe and how my own breathing became his. I recall just as I/we were gasping for our last breath, I was turned in the direction of a woman who seemed to me as old as the earth. She appeared haggard with anger, distraught with anxiety. Her thoughts manifested in my mind as quickly as she spoke them, even without pausing, yet I understood everything she said. She spoke about the misuse of language and how humans have used words to hurt and to harm this world. She spoke about words used to kill, words used to destroy, words used for greed.

Then I recall in this vision state of mind, I was turned once again in another direction where a sacred being robed in red stood before me, holding in his hands an incredible book. The cover was like looking through a portal or a window to the stars. He pointed to a constellation, then he held out the book for me to take, but as he did this, the book of stars became a living pipe.

My uncle would later help me understand how this vision connected me directly to the power of the word. He explained that the books which I teach from and the ones which I would some day write are words in physical form. He said that the pipe which I now keep and protect with my life is the word made physical too. He said that words respected and held sacred would be my source of power as I walk the path of my vision toward my destiny—that words held sacred would protect me and provide for me for as I long as I lived.

From then on, the vision I was granted that one cold night in Minnesota, when I was a young teacher, would become the guiding force and influence of my life. It would enable me to carry a pipe into a state prison so that Native American prisoners, once denied the right to pray in their own way, could smoke their prayers as their ancestors once did and in their minds and hearts reconnect themselves to the powers of the natural world and to the spirit of their own lives. My vision would help me become a better teacher, using books to teach that recorded the old and new stories, that told the real history of the land, the animals, and the People. And I would draw from my vision the strength to write and to give voice among humans to those who have none—the buffalo, the dolphin, the eagle, and the crane; the redwoods, the pines, the willows and the oaks—and to make words that help people remember our common primal roots ... words that help us to see the beauty within ourselves ... words that allow us to acknowledge the seeds of beauty in other life forms as well.

Now, as I face the Direction of my own passing, I stand on the shoreline of Time, still seeing dolphins swim through my sea of memory and still feeling that sense of joy for life that they bring me.

On this shore of memory, I remain still connected to words ... words to tell my own stories and those of others who have tried to walk the path of beauty in this life ... words that describe a world where everything is related, where humans are not regarded as the pinnacle of creation ... words that weave stories and make magic their meaning, as even now, I fall through once again and remember....

THE OLD WOMAN WHO WAS YOUNG...
(from *The Book of Ceremonies* by Gabriel Horn)

The wise old woman of the Turtle Clan sat on the old rock alongside the old river, looking into the doe-brown eyes of her young relative sitting next to her. The girl who was becoming a woman had recently tried to end her short sixteen-year-old life.

"I am puzzled," the grandmother said. "Why would such a pretty and sweet young person want to end her earth walk so soon?" She placed her

hand on her granddaughter's knee. Her own life had seemed so short, she wondered. If only this young one could know how short it all is.... The flash of a firefly in the great scheme of things....

She spoke again, careful not to impose judgment in her voice. "You haven't completed your journey here," she said, and looked in the direction of the tiny Indian violets opened between the crevices of the old stones. "They are the first to bloom in the spring, you know." Then she paused again, appreciating their beauty, contemplating their will to live and their determination to celebrate life by showing themselves even as the last of the freezing rains would fall. "A flower does not turn on itself."

The girl who was becoming a woman glanced up from her sneakers, first at the flowers, then at the source of this gentle, loving voice. Her attention did not focus on her grandmother's long silvery hair, the silky strands lifting slightly in the early spring breeze, but she felt drawn more to the old eyes that still sparkled like a child's ... eyes that were not dark like the deer's as many of the girl's other relatives, but bright green, more like the moss of the old glistening rocks in the middle of the old river, moving past them in the warm noonday sun, or the kind of green that the budding willows wear during their rebirthing this time of year when everything seems new and alive again.

"I have no role model, Grandmother," the girl responded. "No one to look up to ... no one to teach me.... She etched a circle in the dark earth with the toe of her sneaker. It was not a conscious drawing but the expression of a concept etched in her mind. "My mother drinks," she continued. Her voice quivered. One part of her felt angry, the other part just pain. "My aunties drink.... My father I only see once in awhile and when I do he's usually been drinkin'. And my brother was killed in a wreck last year ridin' home from college with his friends. The driver that hit them was drunk."

The girl who had been sitting alongside the old woman sitting on the old rock suddenly stood, taking notice of a pair of cardinals that had just swooped down on a worm. "Look, Grandma!" the young woman who was a teenage girl called. "The male stays so close to the female. It's like

he watches out for her." Then with the flick of a feather the birds returned to the nest.... "Do you think they have babies?"

"Yes," the girl's grandmother replied, "... seems they have young ones to care for." She gazed up at the old elm while she spoke. Its new budding leaves encompassed the nest cradled in one of the tree's strong boughs. "It's like the spirit of new life is all around them," she said. Then she leaned back, stretched, and took a deep breath. She thought, How good it felt to be alive. "You know," she continued, "you mustn't think that people can be your only role models. Look around you. Your teachers are everywhere. They're among the plants and the trees. They're among the animals and birds. They dwell in the earth among the insects. They live in the sea among the dolphins and whales. These are our relatives, and they've been our teachers always. Without them, how would people know how to live?"

The old woman of the Turtle Clan stood and walked to where the young woman who was a girl was standing alone, still gazing up at the elm. "The way we need to live is in that tree ... is in that nest ... is everywhere our Mother Earth provides life that is older and wiser than we are. For many of us have forgotten how to live." She pointed up. "But they have not forgotten. You can learn so much by watching them.... They are your role models. They are your teachers.

"Now come," the old woman who seemed so young said. She held out a deerskin pouch and offered it to her granddaughter. "Take a pinch of this special tobacco kept in this gift from our brother, the deer. Take some into your hand if you like."

The young woman who nearly took her own life but a short time ago reached in with her fingers and took the tobacco. "Now make your prayers of gratitude," the old woman encouraged, "for life.... Sprinkle them like seeds under this old elm in recognition of the spring and the Beginning of Newness."

As time and the cycles of life continued, those seeds of prayer would grow, and the woman who was once young, who was a teenage girl, would one day return to this place by the old river where the old elm still lived and the cardinals had made their nest that spring. This became her ceremony. She would come back every equinox this time of year, every

year for the rest of her long and wonderful life, and she would bring her children and her grandchildren there to still see those hardy Indian violets blooming between the crevices of the old rocks with that same determination to celebrate life, and she would remember the old woman of the Turtle Clan who was always young in her old voice of wisdom and in her old green eyes of spring. She would remember the animals and the birds. She would remember her teachers of the gift of life.

PART 3

CHANGING RELATIONSHIPS

DOGMA AND CATECHISM

MICHAEL MOUNTAIN

Best Friends Animal Sanctuary, in the majestic red-rock country of southern Utah, is the nation's largest no-kill sanctuary for dogs and cats and other animals.

FUNDAMENTALS

Caring about animals means different things to different people. To one person it might mean having a houseful of stray cats, while to another it can mean being a committed vegetarian, or attending demonstrations about a particular issue, or whatever. Animal lovers are often passionate people, and we can become agitated about our particular concerns, but sometimes we don't know that there can be many different perspectives on what's best for the animals.

Nobody has a monopoly on the "right" philosophy or approach, and we can all learn a lot by listening instead of preaching. In fact, at Best Friends we steer clear of telling anyone, including staff people at the sanctuary, what people should believe or how they should live or what they should eat. "Judge not, lest ye be judged," said a famous teacher, and it's pretty good advice. Most people who keep busy by telling everyone else what they should or shouldn't do tend to lack an inner confidence about their own lives and values.

Having said that, however, certain basics are fundamental for an animal lover. (And if it sounds like I'm completely reversing what I just said, I've learned that this is a fundamental right of all animal lovers!)

We live in a world where all life exists at the expense of other life. It is unavoidable that our very existence is going to cause suffering to other species. But there are certain things that people do to animals that are fundamentally and intuitively just plain wrong. The worst of these is vivisection—using animals in scientific experiments.

Vivisection was described by Mahatma Gandhi as "the blackest of black crimes that humanity has visited upon the innocent creation." The belief that we have some divine right to subjugate, torture, and humiliate other species on the basis that we are superior is the quintessential symbol of human pride and arrogance.

There are many arguments against vivisection. Top scientists have argued effectively that experiments on animals have not advanced medical and scientific knowledge. But even if this were not true, it would not reverse our conviction that no possible good can come from the willful torture of another sentient being.

Is the world a healthier place to live in today than it was a few thousand years ago? The epidemics currently sweeping the "civilized" world, for which no cure can be found, are testimony to how little we understand about our relationship to the natural world. The medical community says that the current generation of antibiotics is becoming less and less effective against new strains of stronger and more resistant bacteria. They say no solution to this problem is in sight—no new generation of stronger antibiotics. There is no cure for AIDS, cancer, or heart disease, and trying out more exotic drugs on helpless animals is not going to save the world from sickness.

Animals are used as easy victims for testing more than medical drugs and procedures. Weapons systems, cosmetics, household products, car safety—all are tried out on unconsenting animals. Our great, heroic space adventurers of recent decades made sure that dogs and monkeys were the first to "boldly go where no one has gone before."

Vivisection, sport hunting, fashionable fur coats, specialty foods that cause extra suffering to animals—these and other ways in which innocence is sacrificed to human vanity and the "advancement" of society are the unforgivable sins of a human civilization that has lost touch with nature, the animals, and its own soul.

THE GOLDEN RULE

It is not a moral judgment, simply a fact of life, that wanton cruelty to others destroys something within ourselves. There's a simple law of cause and effect that governs the whole of the known universe. It's known by every scientist, and it translates into the fundamental Golden Rule at the heart of every major philosophy and religion the world has ever known. Here's how it's stated in some of their major texts:

"Do unto others as you would have them do unto you . . . . As a man sows, so shall he reap."—New Testament, Christian text

"Hurt not others with that which pains you yourself."—Udanavarga, Buddhist text

"That which is hateful unto you, do not do unto others."—Rabbi Hillel, Jewish text

"Do not unto others what you would not they should do unto you."—Analects, Confucian text

"This is the sum of duty: do nothing unto others which, if done to you, would cause you pain."—Mahabharata, Hindu text

"A man should wander about treating all creatures as he himself would be treated."—Sutrakritanga, Jain text

"Treat others as you would be treated. What you like not for yourself dispense not to others."—Abdullah Ansari, Islamic Sufi text

It's the simple law of kindness. A friend of Best Friends sent me a poem for which I find a corner every month in *Best Friends Magazine*:

> *Be kind to animals,*
> *Be kind to trees,*
> *Be kind to the earth and everything on it,*

Be kind to children and one another,
. . . and God will be kind to you.
And that's a Promise

When you're kind to others, you feel better. Kindness makes a difference. Some of the stress starts ebbing away. And since, according to many doctors, most sickness is caused by stress, your health may indeed take a turn for the better.

If the predominant drive in our human world were kindness rather than greed and selfishness, much would change, we'd all feel better, and many of the ills that beset our civilization would drop away.

MAKING A DIFFERENCE

Faith Maloney, the director of Best Friends, is to be found every morning at Octagon Three in Best Friends Dogtown at a big kitchen sink where she and the dog staff prepare the dogs' dinners. There are about five hundred dogs at Dogtown and a couple of hundred more who live at other parts of the sanctuary.

Once asked by a newspaper reporter whether she felt that a no-kill sanctuary could really "make a difference," she simply smiled and said, "It makes quite a difference if you're one of the animals here."

Faith knows all the dogs by name. Dogtown isn't just a cute name for where all these dogs live; it really is a town. Dogs are social beings; they create societies, and Dogtown is a complete society. They form their own groups and hierarchies. There are territories and literal "lines in the sand" that one group won't cross over because it would be invading someone else's territory.

The casual visitor to Dogtown can easily miss a lot of what's going on. Beyond the barking and running around, there's a major social interaction taking place. It's a different life from what dogs get in a single-family home. But for dogs who come off the streets, who have been abused and abandoned and are often a bit scared of people, it's a great way to start a new life with your own kind.

Faith says that rather than the dogs becoming more humanized, she's noticed that she and the staff have become a bit more canine-ized! "I find myself a bit more like a dog and relating to them all as a great big pack," she says.

COMMUNICATING WITH ANIMALS

Most of the dogs live in groups in big compounds. Many of them are out of their compounds during the day. "How do you keep track of five hundred dogs?" I once asked Faith. "It's simple, in fact," she replied. "I keep them all in my head. So long as they're in my head, it's OK."

I've read a lot of stuff about "communicating" with animals. Some of it is good, and there are many accomplished animal communicators out there. But here at Dogtown, with five hundred dogs, there's nothing mystical and esoteric about it. For Faith, "keeping them in my head" is a very down-to-earth activity. It means being in tune, in touch, following one's intuitions, being in contact. Losing that contact can have on-the-ground consequences for the dogs who depend on their "alpha mother."

Diana Castle, chief Best Friends cat lady, expresses the concept differently: "Suddenly I'll find myself saying: I wonder how so-and-so is. I have to follow that up at once, rather than just treat it as a passing thought. And I'll usually find little so-and-so is just developing a bad tooth or some other condition that could have escaped notice."

Diana says it's never a waste of time checking out that nagging little question in her head. At the very least, she says, the kitten wanted you to see him or her, and that made a difference.

Catland has about seven hundred cats, ministered to by Diana and her team of cat ladies. Yes, there are some guys who work there too, but Catland always seems to me like an ancient Egyptian cat temple with high priestesses going around making offerings to feline deities. . . .

Everyone who works with the animals develops this sixth sense one way or another. We had a group of school kids visiting last summer. One of them was blind. She spent the week working with the cats, visiting with them, petting them, and giving them lots of love. Three times during the week she "felt" something about them that was a big help.

"This cat doesn't quite 'feel' right," she said to one of the staff. Examination showed that this cat was just beginning to develop an abscess in a back tooth.

Communication with the animals and with nature is a natural part of life at the sanctuary. For first-time visitors, it begins as soon as they drive into Angel Canyon, the home of Best Friends. Some visitors say that the atmosphere was completely identifiable, even when they arrived at night.

That's no surprise to those of us who began Best Friends and brought the animals here from our smaller sanctuary in Arizona. Angel Canyon, at the heart of the Golden Circle of national parks of southern Utah and northern Arizona, drew us here in the face of many logical reasons for choosing an alternative place. For starters, it seemed an impractical place to relocate a small but growing animal sanctuary. It was hundreds of miles from a major city, had no buildings or even power lines, and was far bigger than we could imagine necessary. But from the day Francis Battista, our rescue director, first saw it, the image of what we could build would not go away.

Angel Canyon, Home of Best Friends

Angel Canyon had been a choice movie location for some twenty years before Best Friends came here. The Lone Ranger's bridge is still up there on a cliff, and dozens of famous movies were made here, like *How the West Was Won* and *The Outlaw Josie Wales*. Long before filmmakers discovered the beauty of the canyon, Angel Canyon was known as a sacred place to the Anasazi people who lived here.

The Anasazi culture reached its height about seven hundred years ago, and then the people suddenly left this area. Before archaeologists got busy, all sorts of weird and wonderful theories abounded. Some thought that the Anasazi were actually space people who had been lifted off without warning by UFOs. In fact, it seems there was a prolonged drought, and the people migrated several hundred miles away. When they resettled, they became what are now the Hopi people.

The drought explains some of the legends and tales that surround this extraordinary place. An elder of a local tribe who recently came to bless the canyon sat on the grass under the big dome cave that's called Angels Landing and explained that "hundreds of years ago, this is the place where the nations used to gather to ask for guidance from Mother Nature for their people."

Another tale that's told is about the spring that bubbles up at Angels Landing. They say that during the drought there was a great storm one night, lightning struck a rock, and water gushed out of it. The spring has never dried up since, they say, nor will it ever. Well, the water here is as pure and delightful as you'll find anywhere, and so is the atmosphere of peace and tranquillity that fills the place.

I'm not an expert on sacred places, but I've been told by people who are that each sacred place has a particular atmosphere—a particular kind of energy that emanates from it. At Angel Canyon it is a sense of profound peace. It radiates peace and instills its own peace in all who come here.

It seems, also, that this great peace is a quality which has been here for a long time. The ancient Anasazi, whose forebears came here about six thousand years ago, are known to have been the most peaceful of people. You can see this, say archaeologists, from the drawings and carvings—pictographs and petroglyphs—that they left on the walls of the caves and cliffs. No one knows what the designs mean and whether a whole language is associated with them, but you don't have to be an expert in ancient languages to see the one outstanding characteristic of Anasazi art that differentiates it from every other ancient culture that has ever left its art and language on cliffs, caves, and temple walls.

In fact, it's not what you *do* see in the depictions; it's what you *don't* see. There are no depictions of acts of violence: no war, no killing, no subjugation or slavery, no hunting even. (It's not that the people never hunted animals; it's simply that this was apparently not considered something to elevate into art or religion.) Compare the walls of Egyptian temples, covered in the glories of war and the subjugation of foreign people, or those of the Mayans and Aztecs, for whom ritual violence and disfigurement were the order of the day.

There are also legends of buried treasure left here by the followers of King Montezuma after he was killed in Mexico by the conquistadors. In 1915 a treasure hunter showed up in the local town of Kanab with a treasure map he'd brought from Mexico. He went off to dig in a nearby canyon about twenty miles from Angel Canyon. After several attempts and a second treasure map, he gave up, exhausted, saying he realized he was in the wrong canyon; it was the next one over. Nobody could face starting all over again, so Angel Canyon guards whatever legendary treasures it hides, and everyone who comes here knows that the real treasure is the peace and tranquillity of the place and the animal sanctuary itself

What a place, indeed, for a sanctuary for abused and abandoned animals. What more perfect purpose for a sacred place than to bring life and love to the true innocents of our world for whom the best our society can offer is so often simply a "humane" death.

"This is the place where the nations used to gather . . ." said the elder of his people as he sat at Angels Landing when he came to bless the sanctuary.

THE IN-GATHERING

The late professor Joseph Campbell used to remind his audiences that any place we use for a special purpose and through which we contact the true purpose of life becomes a sacred place. Each of us, he would say, can be the hero of our own sacred drama of life.

All over the world people are hearing the call of their own Muse, their own higher voice, the voice of the animals, of Nature, of Life. We all are being called to the great In-Gathering which must inexorably take place.

Each of us responds in our own way, according to our own inner truth. But we all follow certain absolutes—primarily, the Golden Rule of treating all Life as we ourselves would be treated.

Indeed, we find the Golden Rule at work in the most basic way on our journey. Those innocent creatures who are so helpless and needy turn out to have the key to the sacred place that awaits us at the end of our quest. They can unlock the place in our heart that puts us in touch with compassion, the essence of all spiritual qualities, and brings us closer to Life itself, to nature, and to each other.

The Light and the Darkness

Two distinct trends can be seen in the world of the 1990s. One is the death of the old: a growing darkness that permeates the worldly institutions of government, religion, business, and the whole established social order. Few people have faith in that old order or are any longer even surprised by the daily revelations of corruption at all levels and in every department. For anyone who looks to those institutions for security, direction, hope, leadership, or purpose, the future can only look gloomy.

The other trend can be seen in the growing number of heartwarming stories that we have the pleasure of reading and hearing from all over the world each day here at Best Friends. These are stories of people who care, who go out of their way to help a suffering animal, who see life as sacred, and who nurture it at almost any cost.

We meet these people when they come to visit the sanctuary animals. We know them through the mail, and we read and hear about them in the occasional stories of kindness and compassion that make their way into the news.

They are you—the animal lovers and people of all kinds for whom it is important to practice kindness and compassion to people, to animals, and to all living things.

You may be the only person on your street or in your office or at school who feels and acts that way, and maybe you've often felt alone because of it. But you're not alone; there are thousands, indeed millions of us. And more and more we are all connecting with each other—meeting each other in person, reading each others' newsletters, joining computer networks where people of like mind gather, finding new ways and means to keep in touch. Indeed, the darker the old world becomes, the brighter the light of kindness shines like the proverbial phoenix rising from the ashes.

OUR BROTHER, THE DONKEY

PADRE ANTONIO VIEIRA

(an excerpt translated and adapted by Bill Teasdale)

THE DONKEY'S IDENTITY CARD

Animal, mammal, quadruped, vertebrate, ungulate, perissodactyl, member of the equine family, genus *Equus* and species *asinus*. His four legs end in small hooves. When born, these legs are striped; a cross is traced on his back like the stigmata of destiny. He's tame, patient, and resigned, but like humans he has his moods and humors, and when he sulks, not even the stick brings him to reason. Frugal in appetite and even more so in drink: he can go forty-eight hours without water. When he drinks, the water must be clean. He rarely sweats.

These generalizations differentiate him from the horse. Well-treated, he is more versatile and more useful. The horse is proud; the donkey is humble. The horse has airs and overtones of nobility and is made to be ridden; meanwhile the donkey is everywhere in the life of the family of the *campo*, equal to the most hard and difficult tasks.

We can tell the donkey from the horse by the way he walks, or how he works; by his affectionate neigh; by his docile manner, calm and patient even when a half-dozen children climb on his back; by the versatility and geniality of many of his traits, beyond the scope of the horse.

They are neither friends nor enemies but tolerate each other. That is, except for the stallion of either species, which, like man or the male in general, is protective of his beloveds.

There are few names for the horse, but we must take off our hats to the donkey. We need a dictionary to collect and record all his synonyms. Offhand, I can think of at least a hundred, the most varied, the oddest, the least honorable, the most humiliating.

Nobody today feels, like Ishmael, son of Abraham, happy and honored to be called "Ass," not even by an angel. Instead, we constantly say, "I lead a donkey's life, I work like a mule, I suffer like a blind man's donkey."

ASININE THOUGHTS

The ancient saying is that man is the most noble and sublime creation of God.

Who says so? Man.

Man is defined as a rational animal, as a thinking being.

Who believes that? Man.

It is a fact and perhaps a dogma that man is made in the Divine Image.

Who said such a stupid and heretical thing? Man once more.

The donkey is jeered at as stupid, inept, lazy, cowardly, slow, obstinate.

Who says that? Man.

Let us now reflect and rethink our received wisdom.

Is there not a lack of intellectual and moral honesty in the preceding affirmations?

I have never seen an animal dance on the carcass of another animal. A vulture does not eat another vulture. The animal, once satiated, abandons its prey. It does not kill for amusement, from hate, for revenge, coldly and satanically like the so-called "rational" animals. The peace conferences always end in fiasco. Instead of convening distinguished jurists and eminent diplomats who always nourish the strength of the strongest, the Big Four, or Five, or Six—take a donkey. With his patient and mystic posture, his philosophy of quietude, the donkey is a living prayer—humility, peace, love, serenity.

In the World of the Donkey, peace reigns. He can live without man. But man can scarcely do without the labor, the sacrifice, the suffering of

the donkey. The animals that render the greatest services to man are the most cast-off and deprived, such as the donkey that has accompanied man since the dawn of time, in all weathers, humbly and patiently serving the most brutal of animals. So much dedication and sacrifice are still not enough to please the human heart.

A Jesuit priest, Pierre Charles, wrote these words: "Men are certainly hard to fathom. They fear cruelty, yet ennoble it. They want the services of others, yet despise those who graciously and generously offer it. The lion has never been a benefactor of mankind. He is a distinctly dangerous neighbor. No one ever put him in a yoke or made him pull a plow. He never worked for or was even polite to man. And yet, how we have glorified him and made him the King of the Animals! We put him on national emblems, in coats of arms, we make statues, always with the trappings of grandeur, nobility, and rank.

"And the eagle? He is a cruel and voracious bird of prey, which decimates the flock when he can with that sharp beak and those curved talons. But how aristocratic! One calls to mind the Roman eagles of that great empire of the past. And the Napoleonic and German eagles. Titles, parchments, decorations are ornamented with the figure of that cruel beak. To give someone the sobriquet of 'Eagle' is to award a distinction conveying the highest cultural and intellectual pedigree.

"Dog, horse, donkey, pig, and sheep are derogatory and insulting terms and above all, ass, a creature that never corrupted anyone but always helped us with our burdens and does no more than bray when stricken with hunger or thirst. All foolishness is called asinine, and there is no greater insult than to call someone a donkey or an ass."

THE DONKEY PERSONALITY

Recent psychological studies have investigated the personality of each animal for its more efficient use, starting with temperament, the raw material of individuality, which is different from animal to animal as it is from person to person. The personality of an animal is the result of heredity, alimentation, climate, treatment, acquired habits, sexual equilibrium, endocrine, and so on.

Timidity, aggressiveness, passivity, sexuality, speed of reaction, and activeness are all aspects of the animal temperament. Various studies have shown that their reactions are similar to ours.

The personality of most animals has been drawn in caricature. The dog is diplomatic, faithful, dedicated. The cat, sly and individualistic. The rat, timid but cunning. The fox, crafty, lively, and audacious. The horse, fiery, ardent, impulsive, bold, fearless. The donkey, tame, calm, patient, and willing.

SOCIABILITY

Amazing as it may seem, the donkey is inherently sociable, instinctively affable and docile. This theme can be pursued by way of study of the time when donkeys, onagras, hemionos, kiang, and other related species lived in the forests and wilds. Not predators and lacking means to defend themselves, they created their own *modus vivendi* by establishing a "Code of Honor" to defend each other.

For this reason they moved only in groups commanded by the strongest and bravest stallion. Nature itself, for its part, endowed them with superior instincts and a sense of smell like radar so that they can tell at great distances not only the female in heat but also any fierce animal. One notes that, even today, the donkey has the instinctive habit of raising his head with the upper lips open to taste the air.

In those days, when he sensed the approach of a predator, he brayed at full volume. The donkey has three distinct cries. Hearing the alarm signal, all would rush to a clearing and, placing the young in the center, stand with their backs to whatever was coming. Not even a strong and aggressive animal would dare to come closer, since the kick of a donkey with his small hoof cuts like a razor.

Even today one can observe two atavistic characteristics of the ass: they keep in groups or herds—one rarely encounters a solitary donkey by the side of our roads—and when a vehicle or other object of a certain size approaches, they infallibly turn their backs on it.

I once stood watching the construction of a dam in the municipality of Solonopole and became convinced that humans would not have the

behavior, the sense of responsibility, the discipline that the two hundred donkeys engaged in transporting clay to the dam wall were displaying. Each carried two large empty boxes. Two hundred meters from the wall, there was a bank where workmen dug out the clay and filled the boxes one by one. When the donkey had been loaded, he made his way, without human interference, calmly and in Indian file, to the dam wall where boys pulled the cord attached to the bottom of the box, and the clay fell on the wall. This round was continuous, the donkeys never stopping, straying from the path, or bumping into each other.

It was the most ordered and perfect collective effort that I ever saw in my life. I did see something somewhat similar as a child, when my father took troops of donkeys loaded with bales of hay from the farm to Cedro, forty-eight kilometers away, at a brisk pace with no stopping to rest, in that steady trot and in a sequence ordered with admirable discipline. The troop usually consisted of thirty to forty burros led by one muleteer and one helper.

The experimental farms ingeniously exploit this sense of solidarity of animals. It is common to come across a laden mule accompanied by other unladen burros. The company lightens the task of the laden animal.

American writers describing the gregariousness of such animals relate that it was common at the time of the colonization of the West for herds of wild horses to pass, neighing and prancing, around the corrals in which the domestic animals were penned, and often these last would break their bounds and join their wild comrades.

One could also write more about the docility of the donkey, especially with children, but here I recommend the tenderness of Juan Ramón Jiménez in *Platero e Yo*.

I will dispense with any comparison of the psychology of the horse and the donkey, since there is no portrait more faithful to the arrogance and caprice of the horse and of the humble steadiness of the donkey than Cervantes, when he paints the profile of Don Quixote, so identified with his Rosinante, and Sancho Panza, so well-clothed in his mulishness.

EMOTIONAL REACTIONS

Finally, in his book *L'Ame du Cheval*, Quenon affirms that the ears of the horse, the burro, and the donkey are the mirror of the soul. Every instinctive reaction is indicated by the position of the ears. Facing danger, some disagreeable circumstance, or when adopting a hostile attitude, or in revolt, or again when wishing to show pleasure on recognizing his master, companion, and friend, his ears tell the tale. Thence the saying that every donkey has suspicion in his ears. They are his divining rod, a kind of radar or thermometer of emotion.

It seems that donkeys, possessing as they do larger ears than the burro and the horse, must possess greater sensibility and emotional depth.

Donkeys, burros, and horses are not aggressive animals. If maltreated, they react. It should not be forgotten that the donkey and the burro are animals with powerful and active memories. The Dutch even say that "a donkey never treads twice on the same stone." One can travel with them all day on an unfamiliar road, then release them, and they will return unerringly to the starting point. They retain forever in their nerves and subconscious all they suffered in their early training and in the moments of ill humor of their masters.

Of all the animals, the least aggressive and vengeful is the donkey. But their incredible sensitivity also has unexpected practical uses. For example, in the Paraguayan hinterland (*sertao*) during the summer months the locals follow the dry riverbeds; when they come to a place that has been disturbed by donkeys with their hooves, they dig down and soon find drinking water. The donkey feels the presence of humidity and hence the veins of water through the soil.

My father had many animals, including burros, mules, and donkeys. Some lived in herds, free on the range. Others were kept separately in enclosures with ample pasture or suitably tethered. I learned much from the animals, including a stronger dose of humanity, of social education, of respect and love for others. Even today when I return to the hinterland and live awhile among the animals, I feel more human, while the more I am in the city, the more I feel aggressive, less polite, and exhibit worse manners.

VEGAN KINSHIP

LORRI BAUSTON

In 1986, Gene and I decided we wanted to do something to help farm animals, but we didn't know what or how we would do it. So we started visiting factory farms, stockyards, and slaughterhouses to educate ourselves, and that's when we started rescuing animals like Hilda.

We were investigating a stockyard in Pennsylvania when we found her. Gene and I were walking through the auction pens and discovered the stockyard deadpile in the back of one of the buildings. Mounds of dead and decaying animals were thrown on a cement pad. Cows with ropes tied tightly around their necks. Pigs with large wounds. Goats with twisted legs. The insistent buzzing of the maggots and nauseating smell wrenched my stomach, as did the lingering questions. How long had they suffered? How many days of agony and terror did they endure before dying alone and in pain?

Gene took out the camera, and we walked closer to the pile. The camera clicked, and one of the animals on the pile lifted her head. Gene and I stared at each other, both not wanting to believe what we had just seen. I knelt down next to the animal, and Hilda looked back at me. She was just inches away from a rotting carcass, and flies and maggots were crawling over her body. I held her head in my hands whispering "poor baby, poor baby" to calm her and keep myself from screaming.

Gene ran to get the van, and within ten minutes we were rushing to the nearest veterinarian. Hilda had collapsed because of the brutal transportation conditions. She was not suffering any other injuries or diseases. We learned that Hilda had been loaded onto a truck with hundreds of other sheep. Despite humid, near-one-hundred-degree temperatures, the

185

sheep were severely overcrowded, a standard livestock marketing strategy to get more dollars per load, even when some sheep will die from the stress. Hilda was part of the meat industry's "economic loss" calculations. The meat, poultry, and dairy industries even have a name for animals like Hilda. They call them "downers."

We took Hilda home, and then we knew what we could do to help farm animals. We started a shelter for victims of "food animal" production so that we could care for Hilda and other suffering farm animals, and we started exposing the atrocities of the food-animal industry.

As we continued our investigations, Gene and I learned that Hilda's story was not unique. Every year thousands of animals used for "food" production are abused and neglected because animal suffering is considered part of "normal animal agricultural practices." Blatant animal cruelties, like severe confinement, overcrowding, and abandonment, are deliberately practiced to increase profits, despite the tremendous cost to animals.

We have found day-old chicks discarded in outdoor dumpsters because they do not grow fast enough to be profitable for meat consumption. We have seen emaciated dairy cows dragged to slaughter with chains when they were too sick or weak to walk because they can still be sold for human consumption. We have heard turkeys screaming in terror while they were hung upside down fully conscious and bled to death because poultry are exempt from slaughter-stunning requirements.

People often ask us how we cope with seeing so much suffering and death. Whenever I'm asked that question, I find myself thinking about what inspires me and gives me hope, and I think about a pig I have dearly loved, a pig named Hope.

Hope had been dumped at a livestock market because she had a crippled leg and was no longer "marketable." Hope was just a baby, barely two months old. I remember how frightened she was and how she frantically crawled away when we approached her. Hope had never known a kind touch. Humans had only kicked, dragged, and abandoned her. Gene and I spoke gently to her and wrapped a blanket around her shivering body. She let out one small grunt as we picked her up and then nestled into my arms like she had always known me.

For seven years, Hope was a part of our lives. We cared for all her special needs, and she filled our hearts with love. Hope touched many other people, too. Over the years she taught thousands of Farm Sanctuary visitors that farm animals are just as capable of suffering from isolation, fear, and neglect as a dog or cat or you and me.

I am comforted knowing that Hope reached so many people, especially now that she is no longer with us. Hope passed away at our shelter, surrounded by those who loved her. After two years, I still find myself glancing in the direction of her favorite corner. I will never forget how she rolled over for belly rubs at the touch of my hand, or her distinct thank-you grunt when I placed her food bowl in front of her. Most of all, though, I will always remember how her life inspired us to continue the fight for farm-animal rights.

You might easily lose hope when you've been to a slaughterhouse or factory farm and witnessed so much cruelty. I will never forget the first time I went to an egg factory and saw the horror of modern-day egg production. To produce eggs, four to five hens are crammed into a cage about the size of a folded newspaper. The cages are stacked by the thousands in row after row. Between 80,000 and 100,000 are housed in a single, windowless warehouse. Feed, water, and manure disposal is completely automated, so just a handful of workers oversee the entire production. There is no individual care or attention. The birds endure this misery for two to three years, unable to stretch their wings, walk, or even lie down comfortably.

After months of intensive confinement, the birds lose most of their feathers, because their bodies are constantly rubbing against the bare wire cages. With little feather protection their skin eventually becomes covered with painful bruises and sores. When the hens become too sick or injured to produce eggs at peak production levels, they are literally thrown out of the cage and left on the floor to die slowly from starvation.

We found Lily on the floor of an egg factory, waiting for death to end her nightmare. She was standing in a corner, trying desperately to keep from falling on a mound of feces and decaying feathers and bones. Lily had given up all hope. Her entire body was hunched over, and her head

drooped close to the ground. She was covered with sores, and her left eye was swollen shut. I reached out and gently lifted her into my hands. She trembled as I lifted her. I kept whispering to her, softly telling her that I was a vegan and that her misery was over. My "vegan reassurance speeches" always seem ridiculous to me after a rescue, but no matter how foolish I feel the next day, it's become one of my "rescue rituals."

For two weeks Lily received intensive rehabilitative care. Lily was too weak to walk, and throughout the day I would hold her up to help her regain strength in her legs. She also had bruising over 75 percent of her body, and four times a day we wrapped heating pads around her to reduce the swelling. Since Lily was severely emaciated, she could only eat small amounts of liquid food through a dropper every few hours. On more than one occasion, I wondered if we were doing the right thing, or if we were just prolonging her suffering.

It is the shelter question whenever an animal is near death—but then one morning I had the answer. I opened the door to Lily's rehab pen, and she walked over to me and looked up. I immediately sat down to get as close as I could to "chicken height," and Lily climbed onto my lap. I reached down, and this time, I was the one trembling as I stroked her chin. Lily gave me her love in a way that I could understand, just like a dog talking with his or her tail or a cat purring soothingly.

Rescuing an animal like Lily always carries me through those times when we cannot save a suffering animal, like the time Gene and I visited a California slaughterhouse in the Chino Valley south of Los Angeles. This area has the highest concentration of dairy cows in the world, which means it has one of the highest concentrations of beef production, too. Dairy cows are not being retired to Farm Sanctuary; they are slaughtered and ground for hamburger. The majority of hamburger sold in the United States comes from dairy cows, not rain forests.

We stood near the unloading area, watching the cows come in one by one. Gene was videotaping the scene, and my job was taking photos. Some of the cows were "downers." According to California dairy industry reports, one in four dairy cows becomes a downer due to illnesses and diseases caused by excessive milk production. Dairy cows are forced to produce ten times more milk than they would in nature, and the prob-

lem is getting worse with the use of rBGH (bovine growth hormone) and genetic manipulation.

They put all the downers into one killing pen, and then a worker came around and shot a cow in the head. It was a slow process. Several minutes would pass between each killing, and the ones that were alive had to just lie there and watch. There was one cow who looked a lot like Maya, a cow at our New York shelter. She was shaking from fear, and I wanted so badly to put my arms around her and comfort her. Later, when I was in the car, it was so unbearable. I kept thinking of Maya and how much she loves life. Well, actually, how much she loves my husband, Gene.

Maya adores Gene and is actually jealous of me. She pushes me out of the way whenever Gene and I are in the barn, and since she's an 1,800-pound woman, she's even knocked me down a few times. Of course, Gene has to be careful too. When Maya goes into heat, she tries to mount him. In the bovine family, the females take charge of the mating situation. (Perhaps we humans could learn something from our bovine sisters.) She'll stand there and gaze adoringly at Gene, softly mooing to him, and then turn around and give me the evil eye.

I thought of Maya and her likes and dislikes, her unique personality, and I thought of that poor trembling cow who wanted to live as much as Maya, or you and me. Farm animals are living, feeling animals; they are not "breakfast," "lunch," and "dinner." Americans have drawn an imaginary line and classified some animals as "pets" and some animals as "dinner." Our society is horrified (and rightly so) when we hear of other cultures eating dogs and cats, and most people would never be intentionally cruel to a dog or cat. I have to hope that they would never be intentionally cruel to a cow or chicken either. People who love animals called "pets" would not eat animals called "dinner" if they would only look into the eyes of a suffering farm animal.

The production of food animals is the single largest and most institutionalized form of animal abuse. Billions of animals suffer tormented lives, and millions of people participate in the cruelty. But Hope's life, and now her memory, reminds me that we can stop "food animal" production—one life at a time, one law at a time, and one more person at a time who becomes a vegan because that individual met an animal like Hope.

If you saw a laying hen like Lily, or a frightened dairy cow, wouldn't you do everything you could in your power to stop their suffering? Well, every person can stop dairy-cow suffering, and every person can shut down egg and chicken factories, because every person can be a vegan.

The dairy, egg, and meat industries abuse and kill animals because people buy those products. If you don't buy meat, eggs, and dairy products, they won't produce them. It's that simple and that direct. Food-animal production is entrenched, but that is why we have the greatest opportunity to stop it. Anyone can take immediate action, and maybe that is why being a vegan is such an empowering experience.

When you stop consuming animals and animal by-products, you stop the slaughter of hundreds of animals. Your action saves lives, and it is as direct as going to a factory farm or stockyard and rescuing an animal like Hope yourself. When you become a vegan, you begin to share a special bond with farm animals. Vegan kinship is powerful, and it will touch you and change your life forever. You may notice strange and wonderful things happening to you when you become a vegan—like the time we rescued Jessie. Well, actually, the time Jessie rescued herself.

Gene and I were making a cross-country trip with several turkeys during one of our annual Thanksgiving "Adopt-a-Turkey" projects. Every year, we encourage people to save a turkey rather than serve a turkey for the holiday season. We adopt turkeys into safe, loving vegetarian homes, and the media is invited to report on our unique way of celebrating Thanksgiving.

We were going through Colorado (which is a major beef-producing state) when I spotted her along the interstate. A young Angus calf was just a few feet from whizzing cars. We pulled over, threw on our boots, and started toward her. She was extremely frightened and started running away from us. An injured leg prevented her from moving very fast, and we had her within a few minutes. Our new "baby" weighed about 150 pounds, and as we struggled to get her into the van, we heard angry shouting and saw a man running toward us.

We soon learned that Jessie had jumped out of a trailer while it was traveling sixty miles an hour. When I realized what she had done to escape her fate, I felt like an angry mother cow, ready to tear her horns

into anyone who tried to take her calf away. Finding it difficult to keep calm, I explained to the owner that we were anti-cruelty agents and would be willing to take this calf off his hands because, of course, he couldn't take her to the auction now. To my surprise, the owner agreed. I was gearing up for a major battle, since injured and sick animals are legally sold at auctions all the time. To this day, I don't know if he agreed because he was in shock or because he saw a raging cow in my eyes or because maybe, just maybe, he got a dose of vegan kinship.

The next feat was getting Jessie through the California border, because she needed to be treated at a specialty veterinary clinic in northern California. We drove all night with her and four turkeys through a torturous snowstorm, and just as it was getting daylight, we came to the California border—and the California agriculture checkpoint. Now, every turkey mother knows that daylight is the time when turkeys wake up and start chirping, and we knew we didn't have much time. We turned up the radio and inched cautiously toward the checker. He asked us if we had any apples or oranges. I smiled sweetly and replied "no" and drove on with the biggest grin I've ever worn. Jessie survived and is now a big healthy cow. I've never considered myself a religious person or one who thinks "everything happens for a reason." Still, I can't help wondering if she knew we were behind her when she jumped out of the trailer—at least I'd like to think so.

As a vegan, I have experienced so many incredible things, so many special bonds with farm animals. We all know that people bond with so-called companion animals. Most people have loved and cared for a dog or cat and have experienced many moments of profound understanding and love. I know that whenever I'm feeling blue, my dog friend Suzy can always tell and will come and sit by my side in sympathy. She will look up at me with such a forlorn expression, such concern, that I have to smile.

At Farm Sanctuary, we share special bonds with our farm-animal friends too. Most of the time, it's the little communications that we experience every day, but sometimes we are reminded with a powerful vegan kinship message. Diane, our California shelter coordinator, told me of one of these "precious moments" when she injured her arm while she was in the cattle barn. She was in too much pain to even move and

just sat on the barn floor and cried. Though they were not in the barn at the time, within minutes two of the cattle, Joni and Henry, suddenly appeared. Cattle have a distinct "distress moo," and both cried loudly when they saw Diane on the ground. They approached her cautiously, reaching out their noses. Their urgent mooing turned to soft, comforting moos. For more than twenty minutes, they stood carefully around her, gently licking her face, until Diane could move again.

If you let yourself be touched, animals will touch you, and farm animals are animals. A cow or turkey or pig or chicken is just as capable of feeling joy and sorrow, or pain and comfort, as a dog or cat. Like many people, I am fortunate to have the love and companionship of dogs and cats, animals who are truly a part of my family. But unlike many people, I have also known the love and friendship of cows and pigs and turkeys and chickens—farm animals that suffered horribly at factory farms, slaughterhouses, and stockyards, and I was the one to blame—every time I ate a pizza with cheese or had a muffin with eggs in it, every time I didn't care enough to feel their pain. We need always remember the animals' pain because that is how we feel the love, which translates into the need to stop it.

The next time you want to eat meat or cheese or eggs, imagine living your life in a small, filthy crate, constantly in pain, unable to stand or lie down comfortably. After months of agony, your torture finally ends, but not at the slaughterhouse. Instead, two gentle hands reach down to lift you out of the darkness and bring you to a safe, loving place. For the first time, you can walk through sunny green pastures and rest in a comfortable bed of soft straw. As a vegan, you are providing the sunny green pastures and the soft straw bed. You are providing hope for a needy animal.

I feel fortunate to share my life with animals like Hilda and Hope. I am so thankful that my old friends never knew the terror and pain of a slaughterhouse and that I was able to watch them "grow old" at Farm Sanctuary.

I often find myself glancing out the window to the sheep barn. Hilda is there, quietly grazing in the pasture. Sometimes I wonder what she remembers of that horrible trip to the stockyard. Hilda has remained shy of humans, even after all these years. It is a rare treat when she

approaches you and an even greater privilege when she allows you to scratch her chin.

It took us a while to resign ourselves to this and to one embarrassing moment with Hilda—embarrassing for us, that is, not for Hilda. It happened about a year after Hilda's rescue. I was working in the barn when Gene came running up to me, smiling ear-to-ear. "She likes me! Hilda likes me!" he proclaimed, grinning like a proud father. "She's following me everywhere I go. She won't leave my side." I couldn't believe it, and feeling a twinge of jealousy, I'm not sure if I wanted to believe it. But as Gene walked into the sheep pasture, there was the evidence. Hilda trotted up to him and even leaned up against him. Gene walked toward me and Hilda stayed by his side.

Hours went by, and still Hilda stayed with Gene, following him while he was painting, following him into the barn, following him to the compost pile. True to his nature, Gene kindly remarked that perhaps she had chosen him over me because I was the one who trimmed her hooves. But after several hours of adoration, even Gene started to wonder about this sudden display of affection. Then it hit us, and that day we officially turned from "city slickers" into "farmers." Hilda wasn't in love, Hilda was in heat. Now, after hearing about Maya's story too, you're probably wondering just how charming can one human be? But then you probably haven't met Gene, so how can I, or Maya, or Hilda, possibly explain? We all share a special vegan kinship with him, and there is nothing more I can say.

FISH LESSONS

INGRID NEWKIRK

His appreciation of fishes began when he was snorkeling in Hawaii. There, among the lava rocks, he had seen groupers the size of old English sheepdogs and colorful little fishes, no bigger than hummingbirds, who swam between his fingers. They had looked at him with curiosity, with an innocence you only saw in good children, and, he thought, with affection. Some were boisterous and aggressive while others were shy. It was clear that they had personalities, just as dogs, cats, and people do.

He was still marveling about them when he sat down at the lagoon-restaurant and opened the menu. Inside was a photograph of a large fish he felt sure he had seen only minutes earlier; this one was stretched out on a platter, the eyes no longer dancing with life but as dead as their owner. He had never understood how someone could deliberately spear a fish, indeed, choose spear-fishing for entertainment, but now he couldn't imagine eating the result of someone else's deadly act. He'd detected the fishes' personalities, and they would forever come to mind when he contemplated grilled sole or fried catfish.

I told him about the fish who longed for Saturdays.

The fish had ended up in a house in Maryland. During the week when the house was quiet, he spent most of his time at the east end of the tank, near the window, catching the morning sunlight on his fins and then browsing among the reeds anchored in tubs in the silt. But on Saturday mornings, he swam to the other side of the tank and waited. Here he had the best vantage point from which to watch people's comings and goings: he could see the hallway door through which he knew visitors sometimes materialized. The fish loved visitors.

When anyone entered, the fish raised himself up high in the water and pressed close to the glass, the better to see them and to hear their words carried across the surface of his watery little room. When they left, he and his spirits sank again. He returned to the bottom of the tank and started halfheartedly picking at the gravel, scooping up a stone in his mouth, then spitting it out again, navigating slowly backwards each time to avoid the tiny dust storms created by each disturbance.

He was making time pass.

On weekday afternoons the man came home from work. Like a dog waiting at the gate for the school bus, the fish began "pacing" before the key turned in the door, swimming back and forth with the sort of impatience you might see in a person drumming his fingers on a tabletop. Every few laps the fish would pause and hang in the water, staring hopefully at the door.

Perhaps, Patty Hearst–style, the fish had become infatuated by his captor. Or perhaps he knew the man loved him, as wholly inadequate as a man's love for a fish must be. In fact, the man usually forgot all about the fish until he reached the door, but then he remembered and went straight into the living room to say "hello." The fish jumped and wagged his tail, lifting about a fifth of his body clean out of the water, waiting to be petted.

The man would put his fingers into the water and scratch the fish's back gently while the fish offered first one side of his body, then the other, swishing his fins in ecstasy. The fish didn't know that, sometimes, for a lark, the man and his friends had thrown cherry bombs into the creek when the carp were spawning and then killed them with blows from two-by-fours as they thrashed about on the bank. The fish didn't know that on summer days the man still caught and gutted fishes from that creek and barbecued them just outside the window. The man was kind and good but, like most of us, had a compartmentalized mind. Killing fishes whom you don't know is just part of the culture.

The captive fish tried to make the best of what was otherwise a dreary life. He cleaned rocks by rolling them about in his mouth, swam through the jumbo-size hair curlers fastened together to form a jungle-gym, and tickled his own back in the bubbles from the aerator. Once he swam

purposefully to the west end of the tank, seized a plastic plant in his tiny jaws, and dragged it back to his corner. The next day, when the man tidied the tank and put the plant back in its "place," the fish moved it again to the new spot he had chosen for it.

He also lay in wait for the cats.

In the kitchen, meticulously scrubbed and lovingly filled with water from the nearby spring, sat a ceramic dish the cats studiously avoided. As chocolate-lovers are drawn to Godiva, the cats were drawn to fish-water. By the time a cat was en route to the aquarium for a drink, threading her way along the bookshelves to the point where she could balance on her hind legs and lower her head into the tank, the fish was waiting for her in the tangle of plants.

Before lowering tongue to water, the cat would peer into the depths, looking for any sign of trouble. But the fish stayed quiet as a mouse. Only when a tongue descended did he burst into action, propelling himself up through the weeds like a torpedo, hell-bent on taking a chunk out of that raspy organ. Sensing an underwater eruption, the cat would try to get the first lap in before fish and tongue met.

No blood was ever drawn on either side, but the contest repeated itself daily.

Otherwise the fish kept to himself. He took the presence of new-comers to "his" tank with all the dignity and despair of a librarian who finds a group of young bikers living between the shelves. He would puff himself up and shake his fins at them and give chase if they did anything truly appalling, but he never attacked.

In the end he outlived them all. Some of them died of "seasickness"—the trauma of sloshing around in the bag from ocean to distributor, in the truck to the pet shop, and then in the car on the way home; others succumbed to epidemics of "ick," which destroyed their fins, sending them spinning helplessly to the bottom of the tank, tiny vestiges of their graceful selves; and some suffocated when power failures robbed oxygen from the water.

On the Saturday the tank cracked, there were only two other fishes left. They were African elephant noses, exotic fishes with trunklike pro-tuberances. The fish had spent eight years in the tank when the elephant

noses arrived, and the old fellow had accepted their presence; he and they kept as respectful a distance from each other as fishes can in a modest aquarium.

The man had been at the movies and returned to find water all over the floor. Water was still dripping from a crack in the glass. In the inch of water left in the bottom of the tank, three individuals lay on their sides, dying. Rescue had to be effected without delay. One elephant-nose went into a saucepan, the other into a coffee pot; but this last little fish struggled, caught his long nose in the spout, and suffered a terrible injury. When the substitute tank was set up, the fish could not breathe properly or keep his balance. His companion helped keep him afloat for a few days, pushing him up against the side of the tank so he could reach the food and air. This may have helped him suffer less, but it didn't save his life. Within a week of the injured elephant nose's death, his companion died too. After that, the old fellow was alone again.

When I had first seen him, he had been only about a half inch long, and I was still eating roe on toast and salmon steak. By the time the elephant noses died, he had grown to seven inches. By then I had stopped eating others of his kind. And as he had grown, so had my understanding that there was something wrong with pretending that fishes could be chosen like drapes and kept as living room decorations. My amusement was not worth their barren lives and "accidental" deaths.

When the fish died, I found myself trying to imagine what his ancestral waters were like, where and how he had been captured or bred, and what on earth we were thinking of when we acquired him and robbed him of his little fish destiny. Sorry, old fellow. Truly.

PART 4

RENEWING ANCIENT RELATIONSHIPS

BEING WITH ANIMALS

ALAN DRENGSON

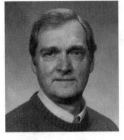

Children are usually quite ready to love other living beings, such as dogs, cats, birds, snakes, frogs, and ants. Our youngest daughter is delighted when she sees a spider on the floor. All of our children love caterpillars and birds. We can learn important things about life by watching children and animals together. They remind us how to use the creative energies of imagination to live fully.

Like many children, my brother and I were given a puppy by our father when we were quite young. Dad loved all animals but especially horses and dogs. He taught us how to relate to the puppy and how to train it. By example and by explaining what he was doing, he showed us the right spirit with which to relate to the pup.

He had an amazing rapport with animals and could attract the most skittish of dogs to come to him. He did not do this by calling them, gesturing broadly, or coaxing, but by being still. He assumed a low, hunkered-down position, and looked to the side of the dog. His overall stance told the animal that he was not frightened, hungry, or aggressive, just curious, friendly, and playful. He taught us how to project to animals (and children) positive spiritual energy, which is welcoming, reassuring, and kind. He didn't call it spiritual energy, but that's a fair name. He said it was an attitude that comes when the heart and mind work together. He said you learned it by controlling your own mind.

In his interactions with our dogs, cats, sea gulls, rats, snakes, chickens, and other animals, we never saw him show impatience or anger. In training our dogs he was soft-spoken. He worked with gesture and continuous praise. He held the dog's attention completely. I remember asking him what he could teach a dog, and he said anything they were capable

of wanting to learn. He said this about horses as well. His confidence was based on his proven ability to work with them, and he told me over and over that we can do anything we set our minds to.

Dad grew up on a mixed family farm with all kinds of wild and tame animals to relate to. He went to Norwegian school in summer, English school in winter. His people were pioneer homesteaders from Norway. He told me that the things he knew about animal education had been learned from his dad, from old-time pioneers, and from animals themselves. His people were hunters, gatherers, and horse farmers. A favorite Norse image is of a man, horse, and dog together going "a-Viking," that is, a-journeying. (In most cases this did not involve plunder and is connected to old Norse shamanism.) These two animals have powerful meanings in the old traditions, and Dad knew this mythology.

What we learned from him was a fraction of what he knew. This was because we did not live on a farm in a traditional community and because his work kept him away from home for long hours and days year-round. What we did learn from him was of central importance, for we learned how to approach and be with animals. Most of the specific techniques he imparted I've forgotten from lack of use.

What Dad taught us about animals was partly a body of knowledge, facts and lore, rules of thumb. More importantly he taught us an attitude, a sense of respect for the values of the animals. It is a state of mind, a way of being, an approach, an orientation, a positive spirit with friendly energy. From this spirit comes rapport and shared learning through imaginative play.

We know that children who suffer from deep emotional difficulties can often relate to animals, such as dogs, and this can help them make contact with humans. A pet dog makes no demands on them. It does not judge them. It accepts them on their own terms. A dog expects nothing from them. It wants to relate to and interact with them. It wants to protect them. A child can say or do anything, and so long as she is kind, she will be accepted.

Dogs are social animals who bond readily to humans, especially when they are shown affection and respect and are fed, brushed, talked to, and petted. Dogs like to be praised and will do surprising things when they

are praised in the right spirit. They are sensitive to human emotions and can respond to genuine grief and happiness in deep sympathetic ways.

Over the years we've witnessed impressive and moving displays of intelligence, sensitivity, and caring from the animals we've known.

Many years ago I spent a summer with a grandfather horseman, also Norwegian by descent, a pioneer. Like my dad, he had grown up on a family farm with dogs, horses, and other animals. He learned to ride by the time he could run. He confirmed everything Dad taught about being with animals, but I'd already seen confirmations of these things over the years. He showed and told me many things about wild animals that I hadn't learned from Dad or on my own. Grandfather Horseman had lived daily with horses and other animals throughout his life, and he was then in his late sixties. He had spent years in the wilderness with wild creatures.

As my father had done earlier, he showed me that working with horses and relating to wild animals requires deep respect and an aura of affection. There were times when he was firm with a horse, but this firmness was not anger. He said to me, "Horses are timid animals. Their teeth are dull. They eat grasses and grains. They have hooves and legs to run fast. They like to run away from danger rather than fight it. They have keen eyes and ears and a good nose. It's important to let them know that you mean them no harm. You must approach them with confidence but not aggressively. Make friends with your horse and pay close attention to what he likes and dislikes." He showed me how to get on with the horse I would ride and care for that summer: Lucky, a big white gelding. He was trained for pack and riding saddle. Lucky and I became friends, as I was able to follow the Horseman's coaching.

Each evening Grandfather Horseman and I sat quietly after supper by the campfire. The horses could be seen and heard grazing a short distance away. Their champing and chewing the grass produced a relaxed, sleepy feeling. Wild animals would come out of the forest into the meadows. Some would come very close. The Horseman showed me that one only has to sit in a certain way, calm one's breathing, settle one's belly into a kind of emptiness, and the various animals would come around. Birds would drop into camp, bear could be seen by the river below camp, deer would browse by, chipmunks would scurry around.

Grandfather Horseman had an endless supply of stories about wild and domestic animals, most of which contained some wisdom or insight. Altogether they showed a keen power of concentration and observation, which comes from an ability to relax and let things be so that they can reveal themselves to us. When he walked the trail with the pack-string, he never hurried, wasted energy, or fought the horses. Although approaching seventy, he could walk from dawn to dusk, unpack and unsaddle the horses, make camp, cut wood, build a fire, cook supper, wash up, all the while telling engaging stories. Much of what he knew was from an oral tradition stretching back to the dawn of domestication of animals in the West. Alas, we are on the verge of losing these traditions. They require sustainable place-based communities. We are destroying such places and their communities.

When I went into adult life, I forgot some of the core lessons my dad and the Horseman taught me about being with animals. Once, when tired, I tried to teach one of my dogs something. I lost my patience and spoke in harsh anger to the dog and struck him with my hand. That intemperate act took some time to work out with the dog. He did not bear a grudge or cringe when I called him, but he became anxious and nervous around me. There was no doubt that my lack of patience and use of negative energy had done temporary damage to our relationship. Eventually, with patience and time, trust was reestablished by practicing what is called blending energy (or *ki* in aikido) with others. In this way, the dog and I worked out the problems caused by my impulsive action.

From experience, then, I have learned that we can generate positive energy that is healing and attractive. I've found that it is inexhaustible, if we dwell in harmony in all of our relationships with animals, plants, humans, our place, and nature. Establishing such relationships is not a theory of animal training. It is an ongoing way of being, a practical activity that enables us to learn and share openness with others. Compassion is a key to this open, positive energy. Through loving attention we learn to complete ourselves in harmony with others, nonhuman and human. In this way we realize the intrinsic goodness of all beings. This is a deep source of insight and understanding.

The natural world is filled with animals all around and within us. The animals have the facts and wisdom we need to solve many of our human problems. Those who can dwell in harmony with animals live in peace because they are peace. With harmonious energy we do not train or condition animals. We let them be themselves. We learn to work together to create something more beautiful from our relationship. The techniques of animal teaching are subordinate to learning how to be in harmonious energy through compassionate attention. This was shown by both Dad and Grandfather Horseman in their actions.

Some of the greatest horse trainers of the nineteenth century learned their skill in the North American West. Among the most famous were the "whisperers." They were called this because they spoke very softly into the horses' ears. According to all accounts, a whisperer could gentle unruly, dangerous horses in a short time, when everyone else had failed. They began working with the horse by spending several hours alone with him in the barn with no distractions. In this way they established an intense bond with the horse, befriended it, let it know they were not going to harm it, that they were going to help it. A whisperer could ride a horse a short distance and tell exactly how it had been trained and treated. Whisperers were said to love horses and favor their company.

The Horseman said that in his family the horsetrainer would bond with colts from an early age. This was accomplished in a number of ways. One of the most important was playing with them. He said that each day his father would go out and play with the colts. He would play with them as if he were a young horse; he would gambol and play their games. In this way he became a member of their "tribe." They would then follow him around. This whole process had nothing to do with breaking the horse or its spirit. Broken horses, he said, are damaged. He remarked, "The secret of being a horseman is to be your best so as to encourage the best from the horse."

These are just some of the things that Dad and Grandfather Horseman taught me about being with dogs, horses, and other animals. Being with one's self and with other people is no different. This way of harmonizing with animals should also be practiced so as to live wisely with the natural world and in the human tribe. If we empty ourselves of desire, ambition,

fear, and urge to control the animal (nature) and match our energy with theirs (it), then we are not of two minds; we meet the other in cooperative harmony. Together we create something more beautiful than we can create alone.

My dad told me that he once watched some Sioux horsemen ride their ponies bareback in a demonstration. He marveled at their ability to remain seated while their mounts were doing all sorts of wild galloping, jumping, twisting, and turning. He asked an elder Sioux standing next to him at the exhibition how the young warriors managed to stay on their mounts. The elder thought for a moment, then smiled and clasped his hands in front of him and moved them vigorously together while saying, "Not two, not two!" In unity the two were one, the opposites become complementaries. When our relationships with animals are an emergent unifying process, then we realize our larger ecological Self and spiritual powers of nature of which we all are a part. Our actions are beautiful.

Grandfather Horseman called my attention to a whole landscape one day. We were resting on a pass and could see a whole watershed. It was then a wild primal landscape. He observed that everything was in its right place, everything fit together harmoniously, and the whole result was striking beauty. He then said that this applies to whatever we do as humans. If we act so that our actions are beautiful, then we act rightly. We should act so as to add to the sum of beauty in the world.

I have thought about these observations again and again over the years. I have realized that he had summarized a whole philosophy and way of life. When I look at the monocultures and clearcuts of both industrial farming and forestry, I find them ugly, out of place, and ecologically irresponsible. When I observe farm and forestry practices whose results are beautiful, I am confident they are right. When I reflect on this in the context of my whole life, I realize that I have gone through deep perceptual changes associated with what I identified as myself.

One of the best ways to articulate this, for me, is to describe it in terms of transpersonal ecology. We start out totally identified with the maternal matrix (nature), and slowly we become aware of ourselves as individuals. This process involves varying degrees of differentiation from the natural matrix. Self-consciousness arises in individuals who are part of a

human community and spend some time outside the community, as in vision quests. They realize both their differences and their samenesses.

Modern Western culture seems to have gotten stuck on a form of individualism identified with ego by sharp separation from nature and from our own wild feelings. This alienation is a problem, but it is also an opportunity, for by going outside we are able to come home with a more expansive sense of self called the ecological Self. The ecological Self is all that we are, including our place and context, without which we could not be, nor could we even define ourselves.

Modernism tried to be contextless and placeless; it tried to reside in abstractions. But when our consciousness is uprooted, it loses reference to values inherent in nature. We cannot orient ourselves. We must come back to place and context with an expanded sense of identification. When we do that, we move to the transpersonal. We start in the prepersonal (preegoic) and then develop a social and personal self (ego). If we mature further, we develop transpersonal consciousness (transegoic). This takes us beyond narrow historical time. It also takes us back to the source, the very primal ground of human self-conscious existence. This is the wild and primal ground that is always creatively emerging. To participate in it fully is to live the secular life in the presence of the holy. It is to honor and respect the sacred in each action, however humble.

When we are with animals in the deep receptive way we have described, we are actualizing transpersonal awareness. This is a timeless, formless, universal awareness in which all sentient beings participate, help to create, and maintain. Even if we still have many unresolved conflicts and deeply buried shadow material, we can still let ourselves be with animals in this way. It is a way to uncover and reveal our own shadow and also ecological depths.

In learning to be with animals, we come to know more deeply who and what we are. We only know animals, nature, and others, in all their intrinsic values, when we know them through the heart of compassion's clear energies. We must love them in their places. This is the wisdom animals have taught me with assistance from Dad and Grandfather Horseman. I thank them all for this wisdom. Let us love the animals around and within us. May they all flourish!

FINDING THE WAY HOME

KATE SOLISTI-MATTELON

I listen to animals. I possess the ability to hear the thoughts and feelings of beings who communicate beyond spoken language. I believe that at one time all human beings possessed this ability to some extent. Since most indigenous peoples around the globe take this skill for granted, I sense that it is not far beyond the grasp of "civilized" people. We have only to remember.

When I was a child, I clearly "heard" animals and plants "talking" with me. I didn't hear audible sound; we simply communicated. Thoughts from other beings chopped into my mind in a comfortable, natural way. Their feelings and sensations flowed into my awareness. This knowledge helped me relate to and "converse" with beings in bodies other than human. When I spoke to my parents about these "conversations," my parents assured me it was my imagination, not animals and plants. Nobody, they assured me, really talked with animals. I began to doubt myself and feel different from the other humans around me. I began to wonder what was real. I was only three years old.

Fortunately someone stepped in to help. He was a cat, an orange-and-cream-colored tabby. I named him Dusty. Dusty "told" me to stop trying to make my parents understand or accept what I was doing. He said I could share these experiences with him, and he would be glad to help me be with and learn from the other beings. I was so relieved and grateful. Finally someone understood!

The next three years were full of glorious explorations and conversations with other cats, dogs, turtles, fireflies, squirrels, and all manner of crawling, swimming, and flying creatures. I learned from the trees how they enjoy protecting us and providing us with oxygen. I learned how the

roses have a love affair with the sun, rain, and earth. I learned how turtles smell the earth to discover what the weather will be doing tomorrow. It was a magical time.

When I was five, I started kindergarten. I enjoyed it but looked forward to coming home and telling Dusty all about the children and what we did together. School seemed much more foreign to me than the garden. Still, it was a new adventure. Before I began first grade, Dusty told me it was time for me to spend more time with human beings. He urged me to listen to them and to dive into human relationships in as committed a manner as I had with nonhumans. I said I would do so as long as I could be with my nonhuman friends, too. He said they would always be there for me.

After our discussion, I began to apply myself in earnest at school. I made human friends. I started to learn how to read. I even began to enjoy myself. Then, one night in October, Dusty climbed into bed with me just as I was dropping off to sleep and told me, "I am very proud of you. You are doing so well. Now our work together is finished." I fell asleep with his soft words and deep love surrounding me.

The next day he was gone, killed by a car on a busy street a few yards away from our own. My pain was immeasurable. I became ill with tonsillitis, and I began shutting down my ability to connect with the nonhuman beings. With Dusty dead, all the joy of opening my heart was gone. No one could replace him. I felt it was better to close my heart and close off my ability to receive the thoughts of other beings than to go through pain that huge ever again. By age eight it was complete. I could hear them no longer; I had become a "normal" child.

So many people remember special relationships with animals, a grove of trees, a meadow, a pond. . . . It is in remembering and accepting this innocent love that we build the foundation to reestablish our ability to communicate beyond words. It is in this willingness to go inside memories so deep, so poignant, and sometimes so painful that we can release the parts of ourselves that hold us back and nurture the parts that know how to listen. And when we listen, we remember once again that this planet, indeed the universe, is alive with loving "sentient" beings.

Through a great deal of personal healing, my ability to hear animals and plants has returned. Now I devote much of my life to reaching out to other species. Mostly I work one-on-one with people and families, giving voice to their companion animals so they can learn more about each other. Often I am a voice for animals undergoing treatment for illness; those animals get the chance to express how they feel or where it hurts just as we do. I offer workshops to help people reconnect to the subtle "languages" of the other beings around them.

This is a process unique and special to each individual who undertakes it. I cannot promise that everyone will learn how to "hear" as I do, but I guarantee that the journey begun and followed will unfold into a much deeper understanding of the nonhuman beings around us, of the wholeness and interconnectedness of life on this planet. This deepening relationship often results in the humans feeling more at one with nature, better in touch with all the beings in their lives, and more at peace with themselves.

What has happened to me as I have "listened" to the nonverbal beings around us is that I have learned that animals are individuals with sophisticated thoughts and emotions. I have learned that they make choices in their lives. I have learned that the animals most in contact with humans (dogs, cats, and horses) on a regular basis have consciously chosen to be with us in intimate relationship, to help us remember, to help us find the love that is our birthright. Through their deep love and commitment, many of us remember how to love.

Other animals help those humans who are drawn to their uniqueness: birds, rabbits, guinea pigs, mice, rats, gerbils, hamsters, ferrets, fish. . . . By living with us and sharing our lives, they support us in specialized and immeasurable ways. As one dog described it, "I am the rug beneath your feet that buffers you from the harshness of life."

Many dogs live with us to provide us a safety net, a daily dose of unconditional love to support us in dealing with the world. Cats generally offer us lessons in detachment and how to heal physical, emotional, and psychological trauma. Horses tend to offer us the opportunity to join with them in perfect love and trust so that together we can touch the ecstasy of Oneness. They remind us that if we attempt to control or

manipulate them for our own purposes, we miss the gifts. All animals teach us that death is simply the end of a body's usefulness. It is not "The End" since the soul continues on in never-ending expression.

One of my clients called me a year after the death of her dog, a young, vibrant vizsla. "CC" was one of those special, unusual companions, and Lisa missed her terribly. She had never gotten over the grief or her guilt. Lisa called me to see if everything was "all right" with CC. Beyond time and space, CC reassured Lisa that everything was OK. She told Lisa that her short time in form was wonderful and that she had learned much. (CC came through to me with almost overwhelming joy and love for her person.) Lisa wanted CC to return to her, and CC assured her that it would be possible. Together we explored the options for CC's new life in form. Lisa decided on an Australian shepherd body and researched breeders. CC chose which mother she felt would be best. CC was reborn, and Lisa made the long trip to see her. With excitement and some anxiety, Lisa chose a puppy. Just weeks after bringing home the puppy, Lisa wrote me:

> I just needed to write to share with you the joy I have in the new love of my life, Cissy. The more she is with us the more I love her, if that is possible. Each day I experience being more and more connected to her. She is so bright, so mature, so smart. And, with each day, I see more and more of my little CC in her. This new little being, though, has taken the best of CC and brought her to me in a way that works even better than before. I sometimes speak to her and thank her for coming back to me and my family. We love each other very much and look forward to our life together.

Through the love of a dog and her own courage, Lisa healed her grief and guilt and opened her heart to an extraordinary possibility—reunion with the same being in another body. Lisa's understanding of life and death changed forever.

I have learned that many wild animals choose to support the planet and the web of life that is Mother Earth's gift. Scientists have admitted that we don't really understand the complex patterns of life on this

planet. I figure it's time to ask the beings who share this planet with us what exactly they are up to. I believe that they may be able to help us understand how to heal the mess humankind has made. They may offer us a glimpse into other ways of being in the world, ways dramatically different from the way "civilized" man now lives. But if we continue to consider ourselves superior to all, if we don't think we can return to them for advice, it is unlikely we will ever stop to ask or listen.

Many have come before to show the way. Henry David Thoreau must have had something valuable to say on this subject or his work would not have survived 150 years. Lao-tzu, Loren Eisley, Emily Dickinson, John Muir, Rachel Carson, Aldo Leopold, George Wald, Edward O. Wilson, and many others wrote about "listening," and countless indigenous elders have spoken about it. There is nothing new here, simply greater urgency for the survival of humankind and countless other species on this planet.

I wanted to give the wild animals a voice in this book, as well, and the elephants came through with a description of their role and an offering.

We are the ears of Mother Earth. We sing to her constantly, lullabies, morning glory songs, celebration songs, songs of grieving.... Through us Mother Earth hears what is happening on the surface, feels the pulse of life she supports and nurtures. We tap into the rhythm of life on Earth—life happening around us and life happening on the other side of the planet. We sing of the passage of time. We sing of new life being born. The lullaby a mother elephant sings to her newborn is the same lullaby sung by mother elephants for thousands of years. The mothers sing:

Oh, my beloved, oh, thou newly born being, thou art the future, thou art the Light in form. Every morning greet the dawn with a song; greet the setting of the sun with a song, and all the world will be made whole. Sing when you are full of joy. Sing when you are full of sadness. Remind the beings walking with you that every moment is precious, every breath is pure. Listen and drink in the rhythms of the Great Mother. Sing back what you learn every day. This is your sacred trust, your reason for being.

In the oceans, the humpback whale sings to Mother Earth. The songs of the whales echo the songs of their terrestrial sisters, the elephants. The whales sing in notes mostly above what the unaided [human] ear can hear, while the elephants sing mostly with notes below. All species have songs, but these two species set the *basso continuo*, the base note that the symphony of all creation weaves around, through, above, and below this planet. This music has a very high purpose. It harmonizes the earth's frequencies. It balances, soothes, and quickens all life on the planet. Without the music, there would be no life as we know it.

We can hear the songs of elephants and whales with our ears and with our hearts. There are many ways of listening, just as there are many ways of seeing. Now is the time. Each of us has the opportunity to change the way we walk in the world. Each of us has the opportunity to shape the future by shifting our consciousness. Look at the reality around you. Is it beautiful? Does it support brother/sisterhood, compassion, cooperation, and love among all beings? Does it make you happy? The world can be remade into a different reality. Eden is within reach, and it will be created by individuals who believe that paradise is possible. If you do not know where to start, look into the eyes of a nonhuman companion and ask the question, "How do I begin?"

MAKING MYTH

JIM NOLLMAN

I suppose "making myth" means that even us generic humans are capable of reinstating a very old protocol that once upon a time defined a harmonious relationship between species.

I arrive at this conclusion as someone who, a long time ago, spent three summers occasionally jumping into the water with so-called killer whales. In those days the species was perceived to be easily as dangerous as lions. In fact, the first time I did it in 1975, almost no precedent existed for such a foolhardy action. And even if there had been, the point is that, at the time, I knew of no other occurrence of a human being jumping into the water with wild and healthy killer whales.

Why did I do it? Easy. The whales simply did not seem ferocious to this unpracticed eye. And even in those days, I didn't believe much of what I read in the newspapers. Nor did I ever call them killer whales. They were always orcas to me, and that conscious choice of nomenclature helped immensely in establishing a friendly protocol between us. Ironically, I felt that if there was ever any risk to such an encounter, it was that the whales would perceive me to be a generic man—the same old story of me getting interpreted as a mean-spirited creature possessed of a long and violent history of harming their kind. The whales might even be forced into taking defensive steps just to protect themselves. In fact, they may have once done that for a minute or two, although, mostly, their sense of trust has always been breathtaking to behold. The event I'm talking about occurred in 1978.

215

A photographer asked if he could shoot me playing music in the water with the whales. I agreed, and so we set off into the straits off Vancouver Island in search of the friendly A pod. We found twelve orcas milling about in a small bay that lies along the northeast side of Johnstone Strait. I slipped on my dry suit and took hold of my instrument known as a waterphone.

The waterphone is named after its inventor, Richard Waters. It is an outer-space-looking device welded together from brass prongs, a pizza pie plate, a vacuum cleaner tube, and a salad bowl. But it floats like a cork and supports my weight superbly. When the prongs are rubbed back and forth with a waterproofed cello bow, the otherworldly sound that emanates into the water and air is both loud and ethereal. The sound has been described as a heavy-metal violin played through a bowl of jello. Keeping to my own convention of never chasing or barging in on the whales, I slipped into the water a few hundred yards in front of the pod and soon started bowing the waterphone. The sound was clear. The whales could hear it.

The first whale to approach was a large bull with a wavy dorsal fin. He advanced on me from underwater. In fact, I couldn't tell he was close by until I suddenly noticed his white eye patch reflecting green right in front of me, four feet below the surface.

It has always taken me by surprise how huge the orcas seem to appear when viewed at water level, with one's eyes never more than eight inches off the surface. The bull orca rose vertically to the surface, his size magnified even more by a six-foot dorsal fin looking like a sky-scraper and staring me right in the face. But I never stopped playing the waterphone. The photographer started whooping and hollering, "Keep playing, keep playing." He was evidently getting some good shots.

The large bull stayed there for no more than ten seconds, then dove, only to be followed by another large male with a straight dorsal fin. This one never came quite as close, although I could see his body passing directly underneath me. This bull was immediately followed by two females who also spouted just out of arm's reach before swimming on in the same direction.

It has been my experience that once the whales pass, they will keep swimming until they finally disappear from view. But this time the

entire pod stopped just a hundred yards from me. I continued playing. Never stopped.

Suddenly, two adolescent orcas turned about and charged me at what seemed like full speed. I saw them coming; they looked like speedboats, leaving a high wake on either side of their bodies. I can't remember how long it took, but just before they should have plowed into me, the two dove together. My heart was in my throat. I stopped playing. But the photographer was cheering and clapping. "This is incredible," he shouted. "Keep playing."

Then I saw the two whales just below the tips of my own dangling feet. They were reclining vertically in the water, looking straight up at me. I looked down at them, and they looked up at me. I couldn't play. My muscles had stopped working. "Come get me," I shouted, "get me out of the water, will you!"

The photographer started his engine and quickly motored to where I floated. He helped me into the boat, complaining all the while that the whales were still here and that we might be able to get even better shots. I could barely breathe, lying there in the bottom of the zodiac for several seconds, shaking all over, and wondering what on earth had I been trying to prove.

Suddenly, the bull with the wavy fin rose alongside us and rolled onto his back so that his pure white belly shone along the entire length of the boat. My mouth fell open as I leaned over the boat and watched him lying there.

In retrospect, I realize that what we viewed as a gesture of vulnerability could just as easily be interpreted in any of several ways. But given the actual context of that particular moment, I immediately read his gesture as a clear sign of friendship. And apology. The whale was insisting to me that there was no danger present here, and furthermore, that if I felt so inclined, I should consider getting back into the water again. Then he disappeared.

I rested another five minutes before getting back into the water again. The whales were still milling about. I began stroking the prongs of the waterphone with my hand and then finally began playing it with the cello bow. The whales moved a bit closer until their bodies rested on

the surface just about thirty yards from my own. I knew from testing the waterphone earlier that the orcas would be able to hear the music quite clearly at that distance. Whatever it was that they heard or didn't hear or felt or didn't feel, they listened for no more than five minutes before moving off down the strait again. I soon came back into the boat. End of session.

OF DOLPHIN DREAMS

REBECCA FITZGERALD

I was in the last year of graduate studies for a master's degree in psychotherapy. Because I'm an abysmally slow reader, I regularly go to bed early and arise at 4 A.M. to study for my courses. I went to work at 7:30, so I used what few hours I could in the mornings and evenings to complete the required reading.

It was during this period that I awoke one night by opening my eyes and seeing, with eyes wide open, the same scene I had just been dreaming. It was turquoise blue water, not very deep, and I was floating on the surface while two spotted dolphins jumped hoops around me. The mood was joyous as I lay happily on the surface while they cavorted, whistled, and somersaulted around me.

As they continued to revolve around my floating body, I had the distinct feeling of physical changes going on within me. Although I was deeply relaxed, I also felt a heightened sense of awareness. I recognized that I was in bed, in the dark, in my bedroom, but I also knew myself to be submerged in beautiful, warm water in the company of two spotted dolphins. Gradually the scene diminished and I felt myself only to be in bed, recovering from a dream.

Although I had no visual perception of the dolphins, I felt their presence keenly. After several minutes of sitting up and staring into the dark, trying to *see* something, I lay down and went to sleep. The dream repeated itself, and I awakened the next morning with a sense of enthusiasm and a kind of *connectedness*. I didn't take it very seriously but was delighted with the experience.

The next evening I turned in early, as usual. After comfortably settling in, I turned on the light next to my bed and began reading. I kept a

notepad and yellow marker on the bedside table and always did some studying before falling asleep. An hour later I turned the light off and cuddled under the covers. The next sensation was being back in the water with the dolphins, only this time there were many more than before.

I was surrounded by a pod of spotted dolphins, and the water was alive with sound. There were noises like creaking doors, whistles, and high-pitched whines. Some of the sounds were like birds and some like tiny kittens. I was enveloped in a complex orchestration of sound, and I tingled from head to foot. I'd never heard dolphin vocalizations before, but the sensation was one of familiarity, and in some way that is still undefined, it made sense. I woke up with dolphin vocalizations ringing in my ears and throughout my body. I was sitting up, wide awake, my bedroom and myself resonating with sound.

Although it was only the second night, I felt completely familiar with this experience and these particular dolphins. Whether awake or in the dream state, I felt their nearness. What interested me was the strong sense of memory that was stimulated. This wasn't at all a "new" experience but an old one. An ancient one, in fact. There was, and continues to be, a timelessness associated with my relationship to this pod, and because of that, I was relaxed and at ease. Events seemed to be revealed rather than newly created.

For the next ten nights I was in close communication with these dolphins. The experiences, however, were not confined to the dreamtime. During the daylight hours the normal perimeters of my reality seemed to stretch and enlarge. I would be driving through town, visually focused on the road ahead, when the air in front of me would open up into a larger space, and I could notice energetic shapes of dolphins swimming around in that dimension. I hasten to mention here that at no time was I using drugs of any kind. I was making mighty efforts to meditate each morning, but my unfinished assignments and basic laziness resulted in fairly impoverished attempts. I have no explanation for this altered state. I did not ask for a relationship with wild dolphins, not consciously, but I was rapidly developing one.

After several days of this ongoing experience, I went to the public library. My curiosity was about the shape and appearance of my dream

dolphins. Like most Americans, the only dolphin with which I was familiar was "Flipper," the television character. As you might remember, Flipper was a large, gray bottle-nosed dolphin with no distinguishing marks. The dolphins with whom I was communicating were covered in spots or speckles. They were smaller, with a head a bit more sleek. My question was whether or not I made them up, or if there actually is a dolphin of this description.

I pulled into the library parking lot, walked straight to the card catalog, and looked up all the dolphin books available. There weren't many. I opened the big one first, with colored photographs and large print. There, to my utter astonishment, was a section on *Stenella attenuata,* or spotted dolphins. The photograph showed a group of smallish spotted dolphins swimming in clear, turquoise water. There they were! It was exactly the same. Truthfully, this unnerved me. Somehow I managed to feel delight and confusion at the same time. I wanted to shout out loud at the confirmation of my dream images, but to be fair, it was distressing to have no idea from where the images originated. I left the library in a daze.

As the nightly exchanges continued, the communication took on the form of words, and the dolphins began showing up before I fell asleep. The process became one of my deeply relaxing, knowing sleep was imminent, and before going completely under, I could consciously feel their presence and then see them. I can only describe this state as a kind of lucid dreaming. As I moved from wakefulness to sleep, I was aware. We went from swimming and basking in each other's company to a more intellectual/emotional relationship.

They began "instructing" me in what seemed like a kind of geometry, a sort of a visceral lesson in time and space. As I hung in the water, they would swim themselves into a shape, perhaps an octagon. I would be at one point of the shape, and they told me to "feel" that shape, to get a *physical* understanding of the octagon. I was able to do so, and when I fully grasped it, they would swim into another shape. We went from triangles to circles to squares, hexagons, pentagons, rectangles, star shapes, and geometrical constructions I hadn't formerly understood or known.

During this dream state I was a mathematical genius! I grasped all the concepts and understood the shapes in a holistic way. It was as though each shape had a sound and a color. It was a great game, and I played with unbounded enthusiasm. It was fascinating how each construct had impact on my physical self. The feeling of a triangle differs greatly from the feeling of a square, and I had definite preferences.

One night, after a particularly exhaustive session, I woke up to hear a voice say, "Write this down! We're giving you specific information, and you're forgetting it all when you wake up." I kept a pen and notebook by the bed, so I dutifully promised to record my instructions and promptly fell back to sleep.

As the nights progressed, I was given specific information about myself and my own life. There were places it was suggested I go and practices I might do to gain further insight into my life here. They offered the idea that we'd known each other for a very long time and that our relationship was far beyond physicality. I'd felt that myself and was comfortable with the depth and familiarity of our connection. When there is a relaxed and thorough integration with another being, acceptance is the natural response.

I was happy and at home with these dolphins. In fact, I was experiencing a unique combination of ecstatic bliss and peaceful fulfillment. The only other time I've felt such a deep sense of completion is when my daughter was born. Although I was pregnant for only nine months, I'd waited my whole life for her to show up, and I knew it the moment I saw her. The dolphins had the same kind of impact—their appearance seemed sudden and unbidden, yet I felt a huge portion of my deepest self finally slip into place. Something had been completed, and a part of me that had for so long been unrelaxed at last found rest. The dreams continued for another week.

What impressed me most during that time in my life was not so much the data I received from the dolphins but the change in my mental/emotional state. I woke up each morning drenched in happiness. My energy level increased, I felt more alert, and although I didn't know it at the time, I'd begun an entirely new chapter in my life. I mention this now because it made my next decision all the more baffling.

I was preparing for sleep in the usual way, collecting books and pens, traipsing around in my white nightgown. I climbed into bed, switched on the light, and after reading a bit, fell into that calm state before slumber. I also, however, felt mentally more clear than usual. As the surrender to sleep began to overtake me, I felt a sharp little click. Without a thought, I announced to myself and to the approaching dolphin energy that it was time to stop the communication. I was due to graduate in less than a month, and I preferred that this altered state come to a halt so I could pursue my career without interference from the psyche or whatever dimension in which this was occurring. Instantaneously the energy was gone. The certainty of my feelings was so strong that I never looked back. That night I fell asleep in the old way, woke up the next morning with little dream recollection, and went on about my life.

The sweetness and closeness that I felt with the dream dolphins was so deep and familiar that it surprises me how instantly I changed tracks. The conclusion I'm coming to at this point, however, is that we know some things very deeply within us. We know them so certainly that we needn't second-guess or ruminate. I believe I knew my future. I knew that this relationship with the spotted dolphins would come full circle and that I had other tasks to complete before we could meet again. And indeed there were.

Four years later I started a project to take small groups of people to swim with captive dolphins in the Florida Keys. I was combining group therapy with dolphin interactions and saw any number of people undergoing transformations. I kept on with my brand of therapy but was feeling some discomfort in this combination. I was always oriented toward spirituality and believed, like Jung, that most of the disoriented and alienated souls who turned to him for help were sick because they were unaware of or cut off from their own spiritual experiences.

My therapy, though, didn't jibe with what the dolphins were offering. One night in September I returned home to New Mexico and, as was my practice, sat in bed meditating before sleep. As I let my thoughts go and drifted into the larger space, I began seeing brief, intense images from my childhood flash in front of my eyes. Each scenario was positive. There were memories of particularly happy Christmases, the day my dad

taught me to water-ski, a secret place in the huge boulder behind our mountain cabin where I'd go to hide and be alone, Saturday mornings in the double bed with my sister when we were little and giggling about everything, looking up into the sky from my perch in our avocado tree in California, helping my mother cook apple pies in my own apron she made for me, Grandma rocking me in her old, tan rocking chair, the box of comic books hidden in the attic that were just for me, and a dozen other obscure, sweet memories. I don't know how long it went on, but after a while I opened my eyes, recognized a good feeling, and just went to sleep. That particular phenomenon went on two more nights. What interested me was that those memories were so obscure that I'd never remembered them before. Some of them were when I was in a crib, less than one year old. On the third night of this pattern I put a stop to the reverie and opened my eyes wide in the dark. I said out loud, "Who's doing this?" I felt that something was being done to me. I didn't set out to remember these childhood fragments. It was as though the memories were being impressed upon my mind, visually and viscerally.

With eyes clear and open, I saw what looked like an energetic pod of dolphins swimming or hanging up near the ceiling of my bedroom. They felt very much a part of what was going on. "What are you doing?" I demanded. It was as if a rolling ball of information swept over me, and I heard or picked out words to symbolize the comprehensions.

I began to understand that the processes I went through in my own therapy and therapy training had focused on pain and concentrated on the behaviors learned through suffering. There was a relentless scrutiny of dysfunctional experiences and repeated reporting of distress and hurt. The dolphins seemed to be saying that they wanted me to have a strong experience of my positive childhood memories so that I wouldn't continue to think that the painful ones shaped me. They stimulated my memories of sweet, tender moments, and I began rethinking my childhood.

The most memorable thing which happened that night was when I heard the dolphins say, "You choose your memories. *Choose again.*" I was left sitting in bed with those words echoing in my head. No wonder

I felt discomfort in doing therapy along with the dolphin interactions. They were offering joy, and I was offering sadness. I was astonished at how much of my youth I completely forgot.

I've had a large percentage of joy in my life, but I convinced myself that my father's alcoholism and mother's depression overshadowed everything and that I was hopelessly involved in sadness and misery. Even more astonishing was that I didn't know I believed that; it had just gradually become a subtle part of my thinking and worldview. That night my life changed again. It took a while for the insight to sink in and become an integrated part of my consciousness, but the shift happened quickly.

By 1988, I'd located a pod of wild dolphins in the Bahamas that matched the description of the dream dolphins. I booked passage on a research vessel to meet them. After a storm that lasted all night, I awakened to the same energy I'd felt in 1983 when the dolphins approached me during sleep. The other passengers were asleep, recovering from a rough night of tossing and turning and vomiting. I'd slept in my bathing suit, and when I felt the dolphin energy coursing through my body/mind, I quickly rose and climbed the ladder to the deck.

Only one man was there, the staff naturalist, who offered to pour me a cup of coffee. It wasn't yet 6 A.M. I told him the dolphins were coming, that I could feel it, and he chuckled as he tried to hide the fact that he was rolling his eyes and shaking his head in amusement. He bent over to grab the coffee Thermos on the floor, and as he did so, I could see, over his bent back, at least twelve dorsal fins cutting through the blue water, heading straight for our boat.

I yelped like a kid and ran over to the side, pointing at the dolphins streaking toward us. Since he was dressed in blue jeans and a heavy sweater, he couldn't get in the water right away. The other passengers were below, sound asleep. After getting his permission to enter alone, I jumped over the side with my mask and fins already on. No sooner did I plunge under the surface than I was surrounded with dolphins and the full effect of their incredible sound.

Just like the dreams, I was engulfed in a wave of dolphin energy and cadence. They swam in fast circles around, below, and above me. As my

mask cleared and I finally managed to quit swallowing seawater, I could see their faces.

Extraordinary! A rather small, brownish/gray eye, giving the impression of utter acceptance and complete pleasure. The upturned mouth, forever in the gesture of a smile: the Mona Lisa smile, enigmatic and compelling. Their skin was beautiful beyond my expectations. White bellies on the young ones, spots appearing as they reached adolescence. The older dolphins become so full of spots that they melt into each other, creating the appearance of granite. I was stunned by their beauty. I still am.

We swam in perfect harmony for over half an hour. We played, dove, did somersaults in tandem; they mimicked me and I them. I was in a state of bliss. I lost all sense of time or limitation. I swam better, stronger, faster, and longer than I ever had in my life. There was no weakness or sense of being tired. I'd never felt more myself than I did for those thirty minutes. If there was ever a sense of "coming home," this was it. Years of discomfort, sadness, confusion, and disorientation fell away. It has never returned. The great sense of wakefulness that I experienced during the dreams in 1983 became my physical reality. It has never left. There, in the turquoise waters of the Bahamas, surrounded by wild spotted dolphins, I was reborn.

I finally calmed down and began to float on the surface. The dolphins stayed very close, swimming less than inches by my side and around my head. They were vocalizing, and I was making involuntary noises in return. I couldn't stay silent, and I have found the same to be true of most people in similar situations with dolphins. The desire to communicate is irrepressible.

As I looked at the white sand below me, I was startled to recognize a pattern of light made by the morning sun on the rippled sand. I remembered it from my dreams. As I looked around, I realized I'd already dreamed these same stomachs and flippers and fins and little flounders hiding on the bottom. I'd seen these same faces, heard this wonderful sound, and felt the sun on my back in this same water. As we swam slowly together, lolling around on our stomachs and backs, gazing into each other's eyes, I clearly and specifically formed a question in my mind. As directly as I could, I telepathically sent a message to these

dolphins swimming so closely to my face and body. "Are you the same dolphins who visited me in my dreams? Was it specifically you?"

I barely finished focusing my thought when all the dolphins who were floating quietly beside me abruptly began leaping joyously into the air. They jumped and spiraled and somersaulted with glee. The water turned to white bubbles, and I couldn't see a thing, but I could hear the high-pitched whistles and clicks. The water was alive and filled with activity. I thought my heart would burst. My whole self was filled with a resounding *Yes*. I swam like a woman possessed!

I dove down and then kicked as hard as I could to propel myself up and out of the water. I curled into a ball as I dove back down and did innumerable somersaults under the water. I squealed with delight and grabbed handfuls of sand at the bottom. I was out of my head! The rejoicing was uncontrollable, and it continued until I was completely out of breath. I'd exhausted myself beyond my physical limits, and it was then that I noticed how far from the boat we'd gone. The vessel looked small, and I realized I had a long swim back.

For the next ten minutes, I dog-paddled, floated, and crawled my way back to the waiting boat. The dolphins stayed by my side and accompanied my crippled efforts most of the way. I wasn't nervous or anxious for my safety. The crew was watching me from the boat, there was a rubber dinghy to come for me if I needed it, and my happiness from the encounter with the dolphins kept me in positive spirits.

As I made my way back, I was filled with messages from the dolphins to return and bring people with me. "We will honor your presence," were the words I heard last as I pulled myself up the ladder to the dive platform welded to the boat. By now everyone was up and watching the activities from over the side. Surprisingly, no one got in the water with me. I was allowed the whole experience by myself.

My Dolphinswim project is now seven years old, and I continue to take small groups of people out to swim with this pod. As the time passes, these dolphins become even more interactive and ready to communicate with people. Many have had several babies, and the pod is larger and more available. The babies are fascinated by people, and most have been swimming with us in utero. I continue my relationship with

this pod and have been contacted by a pod of bottle-nosed dolphins in the same area. In the spring of last year about fifteen of them swam up next to me while I was alone in the water and stayed for about twenty minutes. (This is unusual for the bottle-nosed pod.)

They communicated telepathically that the pod of spotted dolphins is particularly interested in human/dolphin interaction, and now that the relationship has been established, the bottle-nosed pod is also interested in participating. The bottle-nosed then spoke of geometric grids of energy that have been laid down in that area and the impact it has on humans as we swim in and amongst them. They then showed me the grids, and of course, it was the same kind of geometric patterning that I experienced in my dreams years before.

The impact dolphins have on humans is as unique as each person. Some people are impacted immediately; others experience a more gradual change. The dolphins called it "rewiring." For myself, it was an immediate response to a knowing that lay deep within me. The knowing is who I am. The vastness of existence, human existence, is, for the most part, denied or repressed. We aren't sure how to express all it is that we know and are. It's easier to deal with what happens instead of what is.

We are multidimensional beings; we know how to move through time and space without limits. The dolphins gave me this experience while I was conscious, and they gave it to me repeatedly, often enough for it to become integrated into my everyday reality. With that integration, I have become healthier, happier, and more whole.

Today I am receiving impressions from humpback whales. A week ago I dreamed I was floating in a deep, dark blue sea. As I rather "sat" in the water, an enormous humpback whale rose up underneath me and gazed into my eyes for a long while. She seemed to read me, to know all that I am and to consider it. As she stayed by me in the water, I began to feel fear. I noticed that I was in an ocean trench, miles from any land. The depth seemed to be thousands of feet, and as I acknowledged the difference in our two sizes, the whale and me, I trembled.

She instantly felt my discomfort. I could see it register in her body. She gave me one last look and slowly began her descent. I wanted to cry out, to beg her to come back. I trembled because I was afraid of her, afraid of

my own smallness. I remained in the dark water, full of remorse. She was gone. I missed her. I ached to see her again. I woke up.

The next day, the skipper of the boat called me about some logistics for our dolphin expeditions and, in passing, said, "Want to do some trips to see humpbacks?" The dream image resurfaced, and I could feel my skin tingle. I knew that the dream took place below Cuba, somewhere around a trench. "Where would we go?" I asked, excitement mounting. "Turks and Caicos, around the Trench."

I know this: I will meet this whale and her family. Just like the dream, my life unfolds. And just like the dream, when I feel fear instead of acceptance, opportunities disappear. Love leaves. What the cetaceans have taught me is only the beginning. The communications are subtle and complex. The more sincerely I pay attention, the deeper the lessons take me. It requires little more than slowing down and allowing awareness to surface.

We are all connected in an intricate web of life, a web made of consciousness. It is possible to communicate with animals, plants, stars—hundreds of life forms. I began my interspecies journeys with flowers. I've spoken with a wolf spider, dogs, dolphins, and whales. The most subtle nonhuman communication I've ever experienced was with a pattern of light that existed only for a few minutes. It understood its purpose for only those brief moments. Exquisite.

There is a dignity in nature and in animals that we recognize and value. It is this dignity that we must earn and possess ourselves. I am ennobled by my relationship with the spotted dolphins and humbled by their intelligence. There is a wisdom residing within the dolphins and whales, and if we suspend our old ways of thinking and perceiving, we are able to hear the voices of an ancient species who are willing and able to share with us the vastness of their evolutionary understandings.

THE HORNET TREE

MICHAEL ROADS

I was huddled against the trunk of a large elm at Byron's pool in Granchester, England, when the heavens opened with a lashing downpour of rain and hail that promised me an icy drenching. In that frenzied moment of desperation, I remembered the dreaded hornet tree. All of us kids knew about the hornet tree, but none of us ever ventured too close to it. The tree was an old gnarled veteran, its trunk split open in a huge gaping wound that even an adult could squeeze into. The inside was an unknown factor, for a colony of hornets was always active in and around the split trunk, and thus we gave it a wide berth.

A forked flash of lightning seared the air close by, followed within seconds by a shocking clap of thunder that left my ears ringing. Suddenly the air seemed to be solid with water and ice, mixed with a deadly barrage of twigs and branches. The earlier breeze was abruptly a gale, ripping dead wood and life from the trees and spinning it through the air with no concern for a boy. No longer was it a simple matter of getting wet. I badly needed shelter.

I was away and running before I had thought it through, and within a minute of slipping and slithering among the trees, half-blinded by the downpour, I was squeezing my way into the hornet tree. I stood still, frightened by my rash action. Cautiously I looked around me in the dim light, but there was no sign of any hornets. My eyes gradually adjusting to the gloom, I peered carefully into the nooks and crannies, but it seemed that all was clear. I breathed a sigh of relief. I was safe from the storm, and the inside of the tree was big enough that I could turn around and get comfortable.

For a few minutes I listened to the din of the storm and watched as its fury lashed the trees before me. Then gradually another, much closer sound became apparent. I could hear a deep-seated, insistent buzzing, droning in a monotone close by. The hair on my arms and neck prickled as I slowly looked up. There, directly above me, was a huge papery nest, filling the entire space of the tree trunk above my head. I gulped. Around it, a few thousand hornets crawled on the inner tree, their wings slowly opening and closing. They were huge. At least twice the size of common yellow-and-black European wasps, hornets were feared and avoided. And they knew I was there.

I sat down slowly for the simple reason that my legs gave way; my energy expired. Badly frightened, all the horror stories of killer wasps and hornets I had ever heard came surging into my mind. The old man stung to death by wasps in his garden; the little girl stung to death by wasps on the village green; the dog choked by a sting in its throat; a neighbor rushed to the hospital when stung by a hornet. Fearfully, I stared up at the swarm of hornets, waiting for them to descend and attack.

It was obvious they knew I was there, for most of them were facing me, their antennae waving inquiringly, and by now many more were pouring out of their nest to confront me. And all the time their buzzing seemed to get louder and more expressive. Scrunched uncomfortably in the base of the tree, I was in no position for a fast exit. I fervently wished I had stayed by the elm, just getting wet. The risk of flying debris seemed nothing now as I gazed mesmerized at the hornets. They were coming closer. A few of them buzzed around to eventually settle very close to my head, while the swarm crawled ever closer.

I was in trouble. To get out I would have to stand up, and that would mean putting my head in the area that was now thick with hornets. I closed my eyes to block it all out, my heart thudding its message of fear.

Although the droning sound had increased in intensity, I realized with some surprise that it had a soothing quality to it rather than one of menace. Keeping my panic under control, I opened my eyes again. The hornets were now all around me, their dark brownish bodies very close. Yet for some odd reason, I felt less threatened.

As I sat there, unsure of what to do, two things happened simultaneously. In the same instant that a strange, preternatural calm settled over me, I had a clear inner knowing that the hornets meant me no harm. In the years following this incident, I speculated often on just what happened, but I always examined it through logic and reason. It never occurred to me that what happened was not remotely logical; it was mystical.

With startling clarity, I suddenly knew that the hornets were singing to me. In a low buzzing drone, which in some odd way was never drowned out by the crashing fury of the storm, the hornets were communicating with me. This was not a wild daydream by a frightened boy; this was a reality that moved deeply into my consciousness, touching into the ageless wisdom we all hold within us. Their song had a definite physical sound, for I could hear its intense and penetrating monotone, but on some other level of consciousness, it communicated with me in silent pictures. Within my mind, I saw into the nest. I saw the thousands of chambers with their eggs and babies, as though viewing a holograph, and I saw the huge queen of the swarm. I learned that hornets have none of the mindless ferocity of their wasp cousins. Despite being protective of their nest and queen, they are of a more docile nature. Collectively, they sang my fear away, and they sang me into their heart. I cannot fully explain this, but my insight revealed that the consciousness of the swarm accepted me, and I was safe. Not only that, but I felt that the hornet tree would always be a sanctuary for me.

The storm eased away, the downpour becoming a light rain, leaving the ground littered with fresh green leaves and a scattering of branches. In the silence, the hornets continued their song, drawing pictures in my mind of meadows and streams and of hollow limbs in great old trees. I learned that they are declining in number, for while their size threatens and frightens people, their docility does not shelter them from mass extermination. And I learned of their acceptance of this.

Subdued, overwhelmed, I walked home with sadness in my heart. When I left the tree, I had straightened slowly, the hornets quiet. They were only inches from my face as I came upright, pins and needles tingling in my feet. I had been in the tree for nearly three-quarters of an

hour when I slowly eased my way out through the deep split, careful not to squash a single insect, for they were all around me.

I never told my family or any of my pals. Some things do not translate easily, and only now do I feel I have the skill to present the experience just as it happened. Although I was hesitant at first, I returned occasionally, squeezing into the hollow tree to be with the hornets. They never sang to me again, but I always had the feeling that I was accepted.

Sadly, there seemed to be fewer hornets each time I visited, and I felt a real sense of loss. Now I view nature through different eyes, for I have learned of Oneness. In the experience of Oneness, there is no loss. I know now that the consciousness of those hornets continues and that I am connected with their continuity. Within my consciousness, their song lives and continues in the foreverness of Now, not lost in some remote and forgotten past.

IN THE COMPANY OF GREAT TEACHERS

LINDA TELLINGTON-JONES

Interspecies communication is gaining international acceptance and fills a space in the hearts of so many who as children dreamed of a special relationship with animals and who now as adults have realized that telepathic communication with animals is possible and actually quite simple.

I had the good fortune to grow up in a family in which deep love and reverence for animals were part of my inheritance. I learned from an early age to respect and communicate with four-legged, feathered, and creepy-crawly friends. "Do unto others as you would have them do unto you" hung on the wall of my childhood bedroom in framed petit point.

In our household the Golden Rule applied to the animal kingdom as well as to my own species. Grandmother Caywood would never allow a spider to be killed in her house. When I was a six-year-old, Grandpa Hood was frequently awakened by a rescued field bunny who hopped up the stairs to awaken him by rustling around in his beard. Interspecies communication and connection was demonstrated by a mother cat in our farm kitchen who integrated into her litter of newborn kittens three baby ducks my father had brought in from a nest destroyed by a horse-drawn seeding machine. Mother carefully washing a surprised and sticky deer mouse who had fallen into an open jar of syrup in the pantry nestles in my mental scrapbook of memories. Her father, Will Caywood, attributed a good portion of his success as a trainer of race horses to his communication with them. He said he never sent a horse to the starting gate unless it told him it was feeling fit enough to win.

Animals have numerous means of communicating when we learn to listen. Working with horses is as natural to me as breathing, and I learned as a child to know when a horse is thirsty, frightened, trusting, or proud of a prize we may have won together. This knowing was a deep connection developed over many years and went beyond any communication I had with my own species. I did, however, not usually get this knowing in words but rather in feelings.

The first actual communication I remember experiencing in words came from a rattlesnake in 1964. Like all ranchers, I learned to kill rattlesnakes because of the danger to livestock. At the time my husband and I had a ranch and school of horsemanship in the foothills of the Sequoia Mountains southeast of Fresno, California, where two of our horses and one of our Great Danes were bitten by rattlesnakes in the first year on the ranch.

One warm spring day while driving home up our narrow winding mountain road, a very large rattlesnake made its way across my path. I stopped the truck and climbed out with the intention of ridding the countryside of this dangerous snake. Picking up a large rock, I heaved it at the rattler slithering innocently across the track.

At first it paid no attention to me. A wave of sorrow flashed through my being as the stone smashed into the body, but I was convinced it was my duty to carry through with the assassination. As I raised my arms for the third attack, I clearly experienced a telepathic thought coming from the snake, "She means to kill me!" At this moment, the snake turned from its escape route and headed purposefully in my direction. I was stunned! Not from fear of the snake headed in my direction, because it is easy to avoid, but from the conscious thought I had picked up.

Climbing back into the truck and feeling terrible about my unmitigated attack, I apologized profusely to the snake and prayed she/he was not too injured to survive. Several weeks later, I was given a copy of J. Allen Boone's *Kinship with All Life*, one of the most influential books on nature and animals, and read about the respectful relationship between Native Americans of the past and the animal kingdom, rattlesnakes in particular. Because of that mutual respect, rattlesnakes were not considered a threat to them but rather were seen as "little brothers."

I made an announcement to all ranch personnel that in the future, when a rattlesnake was spotted on the ranch, I was to be informed and no snake was to be harmed. Within the month, a nine-rattle snake was spotted in the area of our equestrian jumping course. I headed up in the truck to remove the snake without harming him, carrying two pieces of wood. The snake was moving at a leisurely pace, minding his own business. I approached quietly, placed the end of one of the pieces of wood gently in front of his path, while telepathically excusing the interruption and informing the snake that it was not in a good place and asking permission to accompany it to another location.

The snake stopped and lay still, as though listening. For those of you not acquainted with rattlesnakes, I mention that they cannot strike unless coiled, leaving only a third of their length. I made a very clear picture in my head to accompany my mental communication that we must turn and head downhill about three hundred yards toward the main gate. I indicated the turn with my other piece of wood, and without fuss or hesitation the snake reversed direction and together we proceeded slowly, side-by-side, toward our outdoor jumping arena, with me periodically indicating the direction with the slats.

At this stage I was uncertain how I would get the snake off our property and move it several miles away to a pasture with few cows, but on experiencing our connection, I decided to ask the snake to go under one of the fifty-gallon metal drums we use for a jump.

When we arrived at the barrel, I asked my scaled friend to wait a moment—again indicating the stop in front of his path and communicating a clear telepathic picture of my request. I tipped the barrel on its side and, without any indication of fear on the part of the snake, rolled it in place in front of his nose, gently nudging the rattles under the edge with the wood in my hand.

I drove back to the ranch, found a ten-gallon plastic, high-sided bucket, and returned to the snake. The question was, how could I transfer the rattler from the barrel to the bucket without upsetting it. Trusting that our understanding would continue, I laid the bucket and barrel end to end and indicated that he should slither into the bucket. Without hesitation, in he went. I carefully stood the plastic container on end.

Coiled in the bucket, never rattling or aggressive, he carefully touched the rim of the pail with his nose as though exploring the territory.

I carefully carried the bucket—without a lid—to the truck and drove two miles to a deserted cow pasture. Here I removed the pail from the car and gingerly turned it on its side. The snake moved quietly onto the grass about ten feet away, stopped, coiled, and with its head resting in the center of the coil, turned toward me and began a strange breathing *thhhhhh-thhhhhh* sound. Clearly he was connecting with me. I eased myself down onto the earth, and for twenty minutes or so we sat quietly communicating with our breath. Finally, thanking my new friend for this remarkable experience, I drove home in a state of wonder.

This experience opened a whole new world to me, and I began to see animals from a new perspective. Over the years, rattlesnakes have crossed my path numerous times, usually with specific lessons that were applicable to other life situations. Several opportunities to learn about fear and self-control were presented. On one occasion, a large rattler was coiled in the riding arena during a lesson with a dozen students. We experimented with a nonverbal communication to see how close we could get without alarming the snake into rattling or striking. Of course, we were outside the range that the snake could reach if he were to strike.

Those who could quiet their minds and maintain a slow, regular breathing pattern could approach and stand quietly without upsetting the snake—much closer than students whose breathing, body language, and mental state gave away their uncertainty. The success seemed to depend upon overcoming fear and connecting. A special magic seems to happen when we are touched with these experiences with untamed animals.

Animals, moreover, have many ways of communicating. Gaia had been a laboratory research monkey for sixteen years in the Hunter College psychology department in midtown New York. She had lived in isolation for all those years in a steel cage approximately two and one-half by three feet on a wire "floor" with solid steel sides and three feet of head room. In the small room with no windows were five other monkeys who could be heard but not seen.

When research funds from the National Institutes of Health dried up, the decision was made to sell the six macaques for medical research. Staff

and students of the psychology department began looking desperately for another solution. Carolyn Bocian, who was working toward her Ph.D. in primate studies at Hunter College, called me. We had met some years before when I gave a presentation to staff members at the National Zoo in Washington, D.C., where she had been the primate keeper. Carolyn remembered our Animal Ambassador program and thought perhaps I could help.

I agreed to search for a sanctuary, but after many phone calls and no success I decided to take Gaia and another monkey, Isha, as a "halfway" house. If we could be successful in socializing them, we agreed to take the remaining four.

There had been an unsuccessful attempt at Hunter to socialize Gaia and Isha, a slightly younger macaque. My commitment was to give them an enriched social life with a wide variety of interesting and stimulating fruits and vegetables. They had been living on monkey chow and powdered banana, Jello-like cubes.

Once we got them to my center in New Mexico, we found deep satisfaction in watching them enjoy opening corn husks, splitting tomatoes, spitting out cherry seeds, and exploring new foods.

Using music, visualization, interspecies communication, and much appreciation, it took less than a week before they were grooming everyone on staff and frequent visitors. Within a few months, they had the run of my ten-room center, moving from room to room to take advantage of the sun when their outdoor area was shaded. Amazingly, they paid little attention to visiting dogs or humans, simply skirting around strangers when they went on walkabout.

Gaia was a special being—very different from Isha or the other four macaques who later joined our small troop. Gaia had been captured in Indonesia around the age of four years and had been in constant isolation for sixteen years, able to hear but not to see the other five. I have seldom known so gentle and thoughtful an animal.

There were many instances of interspecies communication that she initiated, but I must share three special cases.

Gaia loved children and would sit quietly on the edge, or sometimes in the middle, of small groups of schoolchildren who came to visit and

learn about the monkeys. Carol Lang, our Animal Ambassador director, was hosting a group of preschool-age children. Among them was a quiet four-year-old girl who stayed toward the back of the class. Gaia was invited by Carol into the room to meet the children. She stopped momentarily at the door, looked around the room, spotted the shy four-year-old, walked slowly to the child so she would not frighten her, carefully took the little girl's hand, brought it to her lips, and gently kissed her finger, all the while looking intently into her eyes.

I had difficulty believing Gaia could be so consciously mindful. But it became clear to us when she had her first kitten that she was indeed consciously communicating. An abandoned gray kitten we named Dusty, about four weeks old, was found by the side of the road near our office and brought to the door. Gaia had already adopted and raised an older kitten named Angel some months before, and Angel had never been fearful of Gaia. Dusty was another matter, however, acting shy and spitting when Gaia came too near.

Gaia "gentled" him as carefully and consciously as a sensitive human would approach a nervous animal. She would sit quietly a few feet away, turn sideways to be less threatening, and "talk" to him with her chin-jutting movements, making a little chattering sound. When Dusty relaxed, she would move a little closer or around to another side. Soon she was able to approach him and pick him up. Gaia did not understand how to pick up her first kitten and would drag her around by the flank. With Dusty, however, some maternal instinct kicked in, and within days she had him sitting against her dry breast suckling.

As he grew, he would pounce on Gaia and play with her like a cat, often clawing wildly at her belly with his hind legs. She would roll on the floor with him and simply close her eyes or turn her head to avoid him. She never returned his attacks but would play with him for hours. We finally put claw caps on him because of his rough play.

Gaia also loved puppies. One day a two-month-old Labrador retriever came to the office for a consultation. Gaia immediately began to make up to him. Once he had overcome his uncertainty about this odd creature, he began to play, biting at her front and hind feet as she sat and tried to cuddle him. At one point he became too rambunctious,

and she mindfully grasped a front paw and carefully squeezed until he backed off. He cooled down a little, and the interaction continued in a quieter vein.

We photographed her being introduced to a blind Chihuahua puppy. She approached him even more carefully and slowly than usual, touched his paw softly with her hand, and carefully reached out with her tongue and touched his tiny mouth. She seemed to have a creative approach for each new situation.

I'll never forget the time she was hanging out on my office floor as I was busy on the computer. I stood up to stretch, sat down on the floor beside her, and for some reason unknown and totally foreign to my normal behavior, looked at her and said, "Kootchee, kutchee-koo." She looked me straight in the eyes, got up, stalked over to me, gently but purposefully groped my bare arm with both hands, held it up to her mouth, put her tooth against my arm without pressure, looked me straight in the eyes, and as clearly as though she had spoken, stated, "Don't you ever kutchee-koo me again." She put my arm down, turned her back on me, and marched out of the room.

From that day on, I realized this was a being far beyond normal intelligence. Her special ability to communicate with other species touched the hearts of many two-leggeds.

Over the years I have come to accept interspecies communication as a part of everyday life. In the past few years I have been inviting participants in my weeklong horse trainings to connect on the spirit level with animals they have known, some still living and many who have long ago crossed through the veils to the other side. Before participating in a group session we sit in a circle. I ask everyone to close their eyes and visualize a pillar of light in the center of our circle, connecting from the heavens into the crystal core of the earth. We then bring that light into and around ourselves. Each person imagines a shaft of light coming from the center of the pillar into their hearts and then passes that light into the heart of the person sitting to the left, until the circle is connected with the light from person to person. We call into the circle the spirits of all the animals we have known; the Spirit Council of Animals; and the

teachers, angelic beings, and guides each person connects to. Almost always an animal communicates by giving pictures, words, or a message of love or forgiveness which brings about an opening of the heart.

Recently an incident occurred in Wyoming at the Bitterroot Ranch weeklong training that affected us all. One morning a moose with twin calves was crossing the river during a flood when one of the twins was swept away by the current and washed up on the bank near the stable. The calf was weak but recovered during the day and hung out around the ranch headquarters for two days, calling for her mother. Several times a day she came close to the lodge, clearly seeking help.

We called Fish and Game Department officials who suggested we leave it alone and hope the mother would come for the calf. This didn't seem likely, however, since the moose had seen her calf disappear into the raging river.

Many of the trainees, naturally, were upset at the dilemma and helplessness of the calf. They sat in a circle to send love to the calf and see if she had anything to relate about the situation.

This is what I received. I call it "Moose Medicine":

That baby moose
came to you today
to show you the way
to a deeper understanding
of the Oneness of All.

That evening, under the guidance of Bitterroot hostess and co-owner Mel Fox, thirty of us gathered and herded the moose calf up the mountain in the direction her mother was last seen. With careful maneuvering, we finally got her to the crook leading to the meadow from whence she came. She leapt across the bank and took off purposefully into the dusk. There were many silent voices praying for her safe deliverance to her mother. Two days later she was spotted by Fish and Game officials safely back with her twin and her moose mom. All who had the privilege of her presence during those two days were deeply touched by that special moose medicine.

In addition to animals, I've had an intimate relationship with trees for many moons. It began with a communication, which occurred in Australia, that I've shared with many thousands of people in many countries. It was my first communication and was completely unexpected. I was visiting Michael and Treenie Roads near Byron Bay and planning to go out to visit with their one-thousand-year-old Morton Bay fig tree at Michael's suggestion. This tree is more than one hundred feet across from branch tip to tip, and the roots are two feet high, thirty feet out from the trunk. I had no expectations. Michael had not told me at that time about his relationship with this magnificent tree.

I headed out early one morning with my journal, intending to record events of the past few days. As I approached the tree, these words came into my head:

Come and sit by me, and I will tell you a story.
Sit on me. Anywhere in the sun.
Once upon a time there were many like me.
We had lived long upon this planet and had acquired much wisdom.
Our understanding and love sent out positive vibrations, which had
far-reaching effects.
Then came man with his lack of understanding.

In order to re-balance and realign the earth, your people
must once again recognize the Kingdoms of the Plants, the Animals,
the Minerals, and the Nature Spirits as One
and as vital to the survival of the planet.

That your race recognize the God within is only the start.
That we are recognized as one with you in the balance of existence
is the key to—not only survival—but to
heaven on earth.

TATTI WATTLES: A LOVE STORY

RACHEL ROSENTHAL

Dear Tatti: I love you, and I miss you. Of all the animals who've lived with me, you were physically the closest. You were on my body so much of the time: on my shoulder, my arm, my lap, in my hand. It was an intimacy of touch, of warmth, of the senses. I loved your ratty smell, your delicate pads, always clean, scrupulously groomed. I loved your long tail that freaked out so many people. I loved your profuse whiskers, your round translucent ears, your little black, shiny eyes, your warm white underbelly.

I loved to watch you stash and eat and wash. I enjoyed your padding around the house, sometimes kicking up your heels and taking off in a loping gallop. I loved your affection, your little tongue kissing me, your little paws with their tiny pink fingers holding my face. I am grateful for your patience with all the activities I involved you in and the people I exposed you to. Oh, Tatti, my little friend, I miss you so. It is an empty shoulder indeed, and my hand searches for the warmth of your little body in vain.

You were a beautiful little creature, Tatti Wattles. I want to tell this to the world, for the world knows your kind as enemy, vermin, anonymous flesh pool used in abominable laboratory experiments or as food for snakes. I have known you as an individual, and I want to open people's eyes to you as an individual—for it is only when we see others as individual, unique, precious, and irreplaceable that we will be ready to assume our full humanity. Only when we are capable of acknowledging that other creatures, human or not, have full rights under the sun—to live and die with dignity, respect, and self-fulfillment—will we be able to claim all of this for ourselves.

Tatti was home!

I couldn't believe it. I was so afraid he'd die in the hospital. He was there three days. I visited him morning and night, before and after hours, alone with him in one of the rooms with the anatomical charts on the walls, sitting with him for an hour or so, giving him healing white light.

He lay in my hand, dull coated, panting, eyes closed, pale. You can tell when a furry animal is pale by the nose, ears, and mouth. I had seen his X-rays. They were frightening. His little heart was so enlarged that it pushed the aorta up against the spine; the negative image showed dark filaments in the lungs—fluid. And then, the miraculous recovery. He came home on Friday, with a pharmacopoeia of medicines. He ate and groomed himself. I made him his favorite—corn on the cob. He ate a bit of whole-wheat bread and half a grape. I was in heaven!

I tried not to touch him too much so as not to tire him. I talked to him a lot. I kept repeating, "Oh Tatti, I love you so!" I had felt so unbelievably guilty about him. Had I been negligent? Did the smell of the paint—I had the facade of my building painted—trigger heart failure? I knew he had a heart murmur. I thought we could catch it in time to medicate and arrest it. It happened so fast. One evening Tatti was sick. I waited till morning. I should have taken him to emergency right then. And what about the air freshener I put in the closet where he slept? Could it have irritated him, too? Perhaps the Canada tour had been too much for him.

I had been too casual about Tatti's health, and he was dying. I couldn't live with this. I had assumed that if I were to accomplish nothing else in my life, I had been good with animals. But here I had failed. Tatti was only a little over two and one-half years old. The vet—a rat expert—said three years was the maximum life expectancy for rats. Yet others had told me four, five, even six. I was confident that Tatti would break records. So it was much too early for Tatti to die. I couldn't accept it.

Tatti made a very modest turd. He hadn't eaten in days and was thin. He was thin and slept a lot. I didn't want him in the closet and kept him in the cage by my bed. Just in case he felt like roaming, I kept it closed for the first time, unless I was nearby. Saturday at noon I was having lunch. I ate sitting on the side of my bed with a tray on a stool, as always. Tatti shared a lot of my meals, but this time he didn't. He became a

little agitated, and I closed the cage door, remembering what the vet said: "No excitement. Keep him quiet."

Suddenly Tatti began to bite the cage door. I opened it. He ran down his usual route to the closet, stopping a couple of times to catch his breath. I didn't know what to do. I didn't want to aggravate him by stopping him. He got to the closet, and I helped him up to his usual nest on my suitcase. He jumped down at once, increasingly agitated. I became anxious, picked him up, and walked back to the cage. By the time I got there, his heart had stopped beating. I became frantic and tried to blow air into his mouth as he gasped. He staggered around a little, his mouth working for air. I felt him again in my hands. The heart was gone.

He didn't want to die. He wasn't ready. His body fought it, but the pump had stopped. A betrayal. An outrage. In my head screamed the words: He's dying! He's dying! I watched helplessly and in despair. His paws flayed the air, his eyes closed, his little mouth opened and closed a few more times and he was dead. I picked him up, limp and flaccid, and keened over him for an hour. I couldn't stop. I felt as if a part of my body had been ripped out.

His fur became wet and scruffy from my tears. I placed him on the bed and arranged his body so it seemed as if he were resting. I brought his tail around close to his paws. I combed him one last time. I put away his bedding, his food, his cage, his litter box, his nest in the closet, all the things that had belonged to him. I got a shoe box and placed him inside on one of his towels. I closed the box and put it in the freezer.

Then I called my friends to tell them about the ceremony the next day. It was August 7, 1982. I felt I had lost my soul.

From *Webster's New Collegiate Dictionary*:

Rat—noun. A contemptible person as a. one who betrays his party, friends, or associates. b. scab. c. informer.

Rat—verb. 1. To betray, to desert, or inform on one's associates. 2. To go back on (as an agreement or statement); welsh on (ratted on her debts).

Rodents were not my first choice of companion animals. I had always been a heavy-duty cat-and-dog person. But Tatti happened, and he

became one of the few of my many animals who transformed my psyche and taught me at least as much as I taught him.

It all started when I left my husband and went to live by myself in downtown Los Angeles. One morning when I stopped by the Los Angeles Contemporary Exhibitions space I saw a sign that read "Homer, the Homosexual Rat," and on the floor, a cylindrical metal cage. I glanced at it casually and suddenly had an adrenalin rush sensing an "Animal Alert!" I approached the cage and saw a tiny black rat, not a baby but a juvenile, looking out forlornly. There was no solid bottom to the cage and the metal mesh sat on the concrete floor of the gallery. In the cage was a tiny piece of soiled cloth, not enough to nest in, a few peanuts, and a saucer with some dirty water.

I felt the characteristic tingling in the back of my neck that heralds an animal-rescue operation and approached the gallery director. "Who takes care of the rat? Does anyone touch him? Did the owner leave any instructions about his care and feeding?" All the answers were negative.

I went to the cage, opened it, and picked the little creature up. He was docile and listless. I stroked him gently. He sat quietly in my hand, watching me with his black beady eyes. His baby coat was sleek and black, and he had a white belly, white socks, and his balls were almost as big as his body.

"How had the owner used him in the performance?" I asked, worried, for he was notorious for having done a piece that consisted in setting four live rats on fire and burning them to death. He was jailed for that, but this work became a *cause célèbre* in the art community—causing a great deal of ink to be spilled attacking or defending his actions, costing a gallery director his job, and making other directors reticent to sched-ule performances by other artists. Sad to say, several performance artists abused animals in their "art," thus shaming the genre.

Though I had no idea how to care for a rat, I immediately acquired Homer. I knew, of course, that "pet rats" is a euphemism for laboratory rats, that the majority of them are used for medical and scientific research or to test every conceivable product unprotected by the U.S. Animal Welfare Act, such as it is. Some of the surplus from breeders go to pet stores where they are sold as snake food. The lucky ones are

bought as children's pets, soon forgotten in their cages after the first fun wears off. I bought rat-care books at a pet store.

Homer turned out to be a most interesting little person. He was extremely serious and very cautious. He was tame and affectionate. He had a huge appetite and was, for the most part, fearless. I began at once to take Homer with me everywhere. He hid under the tent of my then-long hair and never even considered leaving my body. He and I began to frequent art openings, performances, and parties.

When I taught classes and workshops, Homer was the mascot. He enjoyed the attention, the people, the sounds, the smells. With his little pink nose in the air and his sensitive whiskers, he got his bearings by sniffing and let me know by licking if there was a problem. Some licking meant he was insecure—too much noise, too much smoke. Frantic licking came to mean "bathroom." I'd go to the restroom and put him on some paper where he'd dutifully go. After we moved to my new building, I introduced a kitty-litter box and he wasted no time figuring it out.

When he was still growing from a young rat to an adult, there were times when I watched him scurrying around on my bed and thought, "My god, it's a rat!" The most unmistakable characteristic of his rattiness was his locomotion—that peculiar way of hunching his back and tiptoeing high and fast on his tiny feet so that it looked from a distance as if he floated on air, a body with no paws, like a mechanical mouse on hidden wheels.

It was hard getting used to his size. He was so small! How do you pet such a tiny creature? How do you hug it? I couldn't abandon myself to paroxysms of demonstrative love. No—an index finger, the thumb, a few other fingers very carefully perhaps—and that was all. When he grew to a fairly large size for a pet rat, I developed more orthodox methods of venting my passion. But with tiny Homer, I was intimidated.

Homer visited me in bed. When I first adopted him, he had the nasty habit of sinking his needle-sharp teeth into my big toe. I don't think that he connected it to my body and probably mistook it for a piece of knockwurst. I screamed with abandon, and within a short time he stopped doing that. Our trysts in bed became more relaxed. At first I feared that I'd crush him with my body while we slept. But a bed is soft, and so is a

rat's skeleton. These rodents have no bones, only cartilage, which explains how they can squeeze into the tiniest apertures. In any case, he slept in my hand or in the "spoons" position—a huge spoon and a minuscule spoon, and there never was a problem.

A friend of mine used to say to me with wonder in his voice: "He's like a puppy, only tiny! It's like having a minute dog!" I think that what he really meant was: He's a rat, and we're supposed to run from him, but as I get closer it becomes clear that this furry mammal isn't much different from the "accepted" pet animals, only smaller.

I have long felt that to truly communicate with one of another species is something special. We communicate with other human beings through language. Most of our relations with animals are therefore based on attempts to teach them words, for the most part "commands": "Sit!" "Stay!" "Heel!" "Whoa!" "Giddy-yap!" and so forth. We get impatient and angry when animals don't "understand" and think them bad, stupid, or in need of more training. We seldom consider learning their language. Most pets are treated as slaves. They are given room and board in exchange for "services." They must be guards, companions, hunting helpers, mousers, singers, seeing eyes, hearing ears, and decorative, elegant status symbols, loving, devoted, and loyal. It is to cats' credit that a lot of them manage to get away with all the advantages of domesticity while returning none of the expected behavioral payment.

Many people profess to love their companion animals, but how many respect them as completely as they would an equal of their own species? It takes fully accepting one's humanity to be able to bridge the considerable gap that separates us from other-than-human animals. People who achieve this know the full meaning of love—a love that doesn't own or grab, that isn't a projection of our personal needs or neuroses; a love that leaves the other free, that respects and accepts the other's life in its entirety rather than selectively encouraging only traits and behaviors that are convenient or remind us of ourselves.

Above all, such a person has a sense of the sacred. As beautiful and wondrous as is love and total communication between two human beings, love and total communication between individuals of two different species is something that goes beyond—into the numinous and the transcendental.

It would seem that human beings (with a few exceptions) have lost the capacity, wonder, and magic of interspecies communication. Yet animals continue to fascinate us in myths and folktales where they embody spiritual and supernatural powers. They haunt our dreams and symbolize those deepest parts of nature from which we have severed ourselves.

Animals, or rather the idea of animals, are a potent force. We fear animals we almost never come in contact with: bats, snakes, leopards, wolves, rats. These responses are deeply buried in our unconscious where they were imprinted as far back as from our hominid ancestors whose survival depended on cunning. We were part of the food chain then, not the top predator we have since become. We ate and were eaten. We feared, respected, emulated, or shunned other animals. We were constantly on the alert for a dangerous predator or for an animal whose sting or bite could kill. We cannot remember or even imagine what it was like to be in such close symbiosis with such powerful and strange beings. But our unconscious memories remember.

Our children grow up on a diet of fairy-tale beasts: Beatrix Potter's mice, the Big Bad Wolf, the Frog Prince, Br'er Rabbit, and the Roadrunner. But how many of these children are taught to bring a live animal to be dissected in a precocious physiology class that teaches all the wrong life lessons: that it's OK to kill out of curiosity; that to understand life, one must kill it; that a dead frog is more educational than a live frog observed in the wild; that love and respect do not go with science and technology, ergo with civilized society? Happy and lucky are those children whose enlightened parents or teachers instruct them in the patience and empathy needed to really know an animal who is alive and to use this knowledge creatively in the preservation of life.

Death comes. Death is part of the business. I learn about my own death with every animal I know whose death I witness. And I've learned that death, under certain circumstances, can be ecstatic. With this understanding comes acceptance, and with acceptance, peace.

Eventually, my new storefront cum apartment became habitable, after some renovation. Homer and I moved uptown. I attached his large cage to the wall above my bed, and we began to live our lives as a couple!

As I was making my bed one morning and the little rat watched me, resting on the lowered drawbridge of his cage, he looked at me and suddenly announced: "I am Tatti Wattles!" "Yes, that makes sense," I thought, and from then on "Homer" became "Tatti Wattles." I always wait until an animal names her or himself. In Tatti's case, the name surfaced spontaneously when we moved into our new place. Tatti liked his name. When I came back after leaving him at home for any reason, I would open the downstairs door to the apartment, and as I clambered up the stairs, I would call, "Tatti! I'm home!" and Tatti would jump from the cage onto the bed, walk to the very edge, crane his little neck to see me, and greet me with delighted squeaks, lifting himself on his hind paws to be picked up when I came near.

I had begun to detect some deep affinities between Tatti and myself.

Tatti had a problem. His teeth grew too fast. Unchecked, they could prevent him from eating and he would be left to starve. They could even grow through his palate into his brain! Rodents afflicted with this abnormality in the wild can grind their teeth down on hard surfaces. But Tatti was civilized and had lost all such instincts. He liked only soft foods. So he had to go to the vet's every two or three weeks to have his incisors clipped. He hated that, and so did I. He struggled while I held him, protested loudly, and tried to climb up me to get away from the clippers. But *snip-snap!* His little teeth eventually had to go. Not once during these harrowing operations did Tatti attempt to bite, either me or the doctor.

I was amazed until I realized that lab rats are bred to be hyper-gentle. Indeed, it wouldn't do to bite the hand that exposes you to radiation, that injects you with cancer, that implants electrodes in your brain or your tail, that force-feeds you massive doses of poison until your stomach bursts. Lab rats are, in effect, the sweetest little creatures in the world, prefabbed that way for man's purposes by the wizardry of genetic manipulation.

As we drove home from the rat dentist, poor Tatti nuzzled in my ear, relieved after much petting and comforting, and I realized that I suffered from a similar psychological ailment. From childhood I was taught to repress my anger and to view negative emotions as evil and reprehensible.

When I was little, the perception of those violent feelings was so threatening that it would overwhelm me with crippling anxiety and guilt. I developed nervous disorders and facial tics.

My governess had total control over me. She exerted this power abusively, both physically and psychologically. I soon learned the art of passive aggression and became a sulker and plotter of horrendous but never consummated revenge. I never talked back, never cried or cried out, never told on her, never showed in any way that I was hurt or afraid or choking with rage. I was a veritable stoic by age seven. To this day, I have trouble defending myself when attacked. If I detect a barb or, worse, a direct insult, I freeze. If someone has been unkind to me, I will smile assiduously. I have to fight daily within myself to overcome this early training. But one thing was certain: through breeding (either the reproductive or educational variety), Tatti and I both had the bite taken out of us.

That realization gave me the impetus for my next performance, and I decided that Tatti would be my partner. The piece was called "Bon soir, Dr. Schon!" It had some pretty brutal scenes in which Tatti, riding on my head, hung on to my hair for dear life as I detonated cap bombs and screamed. I shouted, "I am a Vampire!"

At that point, Tatti decided to come down to my shoulder where it was safer, via my cheek. As I veered, he hung on with his little claws, and blood began to trickle down on my face. Tatti had a good sense of timing. I had fashioned little vampire bat wings for him. I said, "You, too, are a Vampire!" and "flew" him around the playing area with his shiny black wings. Tatti was relieved when I put him back in his carrying cage after that scene.

"Dr. Schon" was the first of three performances I did with Tatti. He had been a real trouper, and I felt he had contributed greatly to the piece. Interestingly, not one of the reviews mentioned him. It was as if he hadn't been there at all. Did people block? Did they consider him too frivolous to mention in a serious critique? Or did they simply not see him? I was disappointed. I expected Tatti to get good press. But in the following two years, Tatti got a great deal of press and media attention. He was finally seen!

The winter of 1980–81 was fraught with personal financial problems. I began suffering from insomnia, waking up in a cold sweat in the middle of the night. Tatti was in heaven—activity at three, four in the morning! Great. I was dying of anxiety and Tatti wanted to *play*! In those difficult times, Tatti seemed to be my only link to life. Through Tatti Wattles, through the physical and emotional sensation of holding him in the palm of my hand, of my fingers stroking him, I felt connected to life as by a thin but sturdy thread. I said his name and he clucked back. This scanty dialogue was enough to anchor me when it seemed the ground had shifted dangerously under my feet.

Tatti didn't participate in the new piece, "Leave Her in Naxos," although he was there, as usual, in his carrying cage ready for me when I was done performing. He got a serious shock when I returned backstage after the show. I had had my head shaved during the piece as a ritual of letting the old die so the new could grow. It was a deeply healing performance dealing with body and soul. I thought of letting my hair grow back but liked my baldness so much that I have never grown hair since.

Tatti had lost his nest and his shelter, however, and no longer enjoyed being up on my shoulder. After walking around my neck several times looking for my hair, he came down my arm onto my hand. I began to wear scarves he could hide in, but the shoulder definitely lost its appeal after this performance.

After "Naxos," my outer image changed. I kept the bald head for the feeling of freedom, of lightness, of contact that it gave me. And I began dressing at army-navy stores out of pecuniary necessity. I liked the idea of defusing the obnoxiousness of war imagery by wearing army clothes with pink or lavender chiffon scarves, funny jewelry, art buttons, lots of makeup, and purple socks. I didn't realize at the time that my image of military gear, a bald head, and a rat on the shoulder would be quite appalling to people. No matter. It kept some away that I wasn't interested in knowing, and those who got close enough were soon getting the messages that I wanted to send. My rat friend and I were telling the world, "Don't judge a book by its cover, clothes don't make the man (or beast), opposites coexist, gender is a fabrication, respect all life, we were

militant—not military," et cetera. I was a walking paradox, and so was Tatti. We liked it that way. Of course, the new look attracted the media, and Tatti became famous.

We went everywhere together. I taught workshops at Otis Parsons and other schools at the time. When we drove to work in my stick shift, Tatti loved surfing on my knee or my wrist. It was his private roller coaster. He hung on as I shifted and enjoyed himself thoroughly. At Otis, he stayed in his carrying cage while I taught, came to the cafeteria with me and the students, and socialized on the table where we ate.

As we went about town, to openings, to parties, people began to know us. After a while I detected certain patterns in their reactions. Before long I starting rating individuals according to their responses to us, but especially to Tatti. It was like a Rorschach test. There were those who dove for Tatti, with a rapid request for permission to pet him. Many women thought Tatti was OK from the front, but the back side was revolting. One woman shouted as she beat a hasty retreat, "His nose is disgusting! It's like a pig's snout!" That one really puzzled me: first, because a rat's nose is nothing like a pig's snout; secondly, because what on earth is wrong with a pig's snout? What is an aesthetic that declares some evolutionary choices beautiful and others ugly?

Tatti was an educational tool. He converted almost everyone. People would listen to me sound off about rats in general, their special character and adaptations and the dreadful "use" they are put to in biomedical research. Most were fascinated. At the bottom of my list were those who grabbed Tatti without asking first, like the sister of a dear friend of mine. She was an M.D. When she saw Tatti, she picked him off me deftly with one hand and held him dangling in front of her face as she scrutinized him. It was a gesture I could easily recognize—that of the scientist examining an experimental rat for signs of pathology. My skin crawled. The action was eloquent. A lack of respect both for Tatti's individuality and for my feelings. Her words echoed the hands. "Oh, I know those rats." I'll bet you do! I wanted to deck her, but she had immunity by reason of consanguinity with my friend. Frustration.

One night, I was at an opening and an artist approached me. She talked for a while without noticing Tatti. When she did, she hit me on

the chest with such force that Tatti went flying through the air. Luckily, the gallery was crowded and he landed gracefully on someone else's shoulder. When people escaped my vigilance and somehow got close to Tatti in a callous way, I hoped that, for want of biting, he would at least pee on them. Alas, Tatti had a tendency to pee more readily on those he loved.

Our artistic collaboration continued, after "Naxos," with "Soldier of Fortune," a play on words about my calamitous relationship with money. The live performance was accompanied by a limited-edition artist book of the same title that juxtaposed a very bleak text about human brutality and guilt with images of utter hedonism. I was photographed eating seven-course meals at seven of the most trendy and expensive restaurants of Los Angeles. I brought Tatti to four of them. He ate raw salmon at Trumps, potage of spinach at the West Beach Cafe, cheese and berries at Michael's, and French pastries at l'Ermitage. The chefs still talk about it: "A *rat* at Trumps . . . !" The last and best part Tatti had in my performances was in "Traps," a piece about the Bomb. At the end, after an hour of raving and ranting about our human insanities, I brought Tatti out from under a table, saying ". . . as long as there still are sources of affection and tenderness in this world, we are not to give up the day." And I walked with Tatti around the stage, picking imaginary berries and feeding them to him, while a beautiful Chopin étude played and large slides of my hands grooming Tatti were projected on the back wall. Tatti had great stage presence. He loved posing for photographers and video. He loved being in the limelight and never hid or presented his backside. All the photos show him looking handsome and directly into the camera. In performance, he always knew where his light was.

Tatti and I toured "Traps" all over Canada, smuggling him on half a dozen airplanes.

The day he died I was to perform "Traps." I was despondent, but I wanted to honor Tatti. I played the piece up to the time I would have taken him out and, at that point, stopped the performance, explaining that Tatti had died and that I usually did the rest of the piece with him. I then walked around the stage as if with Tatti to the Chopin étude, weeping behind my mask.

Later, I sent an obituary to the *L.A. Weekly*. It was printed then and reprinted at the end of the year under the rubric, "We Couldn't Believe It When We Opened the Mail . . . BEST OBIT." It read:

This is beyond a doubt our favorite obituary of the year:
DIED: TATTI WATTLES THE RAT
WHEN: SATURDAY AUGUST 7, 1982
WHERE: AT HOME
HOW: HEART ATTACK
  TATTI WATTLES THE RAT was 2 1/2 years old and died of a heart attack at home. Famous throughout the art community, TATTI had participated in three performances by Rachel Rosenthal. He had toured Canada, was seen at openings around town, had hosted events and was mascot to Rosenthal's workshops and classes. TATTI escaped the fate of laboratory rats and became a person.

I asked people to send me their reminiscences of Tatti. And I had a service and burial for him—an elaborate ceremony with a few of my best friends attending—chanting, drumming, and creating a very beautiful spiritual circle. Tatti was buried under a big tree with a pink quartz headstone in a beautiful garden.

Shortly after his death, I attended a workshop on shamanic practice. I felt terribly sad and lonesome without Tatti. I simply couldn't seem to get over his death. In the process we were taught for the purpose of discovering our Power Animal, I went on a "journey" in the Lower World, and there I had a reunion with a huge Tatti, as large as I. It was warm and tearful and made me feel that he was close. But the shaman who led the workshop said that Tatti was a specific soul and didn't qualify as a Power Animal because they must be generic: "Coyote," "Eagle," "Bear," and so on. So, I had to go back and search again. The second time, Tatti came back over a hill. As I was going to tell him that I needed to find a true Power Animal, Tatti motioned, and over the hill came a multitude of rats, hundreds and hundreds of them, and soon Tatti melted in their midst until I couldn't single him out any more. He had become generic

like the others. So "Rats" were my Power Animal(s)! They helped me, healed me, comforted and protected me, took no nonsense and gave me joy. Funny Power Animals, they helped me develop irony and humor in my work.

As I continued my shamanic practice, the Rats took me on wondrous adventures. These were deeply healing and I learned a great deal about myself along the way. I began to draw again after many years, recording my experiences. Many years later, I realized that, through this marvelous process, my lifelong anxieties and self-doubts had been lifted. I can't pinpoint the exact moment but I gratefully date it from my activities in the Spirit World.

There are so many memorable moments: Tatti fearlessly backing Mackenzie the black cat off into a cushion and then calmly nibbling on salad with Mackenzie curled up next to him in his cage; Tatti refusing to hide in my pocket for one of the airplane trips, with me diving in and out of the bathroom so many times that an airport guard got suspicious; Tatti dating a girl rat called Riff and proving that his first monicker, "Homer, the Homosexual Rat," was a lie. Riff wasn't quite ready for full-blown sex, but they did a lot of simulation and some spectacular dancing. Tatti was a person, as I said. Every human and animal is a "person" to me, just as even trees and stones are "people" too, embodying a unique spirit.

Spirit, soul, consciousness, and miracle reside in everything. Animals teach us about life and death, if we let them. And in between, about love, hate, tenderness, anger, pain, ruthlessness, loyalty, friendship, craftiness, resignation—every possible feeling with infinite shades and tones. To love an animal truly is to truly love, with no expectation other than to delight in that love. To see and believe that is simple, and yet it is the most radical worldview. Tatti Wattles, a little black Norwegian rat with good karma was here to prove it.

OTHER SENSES

LAVENDER DOWER

I have been involved with the healing of animals by means of Radionic Therapy for the best part of fifty years and have come to appreciate their cooperation and understanding. They are much more satisfactory patients than humans. In many cases I feel they know a good deal more than I do, both about themselves and the world around them. They see things that I cannot see, such as devas and fairies. They retain memory of past incarnations and attachment to human and animal personalities. They live in the two worlds with ease and without question.

I have always been a cat person, but I inherited two small schnauzer bitches when a friend died, and this was my first close relationship with dogs. Tessa, the elder of the two, adopted me as her pet, her charge, and her responsibility. She followed me like a shadow, and I was forever falling over her. If I left the house, she would sit at the window and wait for my return and greet me rapturously when I got back, whether I had been absent for an hour or a week. Sometimes, she would throw back her head and howl like a banshee when I left, which was not too popular in my household.

One day when I took her for a walk across the fields, she suddenly sat down, staring at a tree stump, rigid and shaking with fear, and I, who could see nothing amiss, had quite a job to reassure her and get her home. I am fortunate in having a gifted friend who can communicate with animals, and I asked her to question Tessa as to what she had seen that gave her such a fright. Tessa was reluctant to say, as she said it would upset me, but eventually, after much persuasion, she explained that it was a man who smelt horrible and was hanging in the tree. So she saw not only the tree, which had long been cut down, and the man

hanging in it but also the smell of rotting flesh. I discovered later that in the old days, the Gloucestershire boundaries extended to take in this field and that criminals condemned at the Gloucester Assizes were, indeed, hanged on that tree. When Tessa became sad and senile and was no longer able to enjoy life, I let her go gently and surrounded with love. Her first owner came for her, and Tessa was seen to spring out of her body into the arms of Liz, who had bought her as a pup. Since then they have been seen together walking in the garden.

The other little dog, Tina, was a totally different character. Rather aloof and apt to do her own thing, very much in love with the husband of my gifted friend, with a recollection of having belonged to him in a previous incarnation in the form of a wolfhound. However much her stature had diminished, her love was just as great, and she strongly objected to any show of affection between her erstwhile master and his present wife, of whom she was extremely jealous, wanting the whole of his attention all the time.

When Tessa had gone, Tina's attitude toward me underwent a complete change. She took on Tessa's duties and adopted me as her sole responsibility. She didn't seem to miss Tessa. They had never been close, but she never left my side and was fussy about my well-being, constantly telling my gifted friend that I was not well and would she please do something about it.

She had a love/hate partnership with my Siamese cats. Basil would tease her unmercifully and bounce out at her to prevent her coming into the house. He has a lively sense of humor; she had none. She took life very seriously. Sadly, the day came when I had to say good-bye to her, too. She was thirteen years old, suffered from a bad heart, and the intense summer heat was too much for her. Her only reluctance to going was worry over how I could survive without her care. In dog years, she was ninety-one, but as I was only in my eighty-eighth year and still had work to do, we told her that she could still look after me from another level, which, indeed, she still does, and I often see her about the house. Liz didn't come for her, but her place was taken by a rough-haired terrier, which I did not know, who greeted her like an old friend and took her away, out of the garden but not out of our lives.

I have dealt with all kinds of animals during the course of my practice, including a lion called Boy, who was one of the Adamson pride. He had been seriously injured by a buffalo, unable to hunt or defend himself, doomed to a miserable end, dying out in the bush. George Adamson stayed beside the lion all night to comfort and protect him, and next morning, my friends Tony and Sue Harthoorn, both vets, flew out to see what could be done for him. Having decided to operate, Boy was sedated and maneuvered into the back of a Land Rover and taken to Joy Adamson's camp where a three-and-one-half-hour operation was performed and a thirteen-inch steel pin hammered along the hollow of the broken humerus bone.

The plan was to fly Boy to Joy's house in Nyvasha, where he could be nursed back to health, and after an adventurous flight over the Aberdare Mountains, necessitating a climb to twelve thousand feet, which nearly proved fatal, this was achieved. Sue sent me a tuft of hair from the patient, and I put him on Radionic treatment, which works at any range using a witness, such as hair or blood. The shoulder had refused to heal and the Harthoorns had to perform another five-hour operation, after which he made steady improvement and eventually a complete recovery.

There was, however, a shadow on the horizon. A young Meru called Stanley was engaged to look after Boy. He apparently had treated him without respect when he was weak and helpless, and the lion showed his resentment by growling and following him with his eyes in a menacing fashion. After his release into the wild, Boy became unreliable and took to nipping both Joy and Stanley and other workers when he came to visit the camp. This ended in tragedy, as Boy's resentment of Stanley proved too much. One day he took more than a nip and killed him. George, whose favorite lion he had been, regretfully had to shoot him.

The relationship between human and wild animals is a vexed question. I suppose all animals start as wild ones, but by domestication over a long period, trust and understanding is established, and the two species become interdependent. The truly wild animal has other values, and one cannot blame them for reverting to these when under stress. Man has always tended to use animals rather than to establish a partnership. To a large extent we are dependent on them, rather than they on us, and they

deserve to be treated with respect and gratitude rather than as possessions or tools to an end.

Nature has her own laws, and many of these seem to us to be cruel and ruthless, but I believe that animals are more philosophical than we are. They accept death as a fact; they will fight to the death to protect their young, but they will let them go when they are fit to look after themselves. Indeed, in many cases, they will insist upon this by driving them away.

We have found that animals living in groups appear to have a group spirit, which can be treated by a single witness from any one of them, and we have been able to treat a whole herd of cattle for such things as foot-and-mouth disease or contagious abortion by using Radionic treatment on one hair, whereas a dog or cat is an individual with a unique personality and spirit. Watch a flock of starlings coming into roost, flying across the sky as one, wheeling altogether instantly with perfect timing, controlled by something outside themselves, and you will see what I mean.

For some years now I have accepted only horses as patients. This was originally because I wished to limit my practice in order to have more time for another project. But fate decreed otherwise, and my practice at that time was some fifty individuals. It has steadily doubled and trebled and now averages some four hundred horses on daily treatment.

Making a Radionic analysis is something like solving a whodunnit. The object is to find the root cause of the problem afflicting the horse, be it physical or psychological. Sometimes, these are obscure and unexpected. I had one horse who had a persistent and violent cough, who lowered his head and stamped violently as though he were choking. All the normal veterinary treatment failed to effect a cure. An exhaustive analysis showed self-pity to be the basic factor, and one Radionic treatment served to bring things back to normal. It was his way of showing that he was not receiving the care and attention that he thought he deserved, and this having been recognized and dealt with, he stopped demonstrating.

Horses are sensitive beings, and many of their problems come from their owners, either from thoughtless treatment or from care. A nervous rider reacts instantly on his mount, and his lack of confidence communi-

cates equally effectively. Many racehorses live dull existences with the same daily routine of exercise on the gallops and long periods shut up in their boxes with nothing to do. This may result in cribbing, weaving, or box walking, and one well-known horse therapist gives her horses toys to play with, which alleviates boredom and prevents the development of bad habits.

Some understanding trainers encourage their horses to form relationships with other animals. I know one nervous mare who was only happy when she had a rabbit in the box with her. This presented problems when the rabbit, which came and went, as it would, gave birth to a largish litter. I had a chaser who had an undying attachment to a donkey and could hardly be persuaded to leave, even when going to the races. Some horses take their companions with them when they go racing, and it is not unusual to see a sheep or a goat in the car park with the horse boxes.

Although I spend my days sitting at my desk working out my analyses, surrounded by Radionic instruments and Siamese cats, I seem to build up an automatic rapport with the patients. I seldom meet them, but on the rare occasions when I do, it is as though I am treated as a friend of long standing, often to the astonishment of the owner, who remarks that their horse never behaves that way with a stranger. On one occasion I was called by the owner of a horse that had thrown its rider in the ring and was uncatchable after over an hour's effort. After five minutes standing outside the rails, I walked over to the horse and picked up the reins—to everyone's surprise, including my own.

Horses seem to have a highly developed gift of telepathy, which largely eludes us. I have seen my animals communicate with each other in complete silence, and my dogs could never understand my stupidity in not getting what they were telling me except in the most obvious way pertaining to food and walks, which any fool could understand. Much cleverer than me, my animals. Although they have their own language and means of communication, they learn words in any language, and *walk*, spoken softly, casually and without expression, is instantly understood. My cats know the word *rabbit*, which brings an immediate reaction, whereas *chicken*, for which they do not really care, brings no response at all.

If I pick up a dead rabbit on the road, I bring it home, and Basil will be waiting by the garage, just in case. If I tell him that I have a rabbit, he will go and sit on the garden wall, waiting for me to throw it into the field in the place I call his "dining room." This sets off a ritual that I do not fully understand. He will sit on the wall and shout at the top of his voice for about half a minute before getting to work on the rabbit. I don't know if he is saying "thank you very much" or "this is my rabbit and nobody else's." Twiggy, who is his niece, is very small and quite a different character. She is extremely timid and desperately shy of strangers or any sudden movement or noise and prefers to hunt for her own food. On one memorable occasion, she climbed the wisteria and came into my bedroom carrying a partridge almost as big as herself. This is an unusual way in which to be woken, but as I leapt out of bed and ejected Basil and the dogs from the room, she released the bird, which appeared to be quite undamaged.

Having got its captor out of the room and seeing no future in chasing a disturbed partridge under the bed, I dressed and went down to the kitchen. After breakfast, surrounded by disgruntled animals, who had been looking forward to a lively session and subsequent feast, I returned to my room armed with a landing net, prepared for a lively chase myself. To my surprise, I found the partridge sitting quite casually on my bed, apparently unperturbed and waiting to be rescued. I netted it without trouble, gave it some of Dr. Bach's Rescue Remedy as an antidote to shock, released it back in the meadow, where it flew off as though nothing had happened to disturb its daily routine. I don't know about birds, but if an equivalent trauma had happened to a horse, I feel the reaction would have been quite different.

Horses have a memory center in the spinal cord that retains recollections of instance and emotions, which can affect their entire personality, and, like the elephant, the horse never forgets.

RESTORING THE
ANCIENT ALLIANCE

PENELOPE SMITH

When my husband and I are walking with our llamas or Afghan hounds, people ask, "Are they intelligent?" What do they mean by this question? A few possible connotations are: how do these animals compare in behavior and responses to humans; how much are they like humans; how receptive are they to human training or how obedient to human commands?

The questioners have accepted the model of animals as biological and intellectual inferiors. They distance themselves from animals, looking at them as objects of interest but certainly not regarding them as fellow intelligent beings. They assume that the animals understand nothing or little of the world around them, at least not in the "meaningful, intelligent" way of humans.

They also assume that animals do not understand at all what is being conceptualized or communicated in human conversations. Would they question me about my husband's intelligence in his presence?

Even many people who truly care for animals unconsciously exhibit condescending behavior with members of other species. Inhibited by social blinders, they don't perceive the awareness and intelligence that are present in each being of whatever species unless they outwardly match or at least mimic human expression.

Most investigations into interspecies communication are still mainly concerned with communication with animals indirectly, getting them to learn our symbols and communicate in human language or respond to our cues. However, there is a growing realization, an awakening cultural

awareness, that we all are linked—physically, mentally, and spiritually. This link includes the possibility of direct communication with other species, beyond the constraints of biology, through exchange of thoughts, emotions, mental images, and feelings.

In this profound exchange, we can discover the rich depths of communion and wisdom possible in relationships with our animal brothers and sisters. Humans who get lost in their own mental complexity forget their deeper spiritual nature. Alienated from or "superior" to their fellow species, they become mentally, emotionally, and spiritually disturbed, and this agitation can have devastating consequences for the biosphere.

Members of other species are able to help humans from going "astray." As native peoples throughout the millennia have known, humans must honor the bond with other species to stay in harmony and balance. By learning to relate to animals as partners in life on earth, humans can become conscious, joyful, integrated members of our planetary whole. It is possible that our damage to the planet's ecosystem and our lopsided relationship with the rest of nature, caused by human ideas of separation, dominance, and superiority, might be largely resolved through interspecies respect and understanding.

In my experience of telepathically communicating with animals all of my life and doing interspecies counseling and healing since 1971 with many thousands of animals (human and nonhuman), I have been impressed countless times by the intelligence, wisdom, kindness, patience, and loving understanding of animals in relation to people.

They have exhibited qualities that our society usually extends only to humans, such as sincerity, trust, love, devotion, appreciation, loyalty, empathy, kindness, honor, honesty, patience, integrity, humility, joy, unselfishness, wisdom. In telepathic consultations, over and over again, animals demonstrate their ability to communicate, to understand, and to make decisions by observable, positive changes in their behavior. They ordinarily cooperate generously when their viewpoints are understood by the humans involved.

Contrary to the doctrines of some biologists, I have experienced that animals are not only aware of themselves but of others of their own and

different species as well as the state of their environment, even planet-wide. Let me share a few stories.

Coco, a Tucumán parrot, lived with two other parrots of the same species, four cockatiels, and one human in an apartment in Helsinki, Finland. Their guardian, Eva, had rescued the parrots from abusive situations, and they flew freely together in her apartment.

The birds fought with each other sometimes, especially when Eva left, and I was asked to consult with them. The two younger parrots communicated to me their varying thoughts about their life together and the cause of their disputes. Acting on their information, with some changes in management and Eva communicating with them in a more comprehensive way, the problems were resolved fairly easily.

Coco was a quiet bird. Eva had found her in horrible shape in a pet store, where she had spent many miserable years. Eva wondered if Coco was completely blind, as she flew in circles and bumped into things. I experienced Coco's vision as a white field, with no shadows or shapes. It appeared that she was totally blind.

During our consultation, Coco sat silently on her perch a few feet from me, facing in the opposite direction. I began to ask Coco about her life, and as I translated her answers to verbal language for Eva, Coco flashed her head in my direction in startled amazement. She blurted the thoughts, "Who are you? You couldn't be a human. You listen and understand. You must be a bird. What are you?!"

I explained to her that I was a human who could communicate with animals telepathically and that there were other humans who could listen and understand, too. She craned her head my way, dumbfounded. "This couldn't be," she exclaimed, "humans don't understand anything!"

Coco projected to me her thoughts, feelings, and mental images of how, as a young bird, she had high hopes for having a loving relationship with people but was constantly disappointed. Instead of the companionship she desired, she was mistreated, often isolated, and undernourished. After years of abuse, she gave up on humans and retreated into her own world devoid of physical sight. She had spent her thirty-one years (her own estimation of her age) in one place after another, including years in a pet shop, and now at Eva's.

While she recognized Eva's kindness and nurturing love toward her, she still often felt isolated and misunderstood. The other birds sometimes picked on her, and it made her feel unsafe when they flew around and she didn't know where they would land. We discussed having a safe space in a cage for her when Eva was gone, and Coco approved.

Coco continued to stretch her body toward me, erect and alert, as I demonstrated my understanding of what she thought and felt. She repeated how astounded she was that a human, a *human*, was able to communicate and understand like a bird. She almost cried with relief and strained to see me physically.

When I told her that I would be teaching a workshop while I was in Finland so that other people could learn how to telepathically communicate with animals, she was again amazed. I asked her if she wanted to attend to help teach Eva and the others. She was excited about assisting at the workshop and asked only that the people not touch her.

At the workshop, Coco sat contentedly in her Plexiglas carrying case, after being positioned near me, where she could experience what went on and help when people wanted to communicate with her. We did an exercise in which the participants were guided to softly focus on the animals in the room in order to perceive beyond physical gestures and experience energies, thoughts, and feelings. The room was filled with a tremendous peace, lightness of being, and attunement of all present with one another.

Suddenly, Coco started twirling wildly on the perch in her enclosure. Eva was alarmed at her parrot's unusual behavior and cried out to me. I gestured to Eva to be still and just observe. Coco continued to spin around in a circle for a short time.

After the exercise was completed, I asked Coco what happened. The ecstatic parrot told me that her heart leapt with joy that all these humans could be so full of peace, understanding, and oneness with other animals. Coco perceived that the room was full of intensely bright, white light. She proceeded to look around the room and then down in her box to nimbly pick out morsels of food. Coco could see!

I asked Eva to keep me apprised of how Coco fared. Eva could not detect if Coco could see better when she got home, but she noticed that

the pupil in one eye had more color. Coco demonstrated more confidence and radiated happiness.

While Coco's restoration of eyesight did not seem to be complete or permanent, this was not the most important outcome of her workshop experience. One parrot's renewed hope in humankind abides as a poignant lesson for us all. I don't regard other animals as being humans in furred or feathered clothing. They are themselves—individuals with different senses, forms of thinking, means of expressing themselves, and ways of seeing life. The joy comes when you connect spiritually and share each other's worlds. Then there is no need for categories and hierarchies that separate and lead to condescension or alienation. You celebrate the experience of differences and rejoice in the oneness of your essential spiritual nature. This opens the door for learning from one another, sharing wisdom, and growing together in harmony.

More than any other factor, your attitude toward animals influences how receptive you are to their communication and how willing they are to communicate with you.

Respect and revere animals as fellow beings—different in physical form from yourself but oft the same spiritual essence and potential. If you approach animals with condescension, thinking they are inferior in intelligence, awareness, or substandard in any way, you limit your ability to perceive and understand them as they truly are. As you increasingly see and treat them as fellow intelligent beings, you allow them to express themselves more deeply and fully to you, and your relationship develops, matures, elevates, and expands.

Focusing only on the biological aspect of an animal, while fascinating and wondrous in itself, inhibits true seeing of the spiritual essence and wisdom behind the physical form. Be humble and receptive, and allow animals to teach you.

My experience with Drew, a miniature donkey, was another deeply moving one. He had been rescued from an abusive situation and exhibited some very unusual behaviors: he fell over continually while biting at his legs; he piled all his hay in a corner of his stall; at times he would be trusting and other times run away from people; he often brayed in a harsh, tortured manner.

Drew lived in a small barn corral so that he could do minimum damage to himself and so that his people could take good care of him. He had a wonderful goat companion, who could escape under a bar when Drew got too rambunctious. Even though Drew behaved abnormally, he was affectionate with people and demonstrated his appreciation of their closeness and loving care.

When I met Drew, his eyes were heavily clouded under eyelids that appeared swollen. He gazed at me and got very quiet. As he began to communicate to me about his life and his pain, I could feel extreme spasms in his muscles and painful misalignments in his spine. His people were surprised that during the entire time we communicated, he never bit at his legs, which was his incessant peculiarity, but remained quietly focused with me.

Drew told me how, before being born as a donkey, he came to earth as a spirit from another dimension, wanting to bring love and light to people. Unfamiliar with humans and their behavior, he thought all people were good and would accept his gifts, so he didn't plan carefully his situation with people.

Drew was "owned" by men who were abusive. They wrestled with him in "sport" and routinely handled him roughly, wounding his body, mind, and heart. Drew couldn't understand these people and suffered enormously with them for years. He began biting at his legs when his extremities felt numb after the continual injury to his spine and entire body had cut off a healthy nerve flow. The little donkey learned to make a nest of hay to rest in, trying to comfort himself and ease the pain.

Drew and I worked together, counseling him through his traumas as I did spiritual healing. As the donkey reexperienced painful periods in his life, he let out blood-curdling sounds of deep agony that sent bone-deep chills through my body. With each loud scream, he released more of the pain and confusion. After a twenty-minute healing session, he stood up straighter, looked at me with eyes now sparkling and wide, and thanked me for understanding. We sighed and laughed together with relief.

Drew was such pure spirit—loving, kind, grateful. He had loved people so much and was not prepared for the dark side of humans and their spiritual alienation expressed as brutality for animals and themselves. He

expected people to be spirits like himself, and he had reeled in torment at their cruelty.

After our session, he told me he wanted to be with people and help them as he originally intended, bringing them love and light. He felt he should now be out in the front pasture to greet everyone. His eyes gleamed. I recommended gentle bodywork and possibly homeopathic treatment as a follow-up in a few weeks, after he had integrated the results of our healing session. Drew never acted strangely again. Months later, his people reported that he was trusting, balanced, and happy.

Our attitudes so influence how open we are to the communications from animals all around us. Animals are far more aware than most people assume. Wisdom teachers of other species walk among us daily, patiently watching for those who will reach out and understand. I relay this message from one of them:

It was a cool February night, and my husband and I had just come home. On our doorstep, facing the door, as if waiting to go in, was a tree frog in resplendent green. Picking him up gently, I intended to place him among the plants in the garden. He had other plans. Instead of jumping away, as I expected, he refused to leave my hand, crawling back on as I tried to coax him off.

Bringing him close to my face, I decided to find out why he wanted to stay. He calmly and clearly conveyed his warmth and appreciation of me. I felt an ancient kinship. He said that I should let people know, "We need clean water; we need pure air."

I knew he was speaking for all the earth's amphibians—frogs, salamanders, newts—whose vast numbers are noted to be shrinking at alarming rates worldwide. He wanted to spend a moment with me, feeling we must connect and his message be carried forward.

Now is the time to get back what we have lost, to reclaim the connection, to understand our fellow beings of other species. To regain our inborn understanding, the universal language of telepathic communication, we need to slow down, to be open, to wait, to watch, to love, to listen.

Getting in touch with animals heart-to-heart and mind-to-mind and learning from them is a path to wholeness, leading us to piece together

the giant puzzle of our infinite spiritual potential. We humans can recover the vast reservoir of healing power, wisdom, and love of life with all our relations, and enjoy mutual cooperation and harmony with all the beings of earth.

The animals are waiting, curious, and hopeful.

THE EYES OF THE WOLF

ERYN WOLFWALKER

In a time when the Earth Mother was younger by perhaps a hundred cycles of the seasons, there lived a small community of people in a land that marked humanity's farthest incursion into the North, where cold and snow reigned over the land for much of its journey through time. The village of this tribe rested between the shores of a great lake, which remained in frozen state for extended periods, and a mountainous, dark forest whose vastness could only be imagined. Like sentinels guarding an entry portal, a feathery stand of conifers held back the mighty forest from the edge of the water, and it was within these protective trees that the clanspeople made their home.

The deep forest was habitat for many game animals, large and small, yet the tribe did not develop much of a relationship with the woods, preferring to cast about on the waters of the lake for their sustenance. The forest offered little in the way of comfort to the people, as its sheer immensity and depth was beyond the people's understanding. The woods seemed to be an entity in itself, and as a self, was shrouded in mystery and things unknown. And so the tribe had remained dependent upon the lake for the many things it provided, and most ventured into the woods out of necessity alone.

Most, but not all, for there was one young boy from the village of fisher people who was inextricably drawn to the forest; some wild thing of the ancient woods called out, beckoning to a most carefully guarded place within his heart and his soul. It had been so since he had been a very small child, held to an existence near the lake's shoreline by the same stories of dread and trepidation that girdled his people to the relative safety of the waters.

The forest, which was now summoning him with a greater demand than ever before in his short life, had become the embodiment of fear, the representation of the darkest nighttime dreams for his tribe. Despite this awareness, or possibly because of it, the youth chose to break with the ways of his father, and his father's father before him, and leaving the security of the village, he entered the woods in search of the thing that called to him.

He steeled himself to risk traveling beyond the point within the woods where he could make out the shapes of the tribal lodges between the thick, dark tree trunks. Drawn by an inner calling, though, he ventured far deeper into the trees than even the sounds of the village had carried. And in this place, far from the comfort of the community and others like him, the boy came upon the Wolf and in this first, unexpected meeting felt a welling up of a very special thing within his heart and within his soul.

The animal was large in comparison to the slight stature of the boy, but this did not disturb the youth, and he did not turn away and flee from this meeting as other members of his tribe might have. He actually felt a completeness, some sort of acceptance rising up from within him, and in some way, he knew the encounter had not been by chance. He'd come to the place where his heart and soul had wished him to be, and in that instant he realized the inner calling had vanished. He was now left without guidance or direction to make what he would of the moment.

The animal had been standing in a small copse of trees, so much thicket behind as to render him nearly invisible. His bearing was dignified, well-defined, impatient almost, as though the boy's arrival had been anticipated, and late!

The great beast's body was covered in medium-length black hair, overcasted to a sable tone by the silver that marked the hair-shaft tips. The sun, filtering through the treetops, reached the forest floor where the Wolf stood as a statue, waiting. The almost ethereal light touched the animal's head, highlighting the yellow-gold of his round, intelligent eyes. He blinked slowly once, his canine muzzle relaxed in an almost mirthful expression. His breathing released a cloud of white/gray vapor that wafted about his glorious head before vanishing into the chill afternoon air.

The youth was held motionless, transfixed by the liquid, golden orbs set within the high brow of the Wolf. Engaged by the animal's stare, the boy was compelled to remain still, almost breathless. The Wolf moved forward with a measured step, closing the distance between himself and the human by no more than what would have been for him a full running stride. He settled abruptly onto his haunches, as if demanding full attention from the boy. He blinked his extraordinary eyes again, then once more, in a deliberate manner that gave the movement significance. A thought forked its way into the boy's consciousness with the force and suddenness of a lightning strike, plucking the breath from his chest.

"Your heart is home!"

The Wolf waited a moment, the space of a heartbeat, no more, as if to be certain his message had been received. He turned his grand head back over his shoulder, regarding the place in the woods he had emerged from, and without making a sound, followed his gaze with sable body and was gone.

The young boy stood alone in the woods, hands held over heart, as much to keep the organ from leaping from his chest in pursuit of the animal as to quiet its frantic pounding. His breath would be lost for long moments, this he knew. He noted the gentle movement of the branches before him, marking the path the Wolf had taken. Heart held firmly beneath his small hands, and with only a minute's hesitation, the boy rushed beneath the branches and into the deep forest.

This was not to be the end of the youth, nor the turning away from family and home. Rather, in choosing to follow the Wolf, he became something of a dichotomy, existing in the natural world of the Wolf pack, while a part of him abided in the ways of tribe and family, mankind.

As time moved on, he found a comfort with the Wolf aspect of his divided existence. The pack, which had opened its ranks and social system to accept him, had provided for him as they would have for a natural-born member, for this is how they viewed him. His form was that of a man, yet his energy, heart, and soul were that of Wolf—this the pack was quite certain of. And so his acceptance.

He was educated by them to the way of the woods; they comforted and companioned him. He lay with them upon the sunny rock outcroppings that hung in the sky above the dark green forest. At the rising of the

moon, he joined in their soulful chorus, though his very human voice was painfully out of tune. This the pack learned to endure! And each night, the pack led him to the site of the first encounter so that he could find his way back to his people by the lake.

As he remained for increasingly long periods with his canine family, he became acutely aware of a growing discomfort within his human social group. He was becoming more Wolf-like, this he recognized. Their song pounded through his veins like wild horses. The essence of the Wolf that he carried within his heart throbbed so loudly, he marveled that no two-leggeds could hear it. He became impatient and intolerant of the people he shared the human portion of his life with. He began to think only of the woods and the reality that was decidedly Wolf, not human or something in between.

The village elders wagged their heads and tongues about this strange member of the clan:

"He's more wolf than boy!"

"His eyes are not like those of the family!"

"He carries the mark of the wolf across his face!"

"His relationship with the forest is not natural!"

"He is not one of us!"

The boy's need for the pack and the woods grew, as did his awareness of the dark things that the clanspeople were feeling and saying about him. This made the already difficult task of returning to civilization daily almost unbearable for him.

The season heralded by the spreading of ice fingers across the surface of the lake and the changing hues in the leaves of the few deciduous trees surrounding the lodges was well upon the village. Clanspeople bustled about preparing the dwellings and food stores for the cold time. The nights had begun their deepening into the frigid temperatures that seemingly would deepen their darkness as well. An impossibly large moon, white beyond silver, sailed above the treetops on its way to its perch in the night sky. Below the brilliant giant, a strand of ghostly gray figures slipped silently through the woods to a spot in the forest where the undulating light from the village fires could be seen.

The boy had been pelting through the woods to this point, but now he halted abruptly. Through the trees, he could easily discern the glow from the warming fires of his people, could taste the smoky air, could almost make out what the many voices were saying as the tribe moved about the fires. Where he stood, all about him were wolves of various sizes and shapes, panting companionably after the long run through the woods. Their breath, puffs of light mist, rose into the night air in an aura of vapor. He could taste the muskiness of this family of his, could feel the warmth their bodies gave off as they milled about him. He had determined to re-enter the village this night, to join with his own kind, to be a part of the circle of humans.

As he stood in the circle of wolves, those members of his family of four-leggeds, he found his heart pulling at him, drawing him toward the deep forest and the great white giant rising overhead. He settled onto his haunches on the cold ground, lest he be pulled in either direction unwillingly. His breathing had slowed and had matched that of the wolves. His yellow-green, not-so-human eyes blinked slowly, once, twice. He looked over his shoulder to the path they had taken from the dark woods and, in a moment, no more than a heartbeat or two, had turned from the company of his own kind and disappeared into the forest with those of his heart and soul.

A *National Geographic* documentary on wolves, which aired in the fall of 1964, acted as a trigger for me, activating or igniting a component of myself that I can only guess was an imprint from many lifetimes ago. After viewing the piece, wolves spontaneously became an obsession. I surrounded myself with any and all wolf paraphernalia, from books and statues to jewelry and posters. This was no easy task, as the animal was far less popular then than he is today.

With the assistance of a parent, I crafted a letter to our president, decrying the shameful way the wolf had been treated in this land, as its numbers were reduced almost to the point of extinction. A sincere and serious letter, at least to my seven-year-old mind. Someone at the Department of Interior had the grace to answer my letter. Overnight, I had become a very important seven-year-old, ready to single-handedly

stop the war being waged upon the wolf. At that time, I knew nothing about politics, hunters, bureaucracy, red tape, and the like.

As I grew slightly older and realized how large the wolf issue was, I became a victim of inertia, suffering from an apparent loss of enthusiasm. Without losing my love for the animal, I retreated into the safety of a more normal childhood and surrounded myself with dogs, cats, and horses. I still went off into the woods by myself often, however, and sat at the base of some ancient, wild-looking trees, calling the wolves in to me. I was reasonably sure that in all the forests in Connecticut, there had to be at least one wolf left, and reading my need and sincerity, he would come to me, relieving the ache in my heart.

Though I was aware of how my obsession with wolves made me feel and could isolate the areas of my body involved in the longing to be among the wolves, I had no idea where it had come from. Any glimpse I was given into possible scenarios involving the wolf in my past was due to my overactive and highly developed imagination, or so I was told. Though my obsession became more acute as I aged into my teens, I was relatively sure that I would not live to actually grow up, expiring from a broken heart, which belonged, part and parcel, to the wolf alone.

I had longed for a tangible physical reality among the canids but was disinterested in the conventional or accepted methods of reaching that end. A career in zoo management left me cold; I found most of them to be depressing. The Forest Service avenue was too scientific; I was searching for the Wildness of the animal, its spirit. I could not imagine performing the mechanical routines of tranquilizing, weighing, and tagging or collaring a specimen, while being completely overcome by the sheer magnitude of the animal's presence, his aura, his essence! In some ways I felt I would be doing the species a disservice.

The taking apart of the animals to better understand them trivializes the importance of the *who* that is contained within the wrapper we're wrapped up in studying. I realized finally that I was searching for a career that would allow me my need to commune with the wild canids, provide a safe environment for a spiritual experience and exploration among them, and at the same time, provide the means to support myself financially. The dream job that did not appear to exist.

My path to connecting with the wolves seemed to have ended before it really got started, and bowing to pressure to make a way for myself in a real life, I filed my obsession away in the back of my mind and set off on a rambling course, attempting to assign meaning to a life devoid of wolves.

I made my way through the next twenty years as a student of the horse, primarily as a farrier and then as a bodyworker and trainer. Somehow along the way they managed to teach me quite a lot about myself: spirituality, communication, and purpose. From the rigid confines of farrier science, I made numerous forays into other animal-related fields, from the conventional to the holistic, never really finding an answer to the question of why I constantly carried with me a need to connect with the wolf.

While living in the Vermont farmlands, I attended a lecture and slide presentation by a young explorer who had just taken a solitary "walk" across the length of the Brooks Range in the Northwest Territories. I was hoping he'd managed to capture a wolf or two on film. His presentation was spellbinding. When he began to describe an encounter he'd had with a large masculine wolf across his campfire on a particularly magical night, I found myself sitting bolt upright in my seat, almost standing, as the realization that I had just been struck in my head and chest by a very real force came over me.

He had spoken a word or two, possibly an entire phrase, describing the look in the eyes of the wolf as he'd sat, unmoving and unblinking, just outside the circle of the fire. I don't remember the exact words he had used at the time to define his experience. I do recall the feeling of having the breath suddenly taken from me and the sensation of not quite being able to draw in another breath to replace the one I'd lost.

My face and hands were wet with tears, though I was not at the time aware of crying. My head and heart felt as though they had been levered open, like torn fabric that could not be mended. For some reason, I was unable to stop the tears and the rush of emotion that was pouring through me. I briefly worried that I was losing control of my mind when I realized that I knew every intimate detail of the movement within the soul while staring into the yellow eyes of the wolf. I was certain that I

had experienced it, or at least some part of me that contained memory had! I was also relatively sure that it had not been during this lifetime, not with the kinds of pictures I was getting about the blessed event. I had experienced a soul connection through the very act of facing the wolf, complete and fearless, secure in who I thought I was. And here, possibly lifetimes later, I had been trying to discover the origin and purpose of the Wolf thread that had been woven into my life or lives; that persistent, just-beneath-the-surface piece of the puzzle that would not let itself be found but not forgotten either.

Information was coming through rapidly, almost too quickly for me to assimilate. I had known the Wolf, not in the laboratory or scientific sense but in a deeper, more spiritual way—and also in the way I most longed to act in this lifetime, in the physical. I knew all of the truly important, relevant things: how the animal was put together, every detail of the body of the Wolf, from the moist dark tissue of the nose to the curl and turn of the tail. I knew their expressions and was conversant in their language. I was familiar with their smell, even the taste of them! There was no end to what I had experienced with and about them. I had an understanding of their nature, not of information compiled through months or years of research, of measurable, notable things, but of those aspects of the individual revealed through a melding of separate essences into the awareness of simply One. This was possible through the acceptance of the nonseparation between mankind and wolfkind.

I remembered the unknowable things I could not have learned in my current expression in form. I had a picture of myself, as an individual who was not myself, doing those things with the Wolves that I had always longed for. That self was united with Wolf and all the wonderful, magical experiences contained within that name, that expression of being. It occurred to me then that this other aspect of myself had already lived the life I had been longing for, that of companion to the Wolf. That road had already been walked before me, by me.

The path left before me, that held to the thread of the Wolf, had to be one of spiritual union with the vital principle of this great animal. My lessons this time around would come from the Master Teacher of the Natural Kingdom.

I can accept the fact that I will not be sharing my physical existence in relationship with the wildness of Wolves; I have already been there. I now rush forward to share in their essence. As a teacher myself, being led by teachers, I see the gift of the Wolf's message as a breaking down or casting off of the walls that separate humanity and the world of Nature. They teach of the world of possibility, of imagination, where not all things spoken of by small children come from misdirected minds but from an innocent and untainted understanding of the concepts of reality. The Wolves instruct in the most gentle, subtle fashion, leading humanity to a place of quiet dignity, integrity, resilience, and self-motivation. This particular world is of my making, and here the Wolf is ever present. He holds the key to a complete knowingness beyond the intellect, and I can feel that it is within reach.

Removed from the physical contact with Wolves, I have for many years shared my life with dogs of Wolf parentage. Their unusual intelligence and depth of emotion has been a constant reminder of the higher nature of the Wolf clan, and I acknowledge that I owe much of the richness of my life to their "tutelage."

I run through the conifer forests near our home with Wolflings all about me, united in our response to the song of the Wolf, as Wolf energy pounds through my veins once more, like so many wild horses. I stand with the hybrids at each side, and as our breath becomes synchronized, I feel the oneness possible between Nature and Man. Blue eyes blink slowly, once, twice, and I turn behind me in my mind, looking back to where I've come from. And this time, with the Wolf, the yellow-eyed giant who has carried for me a piece of my soul for all time, I chose the path that leads back to the company of my own kind and know that my heart is once more home.

OTHER ANGELS:
ONE WOMAN'S BIBLE

SUSAN CHERNAK McELROY

It came to me in that twilight between waking and sleeping, a bold, ice-water clear idea, that I would write a book about the healing, life-transforming relationships possible between people and animals. A title even visited the dream: *Other Angels: Animals Teaching and Healing.*

I was four years past my last cancer treatments, past the first laps of an inner reconstruction of my self that went hand in glove with the intense physical transformation brought on by surgeons' knives and radiation machines. That I was still alive made me somewhat a miracle. At work I was a "tremendous example of courage and positive attitude" to my co-workers, a "true inspiration, a miracle." I certainly didn't feel heroic.

The next day I wrote an article that, in my heart, placed credit where true credit was due: I wrote about my dog, Keesha, who had died of a cancerous tumor in her mouth a full six years before a similar growth was discovered in mine. That I was still alive was, I knew, in great part due to the lessons about healing and courage I learned from my old dog.

I wrote my tribute to Keesha in private, spilling tears on the page, sharing the draft with few people. Stricken with shame that I would relate so strongly to a dog and would most likely canonize her if the option were available, I believed myself to be totally alone in my feelings. When I was very young, my mother had told me I'd outgrow it—my "craziness" over animals—and as the years passed, I always thought my enthusiasm about animals was a profound indicator of my lack of maturity.

Looking for acceptance in all the wrong places, I decided to share my Keesha story with my lover, a scientist, who read it in stony silence and afterward said, "This is very sad . . . So very sad that your esteem is so low you aspire only to the success level of a dog . . . a dog." I snatched the article from him in tears and anger, knowing that I'd proudly call myself a hero if the day ever came that I could embrace life with even a sliver of the grace and courage of a dog, of Keesha.

Two years later, I sold "The Angel Who Fetched" to a national dog magazine—two years during which I pressed on with my goal to make my outer life look more like my most genuine inner life, whatever that was. Previously, like a tiny, feathery barnacle, I'd attached myself to whatever, whosesoever, ship was passing by at any given decade of my life. For thirty-six years, I'd dedicated myself to this seemingly mindless, salty drifting, putting up tentative feelers and inadvertently stumbling across sharp flashes of insight that I would quickly dismiss. Gathering, even defining, a genuine life for myself out of the old was the task of my lifetime.

Sifting through my years, searching for pieces that were "true," I heard certain ones call to me. Not loudly at first. Not loudly for a long time, but with a steady, enduring drone.

First, I acknowledged my deep need to live in places that were green, clean, and peopled with birds and squirrels and the reckless, ceaseless chatter of nature. I'd been told for decades that such luxuries as choosing where one wants to live are frivolous. The job, I was told, dictates where and how you are going to exist. This time, though, I stepped off the edge of my own small abyss and moved north, away from family and friends, away from burnt brown hillsides, oily waters, and invisible, smog-enshrouded horizons. I moved to a place of ferns, mossy beaches, and thick, silver rivers. A women's group became my new family. We met with the commitment that we were together to move our lives forward into the land of dreams. In the company of the women, I first shared my twilight dream about a book that would be called *Other Angels*.

Other barely translatable urgings told me I needed a partner, and within a year, I had found and married my life's true companion. "The Angel Who Fetched" was printed a month after our wedding, and letters

began pouring in to me. These were heartfelt tributes to hundreds of "other angels," to animal companions as heroes, mentors, babysitters, "sisters," healers.

In the midst of the wave of letters, we packed up and moved. In honor of the letters, the new move, and the joyful publication of my first article, I brought home the first dog I'd had since Keesha died, a puppy I named "Arrow." The first home I have ever called my own became ours in late winter, and the day we arrived, the mailbox welcomed me with still more letters in tribute to more "angel" animals. Unsure of how to handle the flood of intense words, I hurriedly stuffed them away in a box and hid them under my desk.

That spring, my genuine life, my soul work, began in spite of me. We had moved to a tiny house surrounded by an acre of land. Out back in a field of weeds sat a empty barn, an ancient red structure made of antique wood painstakingly gleaned from an old, crumbled homestead. The loft was quiet, holding nothing but empty air, dust, cobwebs, and old wasp nests. I loved our house, our beautiful green land with its sentinel hemlock and thick umbrellas of Douglas fir, but I loved the barn most. I knew instinctively that it was a place of holy ground, hallowed and consecrated by the spirits of hundreds of animals, animals come and gone, animals who had been born and who had died there on the packed, sacred earth. The barn was a spiritual nation in itself, a church, calling quietly for its own. And so I listened to the gentle, imploring call. I began filling its empty spaces as quickly as my pocketbook and my perplexed husband would allow. First came the family of chickens raised from day-old balls of red and yellow fuzz. Then the cats. Then miniature donkeys, the Zen masters of the animal world, whose sweet voices added to the chicken chorus, filling the rafters with a glorious and inimitable barn symphony. The geese came and added an alto honking section. Phaedra, a frail and sorry-looking llama, turned the carport into an extension of the barn, creating even more holy ground, adding her soft, patient hum to the choir. We got a canary, a cockatoo, another cat. Our kingdom grew.

The nation of animals assembled swiftly in our barn, and letters kept filling my mailbox. As though awakening from yet another dream, I felt

a slow, steady rhythm in my life begin to gather momentum and force. The years of animal work I had dabbled in and then left behind: vet assistance, dog training, horse grooming, kennel work, zoo work, wildlife rehab, humane work—all pieces that had the rough, jagged edges of dreams not pursued—pushed up into my face with honks and clucks and barks and cat cries. The disjointed pieces seemed somehow to knit into a tight and enduring fabric as our farm bloomed into a place of tribes, of families, of cultures and mysterious histories.

Relaxing into the joys and wonders of my first "home," the near-silent whispering to which I had dedicated myself developed a distinct sound. A loud one. An animal sound. In the celestial trumpeting of that indescribable animal music, I had my "moment." Not a moment of new insight, but rather a clean, pure instant of blessed recognition. Simply, undeniably, my life was/is about animals. On that much, I was clear. Animals had been the enduring, connective thread as I barnacled my way through the years, never without an animal companion, never without a keen desire to share my space, my thoughts, my times with them. To me, they were my fondest memories of "home."

That summer I unburied the hundreds of letters and faced the dream I'd been given once again: a book to write. A book that would explore all the mystery, joy, and healing to be found in the human-animal relationship, not with theories but with true stories spoken directly from the heart. I looked closely at my crippling hesitancy to take up such a project. Me, writer of one published article in a dog magazine. Me, cancer patient and self-proclaimed barnacle, whose life looked, to me, like a sack of projects started and abandoned, dreams touched but released before they could ever mature. Me, a woman hunting for her life with the finesse of a child hunting for bugs under a muddy rock.

That there is such boundless grace in this world and that it pours over saints and barnacles alike is a truth that makes my life worth living, worth getting excited and teary-eyed over, time and again. I thought I was given the task of the book because I was the vehicle the universe had mysteriously, perhaps mistakenly, selected to get its message into the world. Perhaps that's true. But what I have come to know is that the book was given to me as a priceless treasure map to my soul's true home.

It wasn't just an outpouring, a gift I was somehow to bring into the world. It was an infusion, a transforming work of the most intense and demanding kind wrapped in a brick-red book cover. I didn't know it then, but I was about to write my bible: what I understand of the universe as it has made itself known to me.

Before the book could be born in any fashion, I had to commit to it. This was no small task for a woman with a lifelong allergy to the word. But I stood fast, and grace washed over me. A publisher literally appeared at my door. As in a dream, I opened my file drawer and showed her some of the earliest, messiest writing. Three days later I had a book contract with national distribution. The real writing began, the letters unfolded into narrative text. I tentatively explored my ideas, laid out my opinions like they were absolutes. The letters guided me, bits of my own life guided me. Yet the part of me that clung to old fears and inadequacies kept me hiding from my own writing like a clam in wet sand. Who was I? Could I move beyond the culturally induced shame of my deep affinity for animals? Tree hugger, animal lover, animal freak, bleeding heart. Who was I? These things, I waited for others to tell me. Curiously, the letters I received during that time were also withdrawn, hesitant.

The first draft came back from my publisher. "A nice start," she wrote. I was more than momentarily stunned. I had convinced myself that I had said all I had to say. The pages of my text were blotched with Post-its, like small, yellow fists, hammering at me to explain myself, justify my blatherings, expose myself, make a case for my flimsy opinions. "I don't believe this: do you?" the stickies challenged. What did I believe? I didn't know. I wavered, questioning again whether the universe had blundered. Surely I was not the woman for this task. Insecure, I looked to other writers, other books, to tell me what to believe about the power of animals in my life and to show me how to say what I needed to say.

Grace intervened yet again. The tribes and nations of my backyard and barn were showering me with "moments" of every conceivable kind: insights, healings, challenges that implored me to revisit my beliefs, my limitations, my imaginings. In stewarding the kingdom in my barn, I was forced to stop looking outside, looking for a better boat to jump. Health crises assailed my animal kingdom and required my immediate, focused

intervention. There was no time for libraries and self-flagellation. There were, instead, choking fits, hard births, and deaths.

Mandy, a gentle and careworn llama of ours, sickened in the cold of winter and died despite my every effort to keep her on her old and tired feet. I knew, even as she went down for the last time in the arching spasm of death, that I had not given her my best, my absolute all. I had given her the resources I was willing to spare, and she had died.

Thrown back inside myself with grief and guilt, I was forced to revisit my ideas about just how far I could—no, would—extend myself for the life of an animal in my care. I looked again at boundaries, emotional limits of time and energy and physical strength, and pitted those concepts against the stiff, cold body of a gentle llama. Mandy, the "white bus" (owing to her size and ample girth), came to me after death in dreams and visions of forgiveness and mercy and left me with another concept to wrestle. What were these dreams? Would I be willing to call them absolute truth in my life and live in accordance with them? Could I say that on paper?

My father died that winter. The loss numbed me. I took on his nursing care in his final days, attending to the most painfully intimate details of his bed care. I wiped his behind and rubbed ointment on his bedsores. When he awoke in a sweat, I bathed him. After his death I wrote and delivered his memorial service and never cried even as the entire chapel wept.

Not until I returned home and faced another animal health crisis did the numbness finally, blessedly leave me. Simone, one of our donkeys, was in the critical throes of a grain-induced choking fit. Over her hunched back, I suddenly found myself wailing out the tears that were for my father. In the kingdom of the barn, I pondered the mystery of grief and how it comes to us and through us. A memorial service, cards, well-wishers, the ash-cold body of my father as I eased him into the hearse: none of these things could reach me. It took a small, pain-filled donkey to help me find my way back to the pain that was waiting for me. I learned then that we find our healing where we need it, whether in a Bible, in the words of a friend, in a funeral parlor, or in a barn, and that we need make no apologies for what moves us, what breaks us, what mends us.

I have never had children and have made certain, as a responsible pet owner, that my dogs and cats never had offspring either. The second summer in our new home, I watched our banty chickens hatch their first broods, and I learned about the sound, the unique and love-precious sound, that a mother saves for her children alone. Putting my ear under a nesting black bantam hen, I listened as a tiny chick deep within a smooth white egg called out to its mother with a muffled peep. The hen answered with a murmured, gentle clucking, sweet-pitched and soft, a lullaby to her yet-unborn infant, and I heard the sound of every mother in that magical, all-loving tone.

SiSi, our first-time-mother donkey, went into labor late one night in deep winter when the winds were bone-cold and strong and rain stung the tin roof. I moved my sleeping bag into the loft and looked down on SiSi for the next five hours, whispering words of encouragement as her body heaved and shook. She paced, sweated, locked her eyes to mine as if to say, "You see? This is how it begins . . ." Her bulging sides rippled as the infant struggled to position itself in its too-tight quarters. SiSi was up and down, turning, stretching, moaning, and vibrating with new life.

Hours later, her baby stuck hard and fast inside of her, I told her to plant her feet against me and *push*. And she heard me and jammed her rear hooves into my breastbone and groaned and shoved. Her baby, Star, exploded in a wet and bloody mass into my lap and instantly began struggling to his feet. The birth sack fell on my legs, his umbilical cord snapped. Instantly, SiSi turned to him, and in the dark of that early morning, I heard it again. This time from a donkey's heart: that tender, sweet-toned murmur of warmth and deep mothering love. Star answered with a throaty honk. Suddenly I knew what it must be like to have a child, to hatch a child, to love a child.

When I began to trust the truth and mystery of my own experiences, my mail reflected changes as well. The stories that came to me were amazing—stories of vigor and conviction standing strong. There were stories of companion animals, wild animals, animals who came to people in dreams. And within the stories were the ideas, rich, delicious ideas I had never tasted.

As I read the pages, my world changed. "We are not fully human unless we are in the context and company of our living wild neighbors, learning from them," wrote Roger Fuchs, an Oregonian who had a "moment" with a red fox decades before. Roger opened my mind a little wider. I saw how empty and restless my days unfolded when I failed to drink in all the life outside my windows: the hummingbirds in the herb garden, the cacophony of starlings at evening, the bees on the daisy bushes. Through his letter and countless others, I discovered that it isn't enough to stop and smell the roses every now and then. I needed to stick my nose into the blossoms and *leave it there*.

I found Judee Curcio-Wolfe, an animal communicator, while seeking stories. We spoke for hours about communicating with animals on a level I had never considered. Judee told me to speak to my animals and craft mental pictures that illustrated what I was saying so that they might better grasp my meaning. The first few times I tried her technique, I felt like an idiot. Over the months, it has become second nature. I speak to bugs, to chickens, to Arrow. I tell them when I'm leaving town and when I'll be back, and I ask them to take care of things while I'm gone. In the spring I ask the moles to please stay off of the lawns. The "animal speak" has become more than just a second language I use around the farm. The simple process of treating animals as beings worthy of consideration and communication has raised my awareness of them, my respect for them, my joy in them, tenfold.

Under the deluge of letters, my shame—my ugly, culture-bound, demoralizing embarrassment—over my deep connection with animals melted away. The hard cell of my self-imposed emotional isolation faded in the onslaught of thousands of words from warm, sane, wonderful people who loved all living beings with a passion that equalled, and sometimes exceeded, mine. I was not alone, had never been alone.

When I had cancer, what I wanted most was to have a minute-to-minute, life-sustaining connection with God. My best friend, Claire, had attained such a connection with the universe years ago, and I envied her. She spoke of her "friend," God, and the "angel-ones" and "joy children," like I might speak of dinner engagements and ironing—just part of every-day life. I never understood how she achieved such a balance with her

inner and outer world, and she could never explain it. In the nation of my barn, and in the creation of my book, I have found it. It would never be the road my friend Claire would have taken to get there, as each one's road home to the soul must be achingly unique; but it is *my* road and it is, after many fits and starts, a magnificent and joyful one.

The book goes out into the world, in accordance with the booksellers' demands. The working title, *Other Angels*, made everyone uncomfortable. And so it was renamed *Animals As Teachers and Healers: True Stories and Reflections*. Its creation has dictated the recasting of my life. Dropping the veil of shame, sharing my days and nights with the nation of animals whose dignity, joy, and wisdom bless our home, I breathe the sweet tang of oregano in an herb garden alive with whirring insects and diligent chickens, and I dance in God's arm—arms that look like wings and cockscombs, donkey muzzles, and dragonfly antennae—every minute of every day. Amen.

HEALING WITH THE WILD ONES

AMAYÉ

The animals were always there for me. Individuals entered my life at times when I needed them most. Snowball, a beautiful white cat with golden eyes, was with me during my early childhood. He was my best friend, a special being who comforted and healed my sadness. Snowball was an embodiment of pure love. Through the years there were so many—cats, dogs, horses, gerbils, mice, fish. My relationship was different with each one, but all provided me with an opportunity to share love.

Wildness, too, fascinated me. I collected shells, rocks, even dead bugs. I wanted to be a naturalist when I grew up so I could spend all my time in the wild with creatures as companions. Growing up in the city, my contact with the wilderness was limited. As I was to discover many years later, a connection with wild beings was a part of my life path, and since I could not go to the wild, it came to me. It came in the form of a bobcat named Junior. I was twenty at the time, going to college and working. My partner announced he was buying a bobcat kitten. I hit the roof. I had a very strong belief that wild creatures belonged in the wild, not in captivity. I begged, pleaded, and even threatened in an effort to change his mind. He didn't listen, and in hindsight I'm grateful.

Not since Snowball had I felt such love for another being. Junior possessed a specialness that I couldn't define. Other people felt it, too. He radiated beauty—not just physical beauty, although he is magnificent, but a spiritual beauty and grace as well. The essence of wildness in Junior was a part of this splendor, but he also emanated a sense of peace. I could not be in his presence without being drawn to him. We quickly formed

a relationship based on mutual love and respect. And though at times it was a challenge to share a home with him, I gave Junior unconditional acceptance, never expecting or wanting him to change his "bobcatness." He was already sacrificing a great deal by living in the demanding confines of captivity.

Despite our closeness, Junior was not "my" cat. So three years later when I moved away to attend graduate school, I went alone. It was hard. Just before I left, Boots, a domestic cat, joined us. He and Junior quickly formed a loving kinship. They became brothers. I maintained my relationship with Junior, visiting as often as I could and looking forward to the day we would be reunited. Being separated from him was difficult. He was in my thoughts daily.

As if to heal my loneliness, wildness entered my life again—this time in the form of an orphaned squirrel. I became her surrogate mother, raising Pita and cherishing her as I had Snowball and Junior. Pita was my adopted daughter, my friend, my companion. She possessed joy and gaiety. Like other squirrels, Pita had a love for life and a special appreciation of the finer things it had to offer: feeling the warmth of the sun, smelling the fresh air, stretching out after a good meal, a spontaneous frolic when the urge hit, and of course pecans! She brought love into our home and into my heart.

Within two years Pita and I joined my partner, Boots, and Junior. Pita died the following year. The toughest part of life is watching a loved one suffer and being unable to intervene. I held Pita as she left, utterly helpless to do anything but love her. I was devastated. The grief I felt was overwhelming. There was so much more love I wanted to give her. All the love, light, and life she shared with me were only memories now. I felt as if a part of my soul had been ripped away.

Though I was incapable of understanding it at the time, Pita's death held a purpose for us both. Years later I realized that for her own reasons she had chosen to go and that by leaving she was giving me the opportunity to look within myself. The anguish and sorrow I felt from her loss were reflections of old feelings that I had hidden deep inside myself for many, many years. Now those feelings were right in front of me, there for me to be destroyed by or confront. They began to destroy me.

I blamed myself for Pita's death and slipped into a state of self-inflicted punishment. I spiralled downward, deeper and deeper into despair, denying myself anything that might bring solace. My life was enveloped in darkness. Junior was holding the light, but I refused to see. Instead I became obsessed with a fear of losing him. Years passed and the pain never ceased. These were the darkest years of my life.

Once again wildness slipped in to try to resurrect me. Allie, a tiny female bobcat, was herself on the verge of destruction from the brutalities humanity had inflicted. I reached out to save her. Unfortunately Allie was typical of what happens to most wild creatures bought as pets. During her short two years of life she had been shuffled through at least four owners. Each bought her as a novelty with no regard for the responsibilities involved in caring for a wild cat. They had mistakenly expected her to behave like a domestic cat. In an effort to force her to be what she was not, her teeth had been filed, all four feet were deformed from declawing, and she had been physically abused. These people had completely ignored the beauty of her wild spirit and instead disdained and sought to control it. When I got Allie, she was being kept in a filthy four-by-two-foot wire cage stuck in the corner of a dark garage. She was understandably terrified of people, and her fear manifested as aggressive behavior. Only her tenacity for survival had kept her sane.

Integrating Allie into our home proved difficult. It took a tremendous amount of patience on everybody's part. Establishing a mutual trust was a slow and at times frustrating process. Her incredible courage along with my acceptance and insight into her fears were what facilitated our eventual bonding. Junior's presence and help were also extremely important. He was providing Allie with a connection she desperately needed.

Allie's past deprivation gave her an appreciation of the care she was receiving. She took nothing for granted. Even though she was still plagued by fears, she seemed happy to be with us. This renewed my patience and encouraged me to continue working with her. Gradually, we began to trust one another, but it would be several years before we developed a closer relationship.

In a very different way, Allie, like Pita, was providing me with an opportunity to look within myself. She was a mirror image of me in so

many ways. Still, I was not ready to see. I continued to be consumed by misery and did not care enough about myself to seek change.

Time slipped by. Again I was faced with moving away. I was leaving to study a group of captive chimpanzees. My plan was to be gone just long enough to collect data needed for my dissertation in six months. I did not want to go but believed I had no choice. I was accustomed to doing what I "should" even when it felt wrong. Junior, however, had other plans for my education. His first lesson was to follow your heart, not your head. As it turned out, I never did leave.

Over a period of months, as I was preparing to move, Junior's health declined very gradually, almost imperceivably. His appetite and level of activity decreased, and he occasionally experienced a slight fever. The cause eluded us, and he didn't respond to antibiotics. The decline continued, and he began losing weight. Junior's veterinarian enlisted the help of a cat internist. Finally, he was diagnosed: histoplasmosis, a systemic fungal infection that can invade every part of the body. By this time it was advanced. The fungus was present in Junior's spleen and his bone marrow and was probably attacking other areas of his body as well. There were only two drug options available for Junior. The prognosis was poor. Junior was going to die.

What was happening seemed unreal. We had not expected anything this serious, this life-threatening. I was being hit with my deepest fear, my obsession: losing Junior. Something inside of me snapped. I was ready to attack this disease head-on. I was adamant. He was not going to die. He would survive. I summoned all my inner strength.

The veterinarian helping us had known Junior for more than nine years. He truly loved him. There was no doubt in my mind that he would do everything within his power to save him. This, however, was not enough. I had to do something. Very quickly, I became knowledgeable about this affliction. I went to a veterinary school library and gathered every shred of literature I could find on the disease, possible treatments, side effects of the drugs, related diseases, medical care of wild cats, and anything remotely related. I pored over the papers. I called veterinarians, zoo personnel, researchers, and professors all over the country, trying to find someone who could offer more information or had dealt with this

disease in a wild cat. I found no answers; nothing beyond what I was being told by the doctors helping Junior.

Two exams within one week had taken a toll on Junior. The stress and necessary sedations had weakened him. He was also dangerously anemic. We tried the first medication. The side effects were severe. It took Junior down to a state close to unconsciousness. We tried lighter doses. He got violently sick and would not eat at all. The only option was a drug not available in the United States. My partner went out of the country to buy it. Like the first medication, this one also posed the risk of permanent damage to Junior's liver. We believed we had no choice but to try it.

We started Junior on the medication. It was heartbreaking. The drug was hard on his system. His appetite remained depressed, and his body was wrenched with vomiting. Despite forced feedings, he became emaciated. At one point his breathing became so labored we had to set up an oxygen tent for him in our home. It brought some relief. During this battle, I was terrified. I stayed up all night watching him for fear he would die while I was asleep. We didn't leave his side. Finally, in the midst of this nightmare, a light came shining through.

I realized Junior was trying to teach me something. I looked at him and asked, "What are you trying to teach me?" That was the single most important question I have ever asked. What followed completely changed our lives.

By recognizing that this ordeal was a learning experience, I had opened myself to receive the message. Junior's answer came through loud and clear, not in words but in the form of an internal knowing, an energetic shift of my being. Once I experienced this enlightenment, I could not go back. I could never be the same person. What Junior told me was that, in order to heal anyone else, I had to be willing to heal myself. Simple yet profound. My rational mind had been exposed to this idea before, but it had not held meaning for me. I had never *known* it within myself. Now, I suddenly understood.

Junior had been willing to die in order to get my attention, to get me to heal, to teach me what I needed to know. The realization that another being could have such love for me and be willing to sacrifice

so much was overwhelming. It forced me to look at what value I had placed upon myself.

For the first time in my life, I made a commitment to heal. It began gradually, first reading one book, then another, each one leading me to more material and a better understanding of what healing was all about. I realized that healing meant moving toward a state of wholeness, not just solving a physical or emotional problem or suppressing symptoms. Unlike the mechanistic approach of conventional medicine, true healing could occur only when the individual was addressed in its totality, working on all aspects of self: physical, emotional, mental, and spiritual.

My exploration led me to the realization that individuals are energetic entities with levels of existence extending beyond what we are normally able to perceive. As energy, we are made up of complex flows and patterns of vibration. It became clear that anything capable of changing these vibrations or altering the energetic pathways would have an impact on the individual. Thus, influences that disrupt the flow of energy or shift vibratory patterns so that there is energetic imbalance create disease. Conversely, any influences that open and allow free flow of energy or shift vibrations so that there is energetic balance create well-being. Finally, here was the answer I had been seeking! The key to holistic healing lies in balancing the individual energetically.

There were many means available for helping the body move toward a state of balance, but the foundation underlying all healing was diet. The life force contained in fresh food was the most important energetic element for the individual. In addition to supplying this essential life force through sustenance, nature held other valuable gifts for healing: homeopathy, flower essences, herbs, gems, elixirs, aromatherapy, work with stones, sunlight, and color. The beauty of these approaches was their gentleness. All allowed the body to tap into its own intelligence to heal. They facilitated and supported the being's efforts to return to energetic balance.

Everything I encountered made perfect sense, and I could feel the truth of it. Junior had led me to my path. I was embarking on my life adventure, acquiring the tools and insights needed to transform myself and help Junior heal.

The first thing I did was to change Junior's diet. This turned out to be the single most significant step in his healing process. All three cats had been eating a commercial food that was formulated for wild cats. It had a reputation as the best diet available. I had never questioned this. Now it was clear that this diet was lacking the most important component of food, the life force. Through cooking and processing, the ingredients had lost their vital energy. In addition, the naturally occurring vitamins, minerals, and enzymes had been destroyed. To make matters worse, ingredients such as preservatives had been added that were detrimental to the body. What the cats had been eating was dead and toxic. How could they have vitality if what they were consuming was devoid of it? It was so obvious, but I had missed it completely. What Junior—all of us, in fact—needed was raw organic foods.

Gradually I switched the three cats to a diet of raw organic meats with the bones, organic vegetables, live wheat grass and sprouts, and small amounts of cooked organic grains. I used digestive enzymes to help their systems make the transition and also added vitamin and mineral supplements. Aside from using live prey animals, which was neither practical nor possible at the time, this diet was the best thing the cats could be eating. I was already a vegan (abstaining from all animal products) for ethical reasons, but I started refining my diet for health benefits as well.

The change in Junior was phenomenal. He began to grow stronger. His activity increased, and he gained weight. Within a month of modifying his diet, Junior was performing athletic feats I had not seen in five years. After giving him the antifungal medication for six months, I finally had the confidence to take him off it. The vomiting stopped, and he continued to improve. His eyes regained their sparkle and brilliance. Junior was receiving the energy and nutrition he needed without being bombarded by toxins. I now knew he would survive the disease, but a very long road lay ahead. Our healing work was just beginning.

I enlisted the help of holistic veterinarians who supported Junior with homeopathy. I was learning that healing took time and patience. Restoring the body's balance was a very different process than the quick fixes offered by conventional medicine. Junior's healing was taking place through the combined efforts of several compassionate doctors. I felt

deep gratitude for each one who lent expertise and talents that saved Junior's life and were fostering his ongoing recovery.

What I had not hesitated to do for Junior I now had to do for myself—reach out for help. This was a tremendous step for me because trusting humans was difficult for me. I didn't feel safe with them. However, I recognized the necessity and gradually opened myself to receive assistance. My work began to shift from an academic orientation to one that was experiential. Altered states of consciousness achieved through hypnotherapy and meditation proved especially conducive to my healing. My exploration continued, and one powerful technique, Holotrophic Breathwork, provided a cathartic breakthrough. I was beginning to feel more comfortable working with others, and I realized that gifted healers are compassionate and gentle individuals who are themselves on a healing path.

Finally I began to look within. Pita and Allie had given me the opportunity years before, but it had taken Junior's insistence to make me confront the pain. Now I was not only ready to see, I was ready to feel.

Two things facilitated the work I was doing. First, by making a commitment to heal, I had opened myself to receive support from the universe. I was finding all the resources I needed at the appropriate time. The magic of synchronicity had entered my life.

Second, Junior was guiding me to use the superb intuitive gift I had been born with. It was quite strong. I easily sensed feelings and information from other individuals and places, but because I didn't understand the ability, it was a source of hardship. I had chosen to ignore it. In fact, I had learned to ignore all my inner feelings in order to survive. Now I began to accept and respect my intuition. I made decisions based on what felt right rather than what I mentally thought was right.

Like Junior, I was undergoing a miraculous change. I had initiated an expansion experience: a process in which my awareness, my being, was extending far beyond its previous boundaries. My partner of fifteen years was not ready to join us in healing. The transformation the cats and I were experiencing was pushing him beyond what he was ready or willing to do. At the same time, his presence was holding us back from achieving our potential.

He left, and for the first time, it was just me and the cats together. It was the best for all concerned. We were free now, and our healing and learning took off at an incredible pace. For the first time, I could see clearly the way I had been living. I began to understand that we each create our own reality. I made the decision to no longer be a victim. Instead, I chose to be a survivor, learning from my past. I took responsibility for my life and set out to create it in a way that included happiness. I was awakening.

My connections to the wild grew, as beings brought messages to aid my growth and understanding. They had always been there, willing to show me the way. I only had to look, listen, and feel, not with my senses but with my soul. Birds, mammals, reptiles, bugs, and plants were teaching, encouraging, affirming that I was on the right path. Even the rocks, with millennia of intelligence locked within, started to share their secrets. A pack of wolves entered my life, leading and directing me past my limitations and protecting me during the process. I began to perceive the universe and my place within it in a different way. I envisioned it as a singular continuum of energy, consciousness, and we, as souls, are different vibrations within it, all connected, all one.

My path led me to a gifted woman who was helping others heal by communicating with animals. While the information I received from nonhumans came as an internal knowing, she had the ability to converse with other beings. Her conversations with Junior, Allie, and Boots provided valuable details for their healing. I was able to refine their diets and decide how to assist them based on the information they offered.

These dialogues proved therapeutic for me as well. Through our friend, Junior and I were able to communicate on a new level. It was a joy to hear his words. His messages were filled with information relevant to my growth, yet the humor and lightheartedness of his personality came shining through.

Junior confirmed the pervasive feeling I had that our connection had spanned many lives. We had done healing work together before, and ties to wildness were deeply rooted within my soul. I discovered that Junior's path of growth and evolution includes touching many others. He is a master teacher who shares lessons about humanity with wild

beings. Ironically, Junior has taught me a great deal about humankind. Snowball, Junior, Boots, Pita, Allie, and I are all serving as links between our respective realms, reaching out to foster understanding, acceptance, and respect between wildness and humanity, both on an individual level and beyond. I asked Junior what message he would like to send out to humanity through this story. He wants to emphasize free choice.

I realize that I have chosen each of my many physical lives. With guidance, I devised the plans for them on a soul level. There were reasons for the choices I made, specific lessons I sought to learn, spiritual goals I set out to accomplish. Junior wants to make clear that humans are not unique in this regard. All beings exercise free choice. Nonhumans are making the same choices as humans. With guidance they, too, create life plans. Each is following a path, living out patterns and circumstances of their own design, which facilitate their objectives for spiritual growth and evolution. Their paths are no less significant than those of humans, no less influential on the planetary unfolding taking place. Every being is a seeker, an adventurer.

Through free choice, lives become intertwined. There is no randomness to our connections. Cooperation occurs on a soul level with our higher selves orchestrating associations that are for the greatest good of all concerned. We choose to interact with individuals whose life work is complementary to our own. In this respect Junior wants to stress the critical importance of cooperation between species, not only for mutual physical benefits but also for mutual spiritual learning and growth.

I believe our own story illustrates this point eloquently. Without each other's help, neither of us would have survived this physical existence. We have quite literally saved each other's life. Beyond that, the spiritual expansion we are experiencing would not have been possible without one another. This is, after all, why Junior and I are together. With this perspective of interrelationship, how can one not cherish all beings and all creation? We need only allow ourselves to become aware, and the value of all life becomes crystal-clear. All of nature, every being, every rock, every molecule of water is a part of the intelligence of the universe and has something to teach, something to share.

This understanding of the cooperative and complementary aspects of relationships has furthered my insight into the dynamics of my own immediate group. Junior, Boots, Allie, and I form an intricate web that we chose to be a part of. In tandem we learn, grow, and evolve on every level of our being. All of the healing work we do is mutually beneficial, and we are, at once, both teachers and students of one another. Each of us brings to the group a unique spirit that allows all of us to expand our awareness and experience life in a different way.

Pita brought many gifts. She was an embodiment of pure joy who gracefully illustrated the preciousness of life. With enthusiasm, Pita demonstrated the importance of living in the moment. She appreciated every instant of life. Though her time was brief, this challenging path allowed her to accomplish tremendous spiritual growth. Pita has taught me to live in the present rather than constantly waiting on tomorrow.

Boots brings balance to our group. His domesticity and acceptance of humans provide a necessary counter to the wildness of the others. Boots exemplifies immense patience and tolerance. Sharing life with Pita, Junior, and Allie has allowed him to reconnect with his long-forgotten past, reminding him of his own ancient wildness. Boots teaches me to be quiet and still.

Allie is the divine essence of wildness, conveying the spirit and energy of Mother Earth. Her courage and incredible desire to learn prompted her to choose the difficult path of a nondomestic creature in captivity. The hardships she endured have imparted her with extraordinary growth and enlightenment. Like myself, she is on a superhighway of change, and we are all helping her along the way. Allie is helping me come to terms with the abuses of my past. She is teaching me how to persevere.

My contribution to the group is dedication and a resolve for providing for our comfort and well-being. I bring compassion and reflect the aspect of humanity that encompasses a commitment to share stewardship of this planet with all species.

Junior is the center around which the rest of us are drawn. He provides protection and strength that unite us, while also guiding us to find our own strength from within. His gifts radiate and reach far beyond our immediate web, touching many souls. As a master teacher, Junior

embodies wisdom and divine truth. His knowledge and understanding of the universe transcend that of humans, and he readily shares his insights. Like Snowball, Junior manifests the healing powers of love. He came into this life to spiritually grow and learn, and we each play a key part in his process. Junior is teaching me many lessons. He is using his own health to teach me to care for myself. Junior knew I would not have learned this lesson on my own. Had I been the one to get sick, I simply would have given up. Junior sacrificed a great deal in order to help me develop self-love. We all share unconditional acceptance and love.

With the help and guidance of my wonderful companions, I have discovered capabilities within myself I never dreamed existed. I am learning to pay attention, to trust life, to feel love for and nurture myself. I am able to embrace change and look upon adversity as an opportunity to expand my consciousness and grow. I can access a state of peace and grace that is an amazing source of healing and strength. I am able to experience joy. Yet I realize this is only the beginning of my path. There are still many steps to take, many lessons to learn, more strength to gather, more love to feel and share. I look ahead with excitement and anticipation for the adventures that await the four of us as we walk our intertwined paths. Our healing will continue because moving into wholeness is an unending journey.

As I write, Junior and Allie are playing a game of chase. Their strength, speed, and agility are amazing. It reminds me of the courage and endurance we have each had to find within ourselves during the past years. We are outside with the brilliant sun warming our souls and the plants' green hues sending us healing energy. Nature is no longer a refuge sought in desperation but our place of peace. Now we are not only living in the light, we are the light.

I am privileged and give thanks every day to be healing together with the wild ones.

AN ADEPT KNOWN
AS FIORINO

SHELLEY DONNELLY

Fiorino, echo of a little Flower,
Spectre of a Master Soul,
Incarnate symphony of movement,
Of knowledge, dignity, and discernment
FIORINO, echo of omniscient JOY

Fiorino del Calcione spent his last lifetime in form—full eighteen years incarnate—with me, in my care. It was clear from the beginning that I had no place in his fields of learning. He knew it all. My only role was to teach him what he had to avoid in terms of society's dangers and the modern hazards of living within that society. For the rest, he made his own decisions.

In his youth, Fiorino allowed me to share his earthly experiences and communicated with me when he chose. He taught both my conscious and unconscious mind. He was and is the best teacher I have experienced. In his maturity he allowed me to share more profound glimpses of knowledge and philosophy, which he recounted to me.

When he told me that he was going to leave his body, reacting with the endemic human panic when confronted with the subject we call "death" and Fiorino calls "a simple change of plane," I asked what I was to do without him to teach me all I still needed to know? He responded with his usual laconic sparsity of words: "All you have to do is contemplate our lives together, and you will know all you need to know. Do not grieve, for I will work better with you out of form than I can now in form." And so it came to pass nearly eight years after his "death" or "change of plane" that we do indeed work together.

"Alive," he was master of himself, his surroundings, and all other dogs, without exception as far as ever I witnessed. His specialty was breaking up dog fights. Not dog fights between miniature poodles, but the pukka war-hound stuff between Alsatians and Dobermans and other more challenging breeds.

Fiorino was a miniature greyhound, an Italian greyhound. But he was a David among the Goliaths, and this could and would certainly be certified by scientists under the heading, "An experiment that gives off the same results, under the same circumstances, with each repetition, constitutes a scientific fact." Fiorino would simply trot straight into the middle of the fight, uttering some startling vocals and effecting an amazingly mesmerizing dance. Both warring canine parties, vociferously engaged in manifesting themselves as sophisticated and efficient shredding machines, would immediately separate and hare into the distance as though attacked by a dervish. Miniature in size, grand in authority, Fiorino would then kick his back legs through the turf and continue on his way without a backward look at either party or me. On no occasion did I ever catch him checking upon the effect of the laws he had so instantaneously enforced upon the warring canines before pursuing his own purposes.

Fiorino had a sense of duty and responsibility that came with the little package—the puppy—and lasted throughout his life, dominated his life. This sense of responsibility took the form of protectiveness and duty before all things.

Communication with Fiorino took place at a mental level; it was not telepathy at a solar-plexus level, which is a different process, and it was always of a serious, philosophical nature. No trivial communication was of the slightest interest to him. It was serious, or it did not take place.

Communication with the animals is not a New Age feat. It is, in fact, an ongoing ability that humans and animals both have: all life has. All that is living has the ability to communicate, for it comes from the same Life Source. Each and every form of life from that source knows each other at the Source.

Saint Francis spent a lifetime reintroducing us to animal-human communications, but just as Jesus reiterated the principles of unconditional love that we have failed to adopt, so have we forgotten what Saint

Francis tried to teach us: communication with all life. J. Allen Boone kindly reminded us of this once again in his perennial classic, *Kinship with All Life*, which has survived decades of reprints. And now there is indeed a renaissance of something that has always been there, incarnating most intensively in America, humans who can communicate with the animals in a direct telepathic process. Again, the two most evident ways are via the solar plexus and through direct mental transmission, the latter of which is the most desirable and usually the least distorted. However, although it brought astonishing results, my own communication with Fiorino was meager when put beside the abilities of the moderns, but it was at a mental level, even if I am forced to admit that I could not switch it on at will. It happened when Fiorino chose to communicate.

After Fiorino left his passage in the manifest, people who had been close to him saw him at least once and sometimes more often. They all described exactly the same phenomenon: "a feeling of expansive peace as though one is being enveloped in a rose-pink glow of absolute love." And others, those able to communicate with him, spoke to him through the subtle ethers after he had gone, including myself. Some time after his death, as we call it, he informed me that it was time I found a human who could communicate with him directly and at will. And so it came to pass.

However startled I was by his request, I set about searching for this special human. After eighteen years with Fiorino, one did not question his requests; one automatically took them seriously and proceeded to act. To my own surprise, it was not long before I did find a human able to communicate with him. Fiorino, however, always seemed to be in a hurry and even downright reluctant at times. So the search was permanently on, and each time I found a lead, it was waylaid and the appointment or rendezvous negated.

Finally Fiorino announced that he would meet me in America where karmic events would happen, and he would start work with me. They did happen just as he related. Once fate or destiny—some are drawn to fate, while others are magnetized to destiny—connected me with Kate Solisti, and Fiorino confirmed that she was definitely the right address, we formed a three-point working partnership.

We call this work "From Animal to Anima."

Our hope is to join the gathering many to help toward creating a twentieth-century renaissance of mutual understanding between the human and animal kingdoms. We aim to extend this renaissance into our daily lives by changing our perceptions so as to meet our mutual evolution with dignity and equality—indeed, absolute kinship—so that we may live together in beauty and harmony and reciprocal gain, for we are all one. In so doing, we will elevate humanity, not the animals—for the animals are already at the point of elevated dignity we sometimes refer to as "noble."

Why all this? Because, as Fiorino tells, and as many, or some of us know, "Each animal species on this planet is the guardian of a cosmic truth, or what might be described as a Cosmic Memory."

We find that each animal species has an activity that is a role which, in itself, completes a part of the Whole of the Divine All. Each and every one of our animal species—the human species included—is a cosmic reality of a part of what *is*.

Let us start with, and honor, the canines that Fiorino chose to represent in his last life in form: an elegant, swift greyhound was he. A sage and a teacher was he in Spirit and in Soul.

All animals potentially have all qualities, as do humans. The canine has chosen to develop specific qualities adapted to his mission of service to humanity and the canine's role on this planet. The canine has chosen the message of love, which is perhaps the hardest mission of all the domestic animals. It is a message that we all seek in the here and now and that we are all getting ready to bring into human cognizance, for without real love, we cannot move into the New Age, nor can we evolve. Without its cognizance we will hold up planetary evolution.

The canine qualities in their pure matrix as established at Source are *altruism, memory, service,* and *unconditional love* through *the knowledge of pure love.*

However, Fiorino points out that

Memory and Altruism are the same for a dog.
Every memory is viewed through Altruistic Generosity.
For a dog, it all happens simultaneously.

What do I mean by "through the knowledge of pure love"? The components of altruism, memory, service, and unconditional love are held together through the knowledge of pure love. If the primordial knowledge of pure love is lost, the rest of these qualities the canine succeeds in blending and maintaining would fall into disarray, just as our own human perception of unconditional love, for the most part, is lost to us. Love and altruism rarely hold hands in our human society today. We see it in a Mother Teresa as an exception, and we do recognize it. The dog holds this in his everyday life, while the quality of human love has diffused into emotionalism.

The existence of this original or primordial memory that the canine holds allows the knowledge of pure love to be remembered as being at the Source of this planetary system. In other words, this intrinsic part of the canine essence allows them to maintain their indefatigable link to unconditional love.

Altruism is a primary, subtle form of generosity through service. The combination of altruism, generosity, and service causes an energetic movement that awakens *memory*, simply because memory is its very source. It is but one of the natural laws of the sequences of energetics completing the circle of life.

We are synthesizing this enormous yet simple concept so as to understand its beautiful fluid existence. We are comprehending and identifying the unique qualities that lie at the original matrix of the evolved canine being. So Fiorino taught me. And says Fiorino:

However, it is important to bear in mind that, for a dog, these actions do not happen independent of each other. They happen simultaneously without intellect, nor can they be obtained through or with intellect. It is about being what actually *is* at the Source.

We are simply showing parts of the Whole. In truth, this is what we, as humans, are striving to develop in the human heart chakra. I realized this only when Fiorino explained how a dog achieved this quality of unconditional love. We are being shown through their example that that is our next step into this New Age.

What we have not been taught is that we need only to look to our canine friends and learn to mirror their qualities—if we can—to achieve our next evolutionary step.

The canine activity is that of a direct, master teacher; that is apparent only once we perceive what he profoundly represents, by recognition of his qualities.

It is no news to anybody that the word *Fidelity* stands for *Fido*, which stands for the dog.

The dictionary defines the word *teach* in one of its meanings as "To exhibit so as to impress upon the mind." In fact, that definition expresses the ideal parental role: the parent constantly acting as a fine example to impress upon the mind of the infant the fine order of life, so that this might be passed from generation to generation. (However, for the moment, in human terms this is but an ideal.)

DK, the Tibetan (of Alice Bailey fame), says:

Pure Love is the Quality or effect of pure reason . . . and the Quality of Pure Love is needed and demanded (even if unrealized) by a waiting humanity.

Little wonder so many of us fall into a state of emotional love and often dependence upon our dogs who, if we became aware of their divine quality, could teach us so simply. So, at the risk of repetition, the canine mission or presence on this planet speaks as the perpetual reminder of unconditional love that, once we have grasped and put into full practice, unintellectually with our spontaneous being, will lead us to pure love. Even the recognition of this concept might serve as an initial step on the long journey toward man's pinnacle of evolution—his return to Source.

One day, when I could resist no longer, rather diffidently, because Fiorino hated frivolous matters, I asked Fiorino whether it is a coincidence that *Dog* spelled backwards reads *God*. And he answered:

The real point of the issue is that the unconditional love that the canines hold through pure love is pretty akin to the way human beings have always defined God.

And of course the human has no further to look for those qualities than their own dogs.

That, in its simplest form, is the message.

He concluded, with his usual economy of words:

The dog is humanity's guardian and gateway. He is the guardian of the cosmic reality that humans have lost: that of pure love. He is the ever present, most perfect exemplification of the gateway to humanity's return to pure love.

In conclusion—as it was then, so it is now—the quality of communication we receive from Fiorino is an animal-human communion of rich philosophy through which we glimpse the light and the beauty and the privilege of sharing a sense of One-ness through interspecies communication.

When a perception of One-ness issues from the blending of heart consciousness, otherwise known as Intelligence, we do all speak the same language, a language of universal quality: the Language of Silence. The instantaneous, telepathic language of Knowing.

And that, and much more, was one of the many themes I learned from Fiorino.

THE ANIMAL IN EACH OF US

MICHAEL TOBIAS

By recognizing our linguistic limitations (most people speak only one language out of the more than five thousand living languages), we should be better, more sensitively poised to appreciate the lacunae of meanings between species. This said, it is equally important to recognize that an even vaster array of human languages have become extinct. In our desire to know each other and the world, we have lost much ground, but an enormous reservoir of undiscovered kinship still awaits us. In English, for example, there are nearly as many words—1.3 million—as labeled species. We know that probably twenty to fifty times this number of species exist in the world. We just haven't described or discovered them yet. Nor is it a coincidence that the average American wields no more sizable vocabulary each day (according to two independent surveys) than between twenty-five and fifty different words, and consumes— from a cornucopia of thousands of fruit and vegetal varieties—fewer than three dozen food types.

I relate such truncations of our communicative life to an equally diminished nutritional palette in order to illustrate the severity of human insularity and the possibilities for enriched experience that are beyond and all around us.

One might argue that our preferences, choices, ideas, expressions, and consumptive behavior are easily attributable to that insistent life-sustaining matrix of needs of which evolutionary nurture/nature is the engine. *Homo sapiens*, knowledgeable, thinking people, accord them-selves unique facilities for expression and free will unmatched, suppos-edly, by any other life form. Yet such hubris—the generally held assertion

that we are a superior biological species with unique cerebral convolutions and neurological sophistication—is all but blinded to the Creation, whose vast assemblage of other life forms are as vocal and no less expressive than are we.

Our near refusal to acknowledge this fundamental fact is conditioned by the same factors contributing to our biological self-centeredness, or *blinding*. Territorial, resource-related, somehow vaguely about survival, at least on the subconscious level (inasmuch as it is difficult to fathom how a cockroach or rat or mosquito could possibly pose a tangible, conscious threat to a human being), this blinding has ensured disastrous consequences for our species, and most other species. Having closed our minds to the possibilities of interspecies camaraderie without respect to "domestic" or "wild," we have driven to extinction one species after another. We have become exterminators or masters, cutthroats and bullies. And—with the exception of those pets that are truly loved— we have lost out on the most spectacular and significant avenues of exploration, meaning, and joy available to us.

Fear and loathing have built conceptual fences and ideological cities to ensure our separateness and advance our dissociation from other species. Rural peoples who remain undifferentiated from the outdoors are deemed primitive. To engage in the language of fences and cities is to acknowledge a narrow gauge upon which we travel, tautologically condemned to repeating an inescapable confine. We have made ourselves into more than a species that inhabits a certain niche. We have become the niche, with most other species relegated to the perilous position of enemy or—at best—tolerated visitor, or pet, or consumable—lower-class tenants with no rights. Where other species are wanted, as in the cases of pets, vineyards, or honeybees, the "want" merely provides a means to exploit other beings for our own pleasure or profit and bears little semblance of a true relationship. Obviously, tens of millions of people do love their pets and derive important love in return: a love that permeates their lives and extends to their behavior in general—not just their behavior to their own family dog but to all animals. But such people, I must suggest, are a small minority. This can be easily determined by examining the number of meat eaters, hunters, poachers, and consumers of

animal products or by surveying the paltry sums that taxpayers have allotted for the protection of habitat throughout the world. Recognizing the interdependent web of impacts upon animals, Jains, for example, are ill-disposed to keeping pets or engaging in any kind of agriculture, horticulture, or forestry.

There are, of course, all kinds of relationships. They need not be intense or intimate, informative or even meaningful. Any number of casual acquaintances pass through our lives, hardly warranting even ephemeral explanation or interest. That we are so easily capable of blocking out the vast majority of other human animals which we encounter, as on any crowded human freeway, says much about our neurological defense mechanism, the limited latitude in our psyches to accommodate excess stimulation.

The same is certainly true of the blocking mechanism we employ to assimilate or tune out the proliferation of data, news, events, and information. We delineate, distinguish, and differentiate with involuntary expertise to sustain at least a modicum of mental and perceptual equipoise. Our retreat from the kinesthetic avalanches that assault our lives is a stratagem for some kind of success. Human beings are surrounded by the white noise of their creations, transactions, causes and effects, memories of the past, anticipations of the future, and the complex haziness of apperception—our perception of our perception.

These mental activities fuel our self-obsessions and, in turn, dictate the scope of our strategic blocking out of nonhuman elements from our inner circles. By that I am neither discounting nor overlooking the history of human relationships with other species—the happy shepherd reclining beneath a shade tree, his sheep dog looking after things across the green sward, rendered so idyllic by any number of Graeco-Roman and Renaissance painters and poets; the ten-thousand-year-old tradition of human domestication of countless breeds of animals. Predating the earliest semidomestication of wild chickens in what is today Vietnam, evidence suggests that the earliest human agriculture, sixty thousand years ago across the Zagros Mountains of Iran, resulted from accidental and then deliberate hybridization of various wild grass species. French courtroom trials during the late Middle Ages pitted pigs and flies and

boll weevils against their human adversaries. The trials were precursors of today's raging legal battles by the few against the many to hang on to what is left of our wild heritage under the attenuated aegis of various endangered species legislation throughout the world. Of course, such trials have scarcely dented the tribulations, the epidemic slaughter, even in those few supposedly sacrosanct oases of biological integrity, namely wilderness areas, national parks, fish and wildlife lands.

In characterizing the many human blocking techniques and dispositions that have accreted into our species-specific prejudices and solipsisms, I am certainly aware of the vast amalgam of human–pet affections, companionships, and dependencies, whose most conspicuous evidence may be the estimated $17 billion spent on pets by their "owners" every year, just in the United States. While humans eat pets in countries like China or the Philippines, one cannot easily doubt the validity of the affection between, say, man and dog along the primeval shores of Lake Turkana, or Heidi and her alpine goats, or of the hordes of New Zealanders who fawn over their roses at annual competitions in Christchurch, the Dutch their tulips, the British their hedgerows. Human beings assuredly "love nature." There is indeed a global community of people who are, unabashedly, incontrovertibly, bravely, sentimentally, by ever so many miraculous accounts, in love with nonhuman individuals. These are people who speak of individuals, not species. This latter term dates to the eighteenth-century Swedish taxonomist Linnaeus, who chose to assemble a hierarchical nomenclature in order to clarify the differences between plants.

But "species," like kingdoms, phyla, taxa, genera, and orders, are about as revealing or compelling as describing Bach's *St. Matthew Passion* as a series of sound waves generated thus and so on the basis of specific cerebrations of one man's gray matter. Nonhuman individuals defy their scientific designations to the same extent that human beings do. To call Jane (my spouse) a *Homo sapien* is of little interest to me. To call Stanley (our dear Mexican parrot friend) a conspecific is equally a senseless vulgarization. Despite some sixty thousand years of systematic human contact with other animals, our overwhelming human collective disposition toward nonhumans has been grotesque and tragic. The

tragedy goes well beyond the magnitude of killing, of torture, of pain and desolation continually inflicted by our kind on most others: it has perpetuated that vast infliction as a generalized function of the way we are, or have become. All those blocking, blinding mechanisms previously described have—in essentially banning all those nonhumans from our biological families and inner circles—divorced us from the most important and majestic mission inherent to the Creation: that of biologically schmoozing. The myth of the Garden of Eden is just that, precisely because our sinister twist of the psyche has insisted on our own literal banishment from heaven and, hence, from all our former plant and animal friends, as well as from the animal in each of us. This is a point I wish to emphasize: the animal in us.

By this historical, psychic alienation we have grown up desperately alone. This fact is all the more ironic when considering our paralyzing frenzy to reproduce, an exponential cold calculus of demographics that is surely no biological success story but, rather, a scorched-earth policy of human growth responsible for the obliteration of most nonhuman individuals under foot. The Creation is being reversed, as shopping malls, high-rises, and new cities are grown hazily across the feverish nights of China, Indonesia, America, Brazil, and nearly everywhere else humans abound.

The tragedy of our neurological self-absorption is not simply that we will, if present patterns persist, extinguish as much as 60 percent of all advanced life forms on Earth by the middle of the next century; the tragedy also refers to the fact that by blocking out, we are blocking in. We have lost the innocence and lack the confidence to break out into intimacy, to let go of our over-humanness, to radically expand our social circle of close friends among nonhumans. By accepting the preconditions of our daily bread and comforts, we have, in essence, bought into the arguments that we use to justify our isolation from Nature and hence, disable the regenerative traits—those long-term survival genes—which, if only acknowledged and nurtured, might yet emerge to gently, firmly guide us away from this colossal brink of aloneness, pain, and infliction.

The alternative to this nightmare—a renaissance of interspecies communication and love—lingers as an ideal, though it also harbors enormously

practical merits and expediencies. Ethical vegetarians often find themselves cornered, resorting to practical, medical (read: narcissistic) arguments in order to at least catch the ear of skeptics and detractors. Yet, in truth, ethics based upon expediency and self-help are not ethics. Similarly, calls for the preservation of rain forests in order to protect the source of future human pharmaceutical agents are economic time bombs that may, in the prudent short-term sense, effect a righteous goal but cannot ultimately guarantee anything.

Only an ethical approach to preservation has any chance of durability, particularly in light of the long demographic winter of development, the fifty-trillion-dollar global economy, the mad dash for jobs and security and income that our doubling or tripling of human numbers is going to unleash. Only if we can catapult a global ethic in conjunction with a sustainable economics is there the slightest chance of halting the destruction of habitat and all that dwell therein. That halting is the only key to undoing the blocking; we cannot aspire to intimacy with other creatures if all that we are doing is killing them.

The tragedy, then, refers to the blinders that our humanity wears in all its dollar-crazed psychotic guises. Our awareness tells us who we are, or who we think we are, at the very moment that it condones the blotting out of whole lives, lineages, and regenerative capabilities (whole habitats). We are bound by the many contradictions of our fragile rules of developmental thumb: a horribly awkward expression that nearly encapsulates an equally impressive blunder, the bidpedal, ungainly carnivore known loosely as "man."

Most ecologists in the vanguard of doomsaying have focused upon what our species has done/is doing to Mother Nature, what I term World War III, a planetary cancer unprecedented in the 3.9 billion years of biological activity on Earth. By Nature, I prefer to think in terms, again, of individuals, not some vague clatter of forces, however exquisitely arranged, exerting, or imagined. A perfect machine is still a machine, which has no more purchase on my own feelings than a forklift or the Golden Gate Bridge. By Nature, again, I invite the reader to consider the totality of other individuals. Nature is the full assemblage of individuals, what the Jains refer to as jiva, independent souls, each of them—

temporarily frozen Alaskan wood frogs and prime ministers alike—equal under the laws of Earth.

To live in the company of other animals—humans and otherwise—to be acquainted with their habits, likes and dislikes, desires, manners, style, nervous energy, their bark and their scent, their wild glints all times of day; to know their fevers, diets, forlorns, and ecstasies; to divine those semblances even in the periphery of what, with any certainty, can or should be attested to, is, then, to know true grief when they suffer or die. Any photographer can capture, more or less, what an animal looks like. But to immortalize who that animal is requires the same level of intimacy that true friends and lovers know. So that—when we are grieving over the loss of a pet rat, turtle, bird, chimpanzee, horse, or parent or child—we know at that quintessential junction where memory confronts the unfathomable voice, and we can, only then, attest to a real Being, unlike any other, that once lived draped in a kaleidoscope of angelic feathers, or fur, or scales, or plain, perfect skin, eyes ablaze, little heart pounding in joy; we can, who knew them thus, only then recall with heartbreaking truth and poetry the fullness of that life, and the unique character that shaped it. Because we are so apt to take for granted the everyday familiar, we often only grasp the magnitude of such individuals—every individual—when we have lost them. A universal cliché, no doubt, but nonetheless a penetrating truth: "There was so much I never told her; so very much he still wished to do; her whole life yet before her..."

These melancholia can be reinvested with a determination to faithfully nurture the living, to do so with the zeal of a new love affair. Nothing short of a gigantic passion is likely to loosen the bolts of our stubborn egocentrism. No other creature besides man is fraught with contradiction. This fact, like no other, separates out our cognition and makes it our freakish fatality to live, to paraphrase Lord Byron's "Manfred." Contradictions that are two verbs describing opposite directions at every instant; so rapid an oscillation. On the left, that ancient utopian reverie where Adam and Eve, the lion and the lamb, commune together, never doubting the full harmony of their perpetual picnic. On the right, a dark tunnel of human separatism, violent expropriation, useless guilt, and unmirroring madness. In the center of this

diseased heaving to and fro, the tenuous balancing act we call rationality, or humanity, or civilization, or ecology.

Yet, rationality or humanity or civilization is not wildness, which is the only trait of any staying power in the world. Wildness, as we have at least come to sense in its evocations, is not merely our conviction of the integrity of ancient habitat and the same biology that drives our insides but the legislation of individuals, down to the one trillion ants and the very mites in our eyelashes. Wildness, for human beings, is a new eye, a reconsidered willingness to be as naked and unblushing as any other animal, to revisit the most familiar as an ultimate challenge of compassion and curiosity. Becoming as wild as any other nonhuman animal is the essential starting point for an empathetic about-face in human affairs.

Enshrouding those few documented cases where humans have confronted human wildness—the wild French boy (Victor) of the Alps in the early nineteenth century, the two girls allegedly raised by bears in India— is the sense of a profound nostalgia swirling around the annals of such situations. This spectacle of lost worlds reaches its zenith in such incidents as that of the early-twentieth-century Native American, Ishi, captured by anthropologist "saviors"; or those researchers still searching for the yeti in the Himalayas; or the tribe without fire in India's northeastern state of Arunachal; or the Gazelle Boy of the Rio de Oro in Mauritania on the western fringes of the Spanish Sahara.

These evocations of the wild man, the half-man, half-animal, are the poetic syntheses of two glaringly contradictory urgings—to live and breathe free and wild in a landscape that supports us generously, and to dwell with equal freedom in a city like Paris, with the fullest access to all which human "reformation" has to offer. Rousseau and Emerson lived torn between these two allures. Spiritual traditions have also debated these two vastly divergent temptations: the wildness of such saints as Mary Magdalene, Onuphrius, and John Chrysostom, and the ostentatious urbanity of the Vatican.

To live freely, to love and be loved, is the evident goal of every being, whether a painter in Paris or a millipede in Malaysia. These biological

dreams are also spiritual. For humans, whose biased brains have condemned us to the uniquely contradictory struggle to reconcile the urgings of our animal individualism and human acculturation, such goals cannot be limited to ourselves. We must extend our hearts to the whole of the biological world, unclogging the communication channels, descrambling the profuse signals that abound everywhere and at all times around us, unblocking the blinders that have tended to isolate a species that is, in fact, quite clearly capable of serving the planet as benign, compassionate members; who, to paraphrase a Jain Tirthankara, might be as an "island of safety," forging a new nature, once again opening to the exchange and respect between all organisms.

That respect would carry forth from one's mate to the distant horizon upon which a wildebeest migration might be occurring, to the owl in the tree at night, to the snake under the pile of rocks, to the rocks themselves. We cannot remake a trout or rhododendron, miracles of the biosphere. But we can remake ourselves, not as superhumans with certain rigid rules or specific, inflexible names of God, but as lovely animals with remarkable wit and patience and curiosity. These are the original habits of mind that transcend the virulent fundamentalism of our historical sense of pathetic superiority over the natural world. By refocusing on those traits every day, with each thought and interaction, we can easily adjust our sights to encompass all other kindred life forms. This process is spiritually, emotionally, and scientifically crucial to the future of life on Earth.

In Zen Buddhism, as in Taoism and Jainism, dew drops, spider webs, grains of sand, and the mist are each endowed with equal shares of needed love, respect, and admiration. This pantheistic sentience is a remarkably meaningful and joyous way of life for those who undertake it. No transaction is excluded between organisms. Everything is possible.

For humans to reclaim their animal origins will take as many guises as there are humans. But one crucial common thread will likely emerge, and this is the commensuralist ability to get along with others in the wild. "Getting along with" is a far cry from the current global holocaust occurring all around us, inside us, whose victims are all those hapless perfect miracles of creation whom we have conveniently labeled nonhuman. To break this evil spell that has marked our species as sure

as the mark of Cain is to finally discover the Earth, an original planet that we have not yet walked, breathed, or truly experienced.

If this opinion seems to overlook the roots of indigenous experience, I would again point out that indigenous peoples were, by self-definition, heavily human, having already eclipsed and usurped the wildness within themselves. We can read the purgatory of transition into the fateful petroglyphs of the paleolithic, where human consciousness seemed to pictorially discuss its retreat from other species, as sure as the glaciers were retreating; occasioning that reversion through the evocative depiction of individual animals with distinct, memorable faces and imputable personalities.

By thirty thousand years ago, the earlier multi-special coalescence had been nearly severed, and humans seemed intent upon going their own way. Once the power in our grip and in our tools had taken to exploiting other animals in our wake, we could not easily turn back; no stopping the inexorable slaughter of innocents, of protohuman contradiction augmenting the divisiveness and destructiveness of the human animal. I do not mean this to be a blanket condemnation or historical assessment of irreversible animal abuse, but rather, an invitation to start anew, one of the basic tenets of "engaged Buddhism," says Tich Nhat Hahn. I believe we can start anew.

Even in a country as contradictory as India, where the "blinders" earlier described are blatantly, hideously manifest, one can single out at least three compelling beacons of enduring ecological nonviolence (ahimsa) and interspecies empathy and love. I refer to the nearly ten million Jains, the more than one million desert Bishnoi, and the fourteen hundred Todas of the southern Nilgiri massif. These three groups are devout vegetarians who revere all other life forms and have fashioned successful, sustainable lifestyles out of that first principle. Their professions, consumerism, behavior, and histories are fully encompassed by a deep ethological bonding or relatedness to other creatures that deserves intense study. And there are other such groups, also challenging us to reassess the possibilities of reunion with other species: the Inner Badui of Western Java; the Hadza of Tanzania; the Drukpa of Bhutan; and the Karen along the Thai/Myramar border, all essentially vegetarian.

It is possible. It costs no money, only patience. We need not think that our deliverance is to be found within the cold confines of a Martian rock or that the mysteries of the cosmos can only be gleaned fifteen billion light-years away. What will make or break our species, and probably most others in our glaring path, is our willingness to confront the fantastic mystery of Earth's wilderness, right here, right now; to fall in love all over again, and again, and again, with the countless, nameless others— winged, hooved, tentacled, long- and short-snouted, tailish, buzzing, murmuring, communicating creatures all around us. That is our only hope. And that should be the true mission of any humanity.

CONTRIBUTORS

JANE GOODALL

The leading authority on chimpanzees, author of six major books and countless articles, and the recipient of numerous prestigious awards, Jane Goodall is one of the most renowned and respected scientists in the world. She has rejected "scientific method" in favor of subjective, emotional, interspecies empathy, and this stance has earned her an added reputation of being one of the most daring field biologists in history. In 1995 Goodall celebrated thirty-five years of continuous research at the Gombe Chimp preserve in Tanzania, East Africa. Established by Goodall after she began her work in the 1960s under Louis B. Leakey, this project represents the longest continuous research program with another species ever undertaken by a human being.

ANTHONY L. ROSE

Anthony Rose earned his Ph.D. in experimental psychology at UCLA where he served as a fellow at the Brain Research Institute and did behavioral research with pig-tailed macaques. Later, with humanist Carl Rogers, he helped found San Diego's Center for Studies of the Person. His work in healthcare, psychology, and animal research came together recently with his founding in Southern California of the Biosynergy Institute, supporting development of programs that foster the reunion of humanity with nature.

MARC BEKOFF

Marc Bekoff is professor of environmental, population, and organismic biology at the University of Colorado at Boulder. A Guggenheim Fellow, he is recognized as one of the world's leading authorities on coyotes and wolves. In the early 1970s he dropped out of a Ph.D.-M.D. program because he was required to kill cats as part of his dissertation research and take part in physiology laboratories in which dogs were used. He is now recognized worldwide as a leader in the field of animal comparative behavior and is the author of six books, among them the first major encyclopedia on comparative animal communications and animal welfare as well as *Readings in Animal Cognition*, published in 1997 by MIT Press.

KELLY STEWART

Kelly Stewart, research associate in the Department of Anthropology at the University of California at Davis, was Dian Fossey's assistant and for two years the head of the Karisoke Research Center in Rwanda, where she wrote her dissertation on mountain gorillas for her doctorate in zoology from Cambridge University. For five years in Rwanda and Zaire and two years in Nigeria, Stewart lived with the gorillas and her husband. Author of more than twenty-five scientific papers, editor of the *Gorilla Conservation News*, and a trustee of the African Wildlife Foundation, Stewart is recognized as one of the few authorities in the world on gorillas.

LORIN LINDNER

Lorin Lindner, Ph.D., M.P.H, is a clinical psychologist in Los Angeles and on the Santa Monica College faculty. A staff psychologist for a homeless veterans' shelter, she serves on the board of directors of Psychologists for the Ethical Treatment of Animals as well as the Fund for Wild Nature. Co-coordinator of Los Angeles Earth First!, Dr. Lindner is widely respected for her outspoken views and environmental activism. She is on the Advisory Board of the Road Removal Implementation Project—noting that road kills account for a staggering 400 million deaths to animals each year. For many years Dr. Lindner has sheltered birds whom she has come to know intimately.

CON SLOBODCHIKOFF

Dr. Slobodchikoff is a professor in the Biology Department at Northern Arizona University. Widely published, he is considered to be the world's authority on prairie dogs, which are so crucial to prairie and grasslands ecology. He is probably the only scientist to have actually broken through the linguistic barriers of prairie dogs and ascertained some aspects of their language.

MICHAEL W. FOX

Vice president of the Humane Society of the United States, Dr. Fox has written more than forty books and writes a nationally syndicated newspaper column, "Ask Your Animal Doctor." A consulting veterinarian, he heads the H.S.U.S. section on bioethics and farm-animal protection. With a Ph.D. in medicine and a D.Sc. in ethology/animal behavior from London University, his most recent books include *The Boundless Circle: Caring for Creatures and Creation*.

RODNEY JACKSON

Rodney Jackson won a 1981 Rolex Award for Enterprise, launching his landmark radio-tracking study of snow leopards in Nepal's remote far West. Today

he is considered the world's leading authority on *Uncia uncia*, the snow leopard. In addition to numerous scientific papers, Jackson has written numerous popular pieces. With his partner, Darla Hillard, he co-authored the June 1986 cover story for *National Geographic* based on their snow leopard expeditions. Jackson and Hillard have continued their research throughout the many countries of the Himalayas where snow leopards are found.

CHRISTINE JURZYKOWSKI

Jurzykowski founded the Fossil Rim Wildlife Center in North Texas, which today provides refuge for more than 1,100 animals representing various endangered species, from lions to giraffes, rhinos, rare birds, zebras, and antelopes. Her life is devoted to raising awareness of the needs and exquisite wonders of wildlife.

STEPHEN R. L. CLARK

Dean of the Arts Faculty at Liverpool University and professor of philosophy there since 1984, Dr. Clark has earned the distinction of having given most of the major endowed lecture series on philosophy and religion in the United Kingdom—at Cambridge, Oxford, Glasgow, and Bristol. His dozen books include *The Moral Status of Animals*, *Animals and Their Standing*, and *Biology and Christian Ethics*. Many consider him the world's leading philosopher of animal rights.

GARY KOWALSKI

The Reverend Gary Kowalski is the minister of the First Unitarian Universalist Society in Burlington, Vermont. He has written widely on animal-related topics and the importance of understanding animals in the context of theology. He has advanced a reinterpretation of the Bible according to its deep ecological roots.

JOSEPH BRUCHAC

Joseph Bruchac is an Abenaki Indian living in Vermont. A Ph.D. in comparative literature from the Union Institute of Ohio and a renowned environmentalist, traditional storyteller, and writer, he has been a visiting scholar at Hamilton College, Columbia University, and the State University of New York at Albany. His poems, articles, and stories have appeared in more than five hundred publications, including *National Geographic* and *Smithsonian*. He has authored more than sixty books for both adults and children. His awards include a Rockefeller Humanities fellowship, the Cherokee Nation Prose Award, the Scientific American Young Readers Book Award, and the Knickerbocker Award for Juvenile Literature. In 1993 he received the Benjamin Franklin Award as Person of the Year by the Publisher's Marketing Association.

TREBBE JOHNSON

Trebbe Johnson is a poet, filmmaker, animal-rights activist, and environmentalist living in rural Pennsylvania with her husband. Her work has appeared in *Harper's Parabola*, *The Nation*, and *Amicus Journal*, and her environmental essays are syndicated by Pacific News Service. She has received the John Masefield Award of the Poetry Society of America and a grant from National Public Radio to write and produce a documentary about the Navajo-Hopi land dispute. Her video, "Only One Earth," was commissioned by the United Nations to open the U.N. Environment Progam's twentieth-anniversary celebration on Earth Day. In addition to writing and filmmaking, Trebbe leads vision quests and creates personal ceremonies for contemporary rites of passage.

GABRIEL HORN

Gabriel Horn (White Deer of Autumn) is a nationally recognized lecturer on writing and on Native American philosophy and its intricate connection to the rights of indigenous peoples, animals, and the welfare of the natural environment. His written works for Beyond Words Publishing include *Ceremony in the Circle of Life*, *The Great Change*, and the Native People, Native Ways series. He serves in the Wisdomkeepers Program in North Carolina, where he has also helped establish a Native American Writers Camp for children on the Cherokee reservation. He has been featured on National Public Radio and has written and read on the American Indian Ghost Dance religion on MS-NBC's award-winning Web site.

MICHAEL MOUNTAIN

Michael Mountain is the editor of *Best Friends Magazine* and one of the founding directors of Best Friends Animal Sanctuary, the nation's largest no-kill sanctuary for abused and abandoned animals. As editor of the *Best Friends Magazine*, he has drawn an extensive following among animal lovers, as Best Friends became the flagship animal-welfare organization in the movement to bring an end to the problem of pet overpopulation. He is currently building the Best Friends AnimalNet on the Microsoft Network. This first-ever electronic publication for animal lovers and pet owners offers news, features, entertainment, and a large database of information from all around the world for people who care about animals.

PADRE ANTONIO VIEIRA

Padre Vieira is a Brazilian animal-rights activist who is the world's leading authority on donkeys. He has written a four-volume treatise in Portuguese on the history, zoology, poetry, folklore, and ecology of donkeys. He has documented

the torment and abuse of the donkey in South America and single-handedly drawn attention to the plight of one of the most mysterious and loving creatures on the planet. In addition to his crusades to help the donkey, Vieira also campaigns to stop the cruel "Vaquejada," a form of bull torture that occurs throughout Brazil for the entertainment of spectators.

LORRI BAUSTON

Lorri Bauston is the president and co-founder of Farm Sanctuary, the world's leading farm-animal-protection organization. She first became involved in animal-welfare issues when she rescued Hilda, a sheep that had been dumped on a stockyard pile of animals left for dead. Over the past several years Lorri has saved thousands of lives of abused and neglected farm animals. Farm Sanctuary's groundbreaking campaigns and programs include establishment of the first shelters in the country for victims of food-animal production, passage of the first state law banning downed-animal cruelties at stockyards and slaughterhouses, initiation of unprecedented cruelty investigations and legal prosecutions of farm-animal abusers, and helping focus national media attention on the plight of farm animals. Today Farm Sanctuary has more than fifty thousand members, including their first supporter, the sheep Hilda, who resides happily at the New York shelter.

INGRID NEWKIRK

Ingrid Newkirk is co-founder and chairperson of People for the Ethical Treatment of Animals, the largest animal-rights organization in the United States, with more than 400,000 members. She appears regularly on *The Today Show*, *Oprah!*, and *20/20*, and occasionally on *Nightline*. Newkirk, the author of four books and countless articles, was a deputy sheriff and a Maryland state law-enforcement officer for seventeen years who recorded the highest success rate in convicting animal abusers. She was also chief of animal disease control for the Commission on Public Health in the District of Columbia. She went on to coordinate the first arrest in U.S. history of a laboratory animal scientist on the grounds of cruelty to animals; to spearhead the closure of a U.S. Department of Defense underground "wound laboratory"; and to achieve a total revamping of the Washington, D.C., city pound, which included prohibiting the government from selling animals to laboratories. In a cover story profile of Newkirk in the *Los Angeles Times Sunday Magazine*, she was hailed as one of the most significant voices of our times for animal rights.

ALAN DRENGSON

Alan Drengson is professor emeritus of philosophy at the University of Victoria in British Columbia. He is founder and senior editor of the influential journal

The Trumpeter: Journal of Ecosophy and also the founding editor of the *International Journal of Ecoforestry*. His many books include *Beyond Environmental Crisis, The Deep Ecology Movement,* and *The Practice of Technology.* He is involved in several nongovernmental organizations focused on wildlife. He is a devoted wild journeyer and also teaches aikido, the Japanese martial art.

KATE SOLISTI-MATTELON

Born with the ability to "hear" animals, Kate Solisti had lost the gift by the age of eight—in order to "fit in." Graduating from Smith College in 1980, she went on to pursue a career in fund-raising for environmental organizations, including The Nature Conservancy, American Rivers, and HawkWatch International. Through a journey of personal healing and self-discovery, Kate reawakened her gift of telepathic communication in her thirties. Kate now dedicates her life to reuniting people and animals, helping redefine human-animal relationships, and assisting others to reawaken. In 1995 she was a guest speaker at the British Holistic Veterinary Conference. Her writing, lectures, and workshops on interspecies communication are helping people and animals around the world; her work with veterinarians to give their patients a "voice" is saving animal lives every day; and her communication with wild animals is allowing their knowledge, experience, and perspective to re-create our relationship with all beings on this beautiful planet.

JIM NOLLMAN

Jim Nollman is the author of four books published in several languages, including *Dolphin Dreamtime: The Art and Science of Inter-species Communication.* He founded Interspecies Communication in 1978 to promote a better understanding of what can be communicated between humans and other animals. He is, perhaps, best known for his remarkable recordings of his music which he performs in the wild in the company of other species. For twenty-five years he has played music interactively with turkeys, frogs, ravens, and monkeys, but he is best known for his improvisational music with various species of free-swimming whales and dolphins, particularly the orcas who inhabit the northeast coast of Vancouver Island. His work has been filmed in countless documentaries in the United States, Europe, and Japan.

REBECCA FITZGERALD

Many years ago Rebecca Fitzgerald began swimming with dolphins off the Florida Keys. They affected her life profoundly, particularly her dreaming. For the past eight years she has been systematically studying the impact of dolphin

pods on the human psyche by regularly taking small groups of people out into the wild sea to swim with various pods of dolphins. Her research into the interactions of humans with dolphins has provided her unique insights, not obtainable in any other way, into the life of marine mammals.

MICHAEL ROADS

Michael Roads is a well-known Australian ecologist, writer, and spiritualist whose books include *Talking with Nature, Journey into Nature, Journey into Oneness, Into a Timeless Realm*, and *Getting There*.

LINDA TELLINGTON-JONES

Linda Tellington-Jones, a renowned horse expert and animal behavioralist, has incorporated her Feldenkrais human-bodywork training with her vast knowledge of the physiology and mental/emotional adaptation of animals. Linda's work is now recognized throughout the world as an accepted, humane form of animal training and communication that significantly transcends domination and obedience. Through the development of TTEAM (Tellington TTouch Equine Awareness Method), Linda has created a method of animal training and healing that allows people to relate to animals in a meaningful, aware, and effective manner.

RACHEL ROSENTHAL

Rachel Rosenthal, a solo theatrical artist–animal-rights activist, was born in Paris and raised in New York. Her teachers as a performer were Hans Hoffman, Merce Cunningham, and John Cage. Since 1989 she has served as artistic director of her nonprofit Rachel Rosenthal Company, which was a recipient three times of an NEA fellowship. She has been a Getty and Rockefeller Fellow, a winner of the OBIE Award, and visiting artist and lecturer at UCLA, NYU, the Carnegie Mellon Foundation, the San Francisco Art Institute, the Art Institute of Chicago, and elsewhere. She was photographed for *Vanity Fair* by Annie Leibovitz. A book to be published by Johns Hopkins University Press surveys her career and her impact on the arts. Rosenthal has been an animal activist for decades and is often involved in rescue and placement of animal refugees. For years she performed in the company of the love of her life, a pet rat, who became the most famous rat in American theater circles.

LAVENDER DOWER

Lavender Dower is a famed British animal sensitive, healer, and veterinarian. For more than fifty years she has championed what is known as Radionic Therapy with animals. Her "clients" have included Joy Adamsons's lions and celebrated British racehorses.

PENELOPE SMITH

Penelope Smith is a telepathic animal-communication specialist. She is renowned in the United States and has a large following in Canada, Europe, Australia, and Japan. Penelope has assisted thousands of animals and their people to increased well-being and understanding. She is the author of *Animals: Our Return to Wholeness* and *Animal Talk: Interspecies Telepathic Communication.* Through her videos, tapes, and workshops, she fills a gap by helping humans develop higher communication skills and assume responsibilities that can dramatically transform their relationships with other species on all levels—physical, mental, emotional, and spiritual.

ERYN WOLFWALKER

A practicing farrier of twenty years, Ms. Wolfwalker's experience in the animal field has included a broad array of positions focusing on alternative therapies and innovative schooling techniques. A guest lecturer at the 1995 American Holistic Veterinary Association's National Conference, she holds a master's degree in the teaching level of the Reiki healing modality and has developed courses and manuals for the application of the modality to animals.

SUSAN CHERNAK MCELROY

McElroy watched her dog die of cancer. Eight years later, she herself contracted the same cancer. By meditating on her dog and its dignity and joy in life, she survived her ordeal. Since that time she has spent years compiling anecdotes and insights from people throughout the world that address the mystical connections between humans and nonhumans. Her first book, *Animals As Teachers and Healers: True Stories and Reflections,* was selected for the Alternate Book of the Month Club.

AMAYÉ

Amayé holds bachelor of science and master of arts degrees in anthropology and is a doctoral candidate in physical anthropology. Working closely with animals all her life, she has a background in primatology, ecology, and the study of felid behavior. Currently Amayé is expanding her understanding of holistic healing, interacting co-creatively with the plant, mineral, and animal kingdoms and Earth energies.

SHELLEY DONNELLY

Shelley Donnelly was led into alternative or complementary medicine through the apparently incurable sickness of Fiorino. The results were so astounding that she studied the methods of Drown, Delawarr, Macolm Rae, and Tansley and

then took a degree in radionics, subsequently receiving an honorary degree for her outstanding work and research in this subject. Shelley presently is engaged in researching and developing a new method for healing animals (in all forms) called Pranamonics.

MICHAEL TOBIAS

Michael Tobias has written twenty-two books and written, produced, and directed more than one hundred films. He has spent many years living in the wilderness on every continent. At his home in Los Angeles, Tobias and his wife, Jane, maintain a small animal sanctuary that feeds several hundred birds (including three endangered parrots), squirrels, rats, mice, and opossums. Tobias's most recent books and films include *A Vision of Nature: Traces of the Original World* (Kent State University Press); *A Day in the Life of India* (Mapin/Collins-Doordarshan); *World War III: Population and the Biosphere at the End of the Millennium* (Bear & Company, and PBS); and *A Parliament of Souls: In Search of Global Spirituality* (co-edited with Jane Gray Morris).

RESOURCES

Best Friends Animal Sanctuary (*Michael Mountain*)
P.O. Box G
Kanab, UT 84741-5001
phone: (435) 644-2001
e-mail: info@bestfriends.org
URL: http://www.bestfriends.org

The Biosynergy Institute (*Anthony L. Rose*)
P.O. Box 488
Hermosa Beach, CA 90254
phone: (310) 379-1470
e-mail: ALR@biosynergy.org

Dolphinswim (*Rebecca Fitzgerald*)
P.O. Box 8653
Santa Fe, NM 87504
phone: (305) 534-4188
e-mail: seaswim@bellsouth.net

Farm Sanctuary (*Lorri Bauston*)

East
P.O. Box 150
Watkins Glen, NY 14891-0150
phone: (607) 583-2225

West
P.O. Box 1065
Orland, CA 95963-1065
phone: (530) 865-4617

Fossil Rim Wildlife Center (*Christine Jurzykowski*)
P.O. Box 2189
2155 County Road 2008
Glen Rose, TX 76043
phone: (254) 897-2960
URL: http://www.fossilrim.com

Humane Society of the United States (*Michael W. Fox*)
2100 L Street, N.W.
Washington, DC 20037
phone: (202) 452-1100

Indigo Quill Healing Arts (*Eryn Wolfwalker*)
P.O. Box 841
Conifer, CO 80433
phone: (303) 838-7698

International Snow Leopard Trust (*Rodney Jackson*)
4649 Sunnyside Avenue N.
Seattle, WA 98103
phone: (206) 632-2421

Interspecies Communication (*Jim Nollman*)
273 Hidden Meadow Lane
Friday Harbor, WA 98250
(360) 378-5186
e-mail: beluga@rockisland.com

The Jane Goodall Institute (*Jane Goodall*)
P.O. Box 14890
Silver Spring, MD 20911-4890
phone: (301) 565-0086

Pegasus Publications (*Penelope Smith*)
P.O. Box 1060
Point Reyes, CA 94956
phone: (415) 663-1247

People for the Ethical Treatment of Animals (*Ingrid Newkirk*)
501 Front Street
Norfolk, VA 23510
phone: (757) 622-7382

Solisti-Mattelon Publications (*Kate Solisti-Mattelon*)
5837 S. Reed Way, Suite 1636
Littleton, CO 80123
phone: (303) 734-1247

TTEAM Training (*Linda Tellington-Jones*)
Animal Ambassadors International
P.O. Box 3793
Santa Fe, NM 87501-0793
phone: (505) 455-2945

Vision Arrow (*Trebbe Johnson*)
P.O. Box 148
Thompson, PA 18465
phone: (717) 727-4272

PHOTO CREDITS

JANE GOODALL
Photo by Michael Nuegebauer

ANTHONY L. ROSE

MARC BEKOFF
with Jethro

KELLY STEWART
Photo by Elizabeth Harcourt

LORIN LINDNER
with Sam and Mango

CON SLOBODCHIKOFF
Photo by Judith Kiriazis

MICHAEL W. FOX
feeding wild boar piglet
Photo by Deanna Kruntz

RODNEY JACKSON
Photo © 1986 by Darla Hillard,
  National Geographic Society

CHRISTINE JURZYKOWSKI
with giraffe
Photo by John Tilley Photography

STEPHEN R. L. CLARK

GARY KOWALSKI
with Chinook

JOSEPH BRUCHAC
Photo by John Pflug

TREBBE JOHNSON
peregrine falcon
Photo by CG Colburn

MICHAEL TOBIAS
with Feather
Photo by Jane Gray Morrison

GABRIEL HORN
swimming with dolphin

MICHAEL MOUNTAIN
with Schnoodles

PADRE ANTONTIO VIEIRA

LORRI BAUSTON
with Gene and Hilda

INGRID NEWKIRK

ALAN DRENGSON
Photo by Gibson Studios

KATE SOLISTI-MATTELON
with Patrice Mattelon, Azul, and Mollie

JIM NOLLMAN

REBECCA FITZGERALD
swimming with dolphin

MICHAEL ROADS

LINDA TELLINGTON-JONES

RACHEL ROSENTHAL
with Tatti Wattles
Photo by Daniel J. Martinez

LAVENDER DOWER
Tessa

PENELOPE SMITH
Photo by Marty Knapp

ERYN WOLFWALKER

SUSAN CHERNAK MCELROY
with Arrow

AMAYÉ
with Junior

SHELLEY DONNELLY
Fiorino
Photo © 1990 by Mary Browning

MICHAEL TOBIAS
Photo by Jane Gray Morrison

BEYOND WORDS PUBLISHING, INC.

Our corporate mission:

Inspire to Integrity

Our declared values:

We give to all of life as life has given us.

We honor all relationships.

Trust and stewardship are integral to fulfilling dreams.

Collaboration is essential to create miracles.

Creativity and aesthetics nourish the soul.

Unlimited thinking is fundamental.

Living your passion is vital.

Joy and humor open our hearts to growth.

It is important to remind ourselves of love.